SHELL-SHOCKED

PRAISE FOR *SHELL-SHOCKED*

"Mohammed Omer could easily have escaped the horror of Israel's impending assault on the trapped and helpless people of Gaza. Instead, he chose to stay, to record, in searing and vivid detail, the savagery of Israel's latest escapade of 'mowing the lawn' and the steadfastness of the victims of a hideous tragedy. Few can match his courage and integrity, but all of us who live in countries providing the arms and diplomatic support that made Israel's actions possible should ponder his words and ask ourselves what has been done in our name and what we should do about it." —NOAM CHOMSKY

"Read *Shell-Shocked*. It's author says, 'I'm a journalist and I owe it to my people and the Israeli people to get to the truth.' Thank you, Mohammed, the truth is like water, a basic necessity . . . without it we will not survive."
—ROGER WATERS

"Written with painful immediacy, these are more than dispatches from a war zone: they convey the human reality of people who manage to survive and endure in conditions that have grown grimmer and more inhumane over the years." —RASHID KHALIDI

"With a terrible and necessary exactitude, Mohammed Omer's war chronicle lets the world know the devastating losses borne by the Gazan people bombarded by Israeli forces in 2014." —JUDITH BUTLER

PRAISE FOR *SHELL-SHOCKED*

"The truth about Israel's crimes in Gaza can never be forgotten, never successfully lied about and covered-up, because Mohammed Omer was there. This great reporter and his family were under fire day after day. When I phoned him, I could hear the explosions outside his front door. Yet, day after day he produced eyewitness dispatches of such clarity and brilliance that, almost single-handed, he reclaimed the honour of real journalism."

—JOHN PILGER

"From the very heart of Gaza, a witness to war: history will record Mohammed Omer's searing testimony about what was done to his homeland by Israel's 'Operation Protective Edge' . . . This is journalism of the highest order."

—JON SNOW, CHANNEL 4 NEWS

"If you only have time to read one book on Israel's 2014 war on Gaza, let it be this one. Mohammed Omer's on-the-ground reporting is stunning and unforgettable, giving access to a daily reality few can imagine let alone endure. Omer describes the landscape of Palestinian life and death in this tiny strip of land during this horrific period. Yet, his accounts are not only about the immense suffering of Gaza's people but about their remarkable resilience and dignity, which cannot be destroyed. An act of conscience and documentation, Omer's book will remain with the reader long after it is read." —SARA ROY

ALSO BY MOHAMMED OMER

Oslo Accords 1993–2013: A Critical Assessment
(co-edited with Petter Bauck)

SHELL-SHOCKED

On the Ground Under Israel's Gaza Assault

MOHAMMED OMER

HAYMARKET BOOKS
CHICAGO, ILLINOIS

Published by
Haymarket Books
P.O. Box 180165
Chicago, IL 60618
773-583-7884
www.haymarketbooks.org
info@haymarketbooks.org

ISBN 978-1-60846-513-2

Trade distribution:
In the US, Consortium Book Sales and Distribution, www.cbsd.com
In Canada, Publishers Group Canada, www.pgcbooks.ca
In the UK, Turnaround Publisher Services, www.turnaround-uk.com
All other countries, Publishers Group Worldwide, www.pgw.com

This book was published with the generous support of Lannan Foundation and Wallace Action Fund.

Cataloging-in-Publication data is available from the Library of Congress.
A catalog record for this book is available from the British Library.

This book is set in the fonts Alte Haas Grotesk and Pobla.
Text design by Bathcat Ltd. Typeset by AarkMany Media, Chennai, India.
Cover design by Eric Ruder.

Printed in Canada by union labor.

10 9 8 7 6 5 4 3 2 1

Introduction

Now, a year since the last war on Gaza, I find myself reflecting on my first meeting with Jalal Jundia. It was during the summer of 2014 when I saw him sitting atop the ruins of his family home, surrounded by dust and rubble. Though he was attempting to remain calm I could see that his face was etched with lines of stress. Like so many in Gaza, he had lost everything during the Israeli assault, the most recent of a series of attacks that arrive with predictable frequency every three to four years. Jalal wondered aloud about his wife and six children. Where could they go now their home had been destroyed? Where was it safe? They were trapped in Gaza and unable to leave. All they could do was wait for the bombings to end and pray for a day when drones no longer occupied the sky. Perhaps then there would be enough peace for his family to rebuild and attempt a return to some sort of normal life.

A year later, Jalal is still homeless. His house has not been rebuilt and his family survives, but is barely alive. As for myself, I try to remain optimistic, no small feat in this ruined shell of what was once a beautiful and self-sufficient costal enclave. Our reality is predicated upon Israel's determination to drive us from our homes for good. After the 1947–48 purge, an ethnic cleansing of non-Jewish residents from territories Israel coveted but had not been granted by the United Nations, Gaza became a safe haven for tens of thousands fleeing the massacres at the hands of the Irgun, Stern and Lehi gangs. Self-admitted terrorist organizations, these were the forerunners of today's Israeli military, police and Shin Bet. Meanwhile our elders today, the men, women and children who fled before the Zionist militias, still hold on to the keys of the homes they lost. These keys represent hope and a determination. One day they hope to return home.

In the wake of this latest attack, the vast majority of Gaza's children remain traumatized. We continue to live under siege, limited in what we can buy, export or import. We can't leave and it is very difficult for people to visit us. We listen resignedly as human rights activists laud the fact that we "Palestinians can withstand the aggression" simply because we have survived it for so long. That may be true but it begs the question: why should we be forced to continue to put up with this misery? The Second World War lasted six years; the Third Reich's assault and ethnic cleansing of those it deemed undesirable lasted twelve. Our oppression has lasted sixty-seven years, making the Israeli occupation of Palestine one of the longest in history.

Every minute of every day we live in a distorted reality, a man-made catastrophe crafted to protect and enshrine a peculiar manifestation of overt racism that grants privilege and life solely on the basis of religion and race, and then denies it exists. Its purpose is to make the lives of those of us who belong to the non-favored race and religion unbearable. Its objective is to force us to "volunteer" to abandon our country, businesses, family, homes, ancestry and culture. The tool of this persecution is systemic and infects all aspects of life. It ranges over preventing us from rebuilding our homes to military aggression, targeted killings, imprisonment, starvation diets enforced by siege and an array of punishments that dehumanize and strip us of our rights. And then there are the obstacles to our movement—walls and checkpoints for "security."

And yet, despite all this, we're still here. It's true: In Gaza we find ways to survive. Our women recycle the spent tank shells that have destroyed our homes into flowerpots. Students return to bombed-out schools determined to complete their education. Torn books are taped together, pens are jerry-rigged back into service. At night we often study by candlelight. The frequent cutting off of gas, water and electricity is another daily reality of life in The Strip. And so we carry on, focusing on the basics and muddling through with proud determination. We are human, with dreams and nightmares, equally strong and equally vulnerable. We pride ourselves on our self-sufficiency and humbly thank God for the help of others as we hope and pray for justice.

That justice has yet to arrive. Each time he sees me Jundia asks when the West, with its pontificating about democracy and existentialism relating to human rights, will take action in keeping with its ideals. Do they not hear of Israel's attacks on Gaza? His eyes search mine in hope. He knows I've been outside of The Strip and speak regularly with influential people in the West. Often, I am unable to meet his gaze. I'm aware that Western powers care little of human suffering if it happens in Gaza. Here it often feels as if we, the two million inhabitants of The Strip, don't exist. I can't relate this disturbing truth to Jundia. Rather, I bolster his hope, assuring him that I will continue to share his story with the world. I promise him that his voice will not go unheard.

Like Jundia, I am a resident of Gaza and suffer through daily local attacks, as well as the major assaults every few years. This has been my experience of life, first as a child, then as a young man, and now as a father and husband; I was born a few years prior to the first intifada. Today four generations have lived under this occupation. The majority of us in Gaza have known nothing else. Now the latest major attack is a year behind us. For fifty-one days last summer we endured unspeakable devastation. With each attack we emerged more tightly squeezed together, more resilient and determined. We are united by this will to survive and to rebuild our lives. There is a hope now that perhaps last summer's was the final major attack—that never again will the people of Gaza be forced to succumb to such suffering. Hope, but not much faith.

This book illuminates various aspects of the war, drawing on many of the articles I wrote reporting on Israel's occupation. Social media made the difference in this latest attack. Censorship, be it the policy of media corporations or imposed by the individual journalists themselves, is prevalent when it comes to dealing with the state of Israel. But what was once passed off as news is now questioned. The sheer brutality of Israel's attacks was impossible to ignore because of social media. The networks felt compelled to send their reporters. This was an improvement, although the media in Europe and the United States has continued to slant the story. Human voices like Jundia's are rarely aired. Instead talking points issued through Israel's Electronic Hasbara Force, a network of volunteers dedicated to represent the positions of the Israeli government on social media around the world, are repeated ad nauseam. These include Israel's "right to exist as a Jewish-only state" and its "right to defend itself" through pre-emption, which is the ultimate oxymoron.

Israel's security nearly always stands as priority in the media. We hear of the need for the security of Jewish settlers, security of Israeli workers, security of Israeli students, security of Israeli military personnel, security of Israeli police and security of Israeli diplomats—but no one ever addresses the security of millions of Palestinians under constant attack or expelled from ancestral homes and lands well-tended and cherished for millennia, prior to the state of Israeli in 1948. This absence of recognition—or selective ignorance—feeds and reinforces the oppression experienced by millions of Palestinians.

Very few in the mainstream media ever talk about the right of the people of Gaza to defend ourselves, or even just to exist. After all, we're not the ones with the navy, air force, army and nuclear weapons. We haven't set up the checkpoints. We don't bulldoze Israeli homes, take their businesses or imprison their people, including children. We don't build walls around their cities, uproot their crops or withhold their taxes. We don't determine the minimum caloric intake required to survive and then enforce that diet through checklists of prohibited items. We don't prevent Israelis from leaving Israel whenever they want or keep them from going to school. We don't cut off their electricity, bomb their water treatment plants and flood their streets with sewage. We don't withhold shipments of drugs to their hospitals, shoot at their fishermen if they stray beyond an artificial boundary or allow people to die at checkpoints awaiting medical leave. And we certainly don't prevent Israeli husbands and wives from living together because they're in two different parts of the country. We don't do any of these things, they are done to us by Israel. They've been doing it for decades, and that doesn't include the military attacks every 3-5 years.

It's clear that the Palestinian narrative is under-represented in the media and when it is to be found, it is generally as an addendum to a defense of Israel's rights. This tiny nation-state spends enormous sums of money on media spin. The Palestinian Authority attempted, for a long time, to reconcile with Hamas. Upon doing so, they were threatened by

Israel and the United States with the withholding of tax revenues collected by the occupier on their behalf. Most of the time the Authority is near to being broke, hardly able to find the money to pay employee wages let alone counteract the expensive media barrage mounted by the Israelis.

By not providing the full story, it's easy for much of the media to de-humanize Palestinians and therefore control the narrative in favor of the oppressor rather than the oppressed. We are an occupied people. We've been occupied officially since June 6, 1967 and on the receiving end of ethnic cleansing since November 30, 1947. The land set aside to create Israel by the United Nations in November 29, 1947 is one third of what the new nation took by force in the six months leading up to its statehood and the months following. The remaining land was acquired by military conquest in 1967. This usurpation of the land, the occupation, represents the root of this conflict. This isn't about religion and never was. Religion is simply used as a means to segregate by assigning an ethnicity to it.

This occupation is not about religion, biblical history or any of the other excuses used to justify it. It is about water: headwaters, rivers and aquifers. It is about who controls and prospers from natural resources ranging from arable land to the natural gas reservoirs under the West Bank and beneath Gaza's coastal waters. And it is about economic and political power: who has the most clout financially and militarily in the Middle East. That's it. The rest is spin.

The fact is that for over 1,400 years all three faiths—Christians, Muslims, and Jews—coexisted in the Holy Land in relative peace and harmony. Occasionally conflicts erupted, but in most cases these were created by invaders, whether the crusaders of medieval Europe, the Ottomans, the Romans or the Zionists of today. Left to our own devices the different groups in Palestine generally get along fine. And, as history proves, we even like each other!

Social media is changing the narrative of the Israel Palestine conflict from glossed-over, one-sided idealism to multi-faceted, fact-driven truth. Slowly the narrative is shifting from fantasy to reality. I hope this book, too, will assist in that end.

I've written this book as a way of preserving and passing on stories that need to be told. Some are positive narratives, like the reporting of the 4,500 babies born in Gaza during the last assault. Some are more poignant, like the story of young Ahmed, a boy who did not survive the Israeli attacks. He is remembered through his sister Narjes al-Qayed's words and memories. I also seek to honor the steadfast spirit of solidarity between Gaza's Christians and Muslims. The priests and imams opened their churches and mosques for all, regardless of faith. People forget Palestinians are of all religions, including the Jewish faith. Palestine has existed for more than 3,000 years. It is noted in ancient Roman records, within the writings of Hebrew scribes, on historical maps from Europe and Asia. It is written on the tombstones in Old Jerusalem marking the graves of fallen British soldiers pre-1948. To be Palestinian simply means to be from the region of Palestine, which includes parts of modern day Lebanon, Iraq, Jordan, Israel, Egypt and the Occupied Territories. Our race isn't Palestinian. Our race is Arab, though many of us share Caucasian, Asian and/or African backgrounds as well. Our religions, which are not races, include, but are not limited to, Muslim, Jewish, Druz and Christian.

In Gaza, Christians and Muslims live and suffer together. Palestinians of both faiths have seen their schools and places of worship bombed by the Israeli military. Palestinians of both faiths are arrested, starved, humiliated, separated from family, prevented from leaving and killed by the Israeli military and zealous settlers in the West Bank. And Palestinians of both faiths remain united in a spirit of common humanity despite the Israeli narrative and systemic dehumanization.

These are important facts to remember because one of the primary tactics used to prolong the occupation is creating divisions where none exist. These supposed divisions are often at the heart of the support by Western governments for a "two-state solution." Two state. One state. Neither is much of an issue in the Middle East and certainly not much of one in Palestine or Israel. The argument is another layer of lacquer slathered over the issue to make it look like something is being done to end the occupation. But the occupation will end only when it costs Israel more in political and economic capital than it is worth. Forcing Israel to pay that price is the purpose of the Boycott, Divestment and Sanctions (BDS) movement, and the beauty of it is that it takes a legal route that doesn't use guns or kill people to make a point. It is completely non-violent, and as South Africa showed, quite effective.

Speaking personally, I would like to see a single state where equity and tolerance are the only way forward for Israelis and Palestinians. On April 2, 2015 the Pew Research group released a report, *The Future of World Religions: Population Growth Projections, 2010–2050*. By 2050, the study predicts that nearly 80 percent of the world's Jewish population will be in just two countries: Israel and the United States.

It's interesting that even today, in one of those countries, the United States, Palestinians and Israelis, Muslims, Jews and Christians work together, often live in the same neighborhoods, go to the same stores and are sometimes even friends. Each group has its own faith communities, customs and traditions and each group is able to live with the other, absent walls, checkpoints, bombs, laws of segregation and all the other means of oppression deployed against the people of Gaza and the West Bank. It's only in Israel that a state of permanent war exists. This suggests to me that the problem isn't one of race, religion or ethnicity. The problem is policy. Change the policy. Change the dynamic.

Strength lies in mutual peace. If Israel feels threatened by its neighbors it's going to need Palestinians as a mutually respectful partner. If we look back—to just before the intifada of 2000—we see a time when Palestinians and Israelis lived alongside each other in relative peace, with Palestinians employed inside Israel, often staying overnight for their work and returning peacefully to their homes. Such were the days when Palestinians could, at least, earn a wage to feed their families and maintain their homes, before the current situation in which they are forced to rely on the international community for aid, charity and handouts while Israeli is allowed to loot the land, set up closed zones, lock down the borders, and attack at whim. These realities have turned 80 percent of Gaza's Palestinians into refugees, dependent on UN relief agencies. When UN resolutions call again and again for the end to Israel's collective punishment and occupation and Palestine's self-determination, these are blocked by the United States and Israel doubles down on its oppression.

International law has always been in the background, somewhere, gathering dust, when it comes to war crimes and human rights abuse against Palestine. Every war in my relatively short life, so far, has taught me that the reaction of the international community is hopelessly weak when it comes to preventing innocents being killed. Consider the refusal to declare a no-fly zone, like the one that was imposed over Libya in 2011, to defend Palestine from Israeli bombing. I don't see the difference between defending innocents in Libya or in Gaza, especially when UN agencies are there, on the ground, working to provide relief.

I conclude on two positive points: the resilience of Palestinians is intact, despite being constantly hit hard with daily despair and huge unemployment throughout the Gaza Strip. The younger generation do all they can to hold on to their lives and human rights—they attend schools and colleges, and continue to value education highly as a foundation for their future careers, even if very few have been allowed by Israel to leave the Gaza Strip and pursue their dreams. This is the new generation that Israel should be seeking to make peace with, rather than setting up as an enemy.

The second positive point relates to the United States. I can recall my first talks at Harvard and Columbia universities, and in several synagogues across the USA, where most people listened but some came to heckle and shout against the truth being told. This trend is now changing and there is a stronger connection with young Jewish American people. The tide is turning toward justice and equitable peace. I know it is a slow process, and may take years, but it feels right. Change is coming. And that is a good thing.

—Mohammed Omer

When my son screams

We don't even seem to have a right to exist or defend ourselves. That right, according to the United States, belongs to Israel alone.

At just three months old, my son Omar cries, swaddled in his crib. It's dark. The electricity and water are out. My wife frantically tries to comfort him, shield him and assure him as tears stream down her face. This night Omar's lullaby is Israel's rendition of Wagner's *Ride of the Valkyries*, with F-16s forming the ground-pounding percussion, Hellfire missiles leading the wind instruments and drones representing the string section. All around us crashing bombs from Israeli gunships and ground-based mortars complete the symphony, their sound as distinct as the infamous Wagner tubas.

But unlike a performance, this opera of death lasts days. Audience applause is replaced with the terrified cries of babies and children shrouded in smoke. Shrapnel zings off buildings and cars as another missile finds its mark, landing on another home. Six more are now dead. A doctor's house next door was hit by three Israeli F-16 missiles. It's hard to know what the target was. The doctor was killed, joining his mom and dad, killed in the previous war in 2008–09. The air strikes are buzzing in my ears and Lina's. Omar's crying continues. Now the death toll is at 186, with 1,390 injured. The majority of them are civilians, as reported by the UN.

There is no end in sight. Beyond the border we see tanks amassing, preparing for a ground assault. Above, the ever-present *thwup-thwup* of hovering Apache helicopters rocks Omar's cradle through vibration. Warning sirens pierce the night—another incoming missile from an Israeli warship. The border is not far. But we cannot leave. The Gaza Strip has been under siege since 2007. Unlike Israel, we do not have bomb shelters to hide in. The 1.8 million citizens of Gaza, over half of them children under the age of 18, are packed into an area the size of Manhattan, unable to leave. We must stay and pray, pray that we don't get hit.

I've been through this before. I grew up in Gaza. But this is my first time under fire as a parent and husband. It is a wholly different experience. I wish I could airlift my wife and son out of here. But this is my beloved ancestral home; what else can I do? The air strikes are too loud and unending, it seems. In a moment of nervous quiet, Lina breast-feeds Omar and quietly prays.

Crash! Boom! Another air strike smashes into the ground outside our home. Lina darts out of the room, shielding Omar in her arms as she seeks safety on the other side. Omar screams, and screams and screams. It's piercing, enveloping me in a horror only a parent can understand. I find it impossible to comfort him, holding his tiny hand as he lies in my wife's arms. Lina is clasping Omar tight. We nervously jump from room to room scanning the skies for incoming missiles. Israel always claims they are precision. Precision? Then why are so many children, women and elderly injured, maimed or killed by them each time? Why is the hospital bombed? Why schools, bridges, water treatment facilities, greenhouses and other civilian targets? The statistics always tell a different story.

Boom! A flash of white and another crash. The stress is debilitating, fostered by the constant buzz of drones. It haunts us as we search for anywhere safe, but there is nowhere safe. We watch, waiting. Another volley of Hellfire missiles shakes the building. No rest. No sleep, but we are lucky we are still alive.

I open and close the refrigerator door. The electricity is out, but it makes me feel normal. Lina tries to sleep, catches a few minutes and wakes up trembling. This is what it is like to be under attack in Gaza, and we don't know for how long or when it will end.

We talk, looking for distraction, wondering how the Israelis are doing on the other side of the segregation wall. They are free to come and go as they please without restrictions. Do they feel safe, with their warning sirens and bomb shelters to hide in? They don't have to worry about warships pounding their homes, tanks smashing through their streets, bulldozers destroying their homes, jet fighters dropping bombs on their neighborhood or drones hunting them down. Israel has the fourth-most-powerful military in the world, with a full army, navy and air force as well as their Iron Dome, which is quite effective against the homemade rockets lobbed from Gaza. We have no navy, no air force and no army. We have no checkpoints for security. We don't even seem to have a right to exist or defend ourselves. That right, according to the United States, seems reserved for Israel and Israel alone.

Pondering this hypocrisy elevates the cognitive dissonance of the situation to new heights. We're a mere hour's drive from most major cities in Israel, yet we live in a completely different world. Gaza is the Łódź, Kraków and Warsaw ghettos rolled into one. We cannot leave or enter without Israel's permission. Israel tells us what we are allowed to eat, raids at will and often decides which products we're allowed to have, down to toilet paper, sugar and cinderblocks. It arrests our children, fathers and mothers, and can hold them as long as it wants. Its snipers amuse themselves at the expense of our children. How can Israeli society not know what we are suffering or what they're paying to have done to us? Didn't their parents or grandparents go through the same horror before coming to Palestine? Wasn't Zionism created to prevent these horrors from occurring ever again . . . *to any people*?

Shakespeare said it well, with a slight modification: "Hath not an Arab eyes? Hath not an Arab hands, organs, dimensions, senses, affections, passions, fed with the same food, hurt with the same weapons, subject to the same diseases, heal'd by the same means, warm'd and cool'd by the same winter and summer, as a Jew is? If you prick us, do we not bleed? If you tickle us, do we not laugh? If you poison us, do we not die? And if you wrong us, shall we not revenge? If we are like you in the rest, we will resemble you in that."

Despite the desperation, Gaza is my home. Wherever I go, however long I have to wait at checkpoints, to leave or return, sitting under the hot sun or arguing with officials about the abuse of travelers and victims, I feel a deep joy and love when I pass through Rafah gates, for I am home.

I have options, given my Dutch citizenship. As the bombs continue to fall, I ask myself if I should take my family to the Netherlands, where my son was born, press on with my PhD studies at Erasmus Rotterdam and Columbia University and try to forget the F-16s and nightmares Israel reserves for us.

But I'm a journalist, and I owe it to my people and the Israeli people to get to the truth. I choose to stay in Palestine, my beloved home, with my wife, son, mother, father and siblings. I am not willing to let Israel or Zionism exterminate me.

Since 1947 Israel has disrupted our lives. My family and I are the wrong race and wrong religion, so the state doesn't want us here. This is my home and, steadfastly, I will stay. It is my right as a human being and our right as Palestinians or Israelis, whether we're Jewish, Christian or Muslim. Ultimately, we're all human.

Darkness falls on Gaza

Gaza under Israel's onslaught

Ramadan, when night descends, is usually a joyous time. Friends and family gather to break their fast at the *iftar* meal. Not this year.

Nights are the worst. That is when the bombing escalates. Nowhere is safe. Not a mosque. Not a church. Not a school, or even a hospital. All are potential targets.

On Monday, the Israeli military fired artillery rounds at Al-Aqsa hospital in Deir al-Balah, central Gaza, claiming to target a cache of anti-tank missiles. Dr. Khalil Khattab, a surgeon, was operating on a patient when the first shell struck. He ran to the floors below to discover at least four dead and dozens of colleagues—doctors, nurses, orderlies and administrators—injured. The medical staff had become patients.

The Gaza Strip—a little less than half the size of New York City—is home to 1.8 million people, mainly Muslims, with a small Christian minority. Its population is cut off from the world, living under the blockade imposed by Egypt and Israel in 2007. For anyone over the age of seven, this is the third time they've lived through a sustained attack.

In two weeks of bombing and shelling, more than 600 Palestinians have been reported killed. Since the Israeli ground invasion began, 28 Israeli soldiers have died; the conflict has also claimed the lives of two Israeli civilians.

Here in Gaza City, the electricity was gone; it was dark everywhere. The water supply was foul, food was rancid, and fear permeated the summer night.

On Eighth Street, I visited the al-Baba family. For this family of 15, a corrugated tin roof was all that stood between them and the bombs. Hani al-Baba, 23, heard the hum of a drone. Some are for surveillance, some are weaponized. Which is which, one never knows. The sound was enough to send the children scurrying into corners, trembling and praying. Nervously, Hani scanned the night sky.

Israeli strikes have taken out entire families. In a town near Khan Younis on Sunday, more than 20 members of the Abu Jameh family died when their home was hit. For safety, Hani's father split the family into different rooms—a scene played out in nearly every home in Gaza, a grim shell game of family members.

Suddenly, a bomb exploded in the field behind the al-Babas' house: a boom followed by a flash of light. Everyone screamed. The ground shook, the air seemed to implode, sucking the breath from lungs.

Then it was dark again. Why this area was being bombed was unclear. There were no "terrorists," no rockets. It was a neighborhood of families, scared and cowering in the dark.

The long siege has bled the Gaza Strip dry. There is no money for public services; the majority of the population lives in abject poverty. And now at least 120,000 Gazans have been displaced by the fighting, thousands taking temporary shelter in United Nations schools. Many will return to homes damaged or destroyed, with little or no means to rebuild. Cement is especially severely rationed because Israel suspects it is diverted by Hamas to build tunnels for fighters.

At Shifa Hospital, what struck me was the resilience and dignity of the families. Forced to evacuate under gunfire, they had become refugees in their own land. I watched a grandmother who'd fled the east of the city comforting her four grandchildren and two daughters. The family broke their fast with slices of bread, two yogurts, cucumber and tomatoes. This was their *iftar*.

A cease-fire agreement is possible, but all parties need to be at the table; Hamas was not consulted over the one proposed by Egypt last week. Even peace might be possible—if the international community has the courage to engage in dialogue with Hamas. The terms outlined by Hamas for a cease-fire are the same as those the United Nations has called for repeatedly: open the border crossings; let people work, study and build the economy. A population capable of taking care of its own would enhance Israel's security. One that cannot leads to desperation.

In January 2008, barriers along the Gaza–Egypt border were knocked down. Thousands of Gazans poured into Egypt to acquire much-needed supplies. I remember the relief within the Palestinian community. This transient glimpse of freedom was a treat.

A neighbor of mine was simply delighted to drink a Coca-Cola. The freedom to move, fresh food and clean water, and the simple pleasure of sipping a soda, this is what Gazans need: the normal life everyone else takes for granted. During the first days the border was open, Hamas suspended rocket attacks from Gaza. Israeli politicians should take note.

Whatever its official statements, Israel has no interest in destroying Hamas; it seeks merely to weaken and isolate it. Hamas gives Israel an out, a convenient villain, someone to blame. Yet the siege of Gaza serves no purpose other than to radicalize the next generation.

Families like the al-Babas shouldn't have to move their children around the house in the hope that some may survive. Nor should families in Ashdod, over the border in Israel, have to hide in bomb shelters from the militants' rockets.

Without a process that includes all parties at the negotiating table, though, I fear this cycle of violence, punitive and disproportionate as it is, can lead only to an Islamic State in Iraq and Syria-type extremism among the Palestinians. Only the darkest cynic would wish for that.

Our bodies are spent, but our spirit endures

"Unlike international reporters, those of us from Gaza don't simply report," says journalist Mohammed Omer. "We live and die here."

The days flow from one into the next, punctuated by breaking stories, covering one massacre to the next. Each day another home is bombed. Homes with children sleeping inside.

Even soccer isn't safe. A highly accurate Israeli missile obliterates a few young boys watching the World Cup. They'll never know who won.

We are labelled "human shields" by Israel, though no proof has ever been offered supporting this. There isn't any. We're targets to Israel and yet they are the victims.

It is surreal to watch, but a nightmare to live. Each person killed here had a life, feelings and memories. Their death affects parents, children and spouses, none of whom can mourn as they must continue running for their lives in an increasingly shrinking cage. To put this in perspective, the number of people killed in Gaza, given as a percentage of the population, translates to 120,000 Israelis or three million Americans murdered within three weeks. We are an occupied people, who are told what we may eat, where we may go, how to live and even with whom we may associate. We have few choices.

I am one of these people and Gaza is my home.

As a journalist, no horror has affected me more than witnessing a mother nursing her baby killed by an Israeli missile, something my own wife does daily with our four-month-old son. Miraculously, the woman's baby survived, but she died instantly.

I see this, live this and desperately tweet and re-tweet because I am offended, not only as a human, as a Palestinian in Gaza, and as a father, but also as a journalist in Gaza. To get a story, I navigate a sea of body parts and blood each day, much of it the remnants of people I know: my neighbors, friends and community. Unlike international reporters, those of us from Gaza don't simply report. We live and die here.

When global journalists arrive to witness another bloodbath here in Gaza, one can only pray that they are humbled by the blood and the body parts around them that were, just moments before, ordinary people, children, babies trying to exist, live and survive under such degrading, inhumane circumstances. With each report filed, the people of Gaza pray these messengers of news will transfer the truth to the media world outside Gaza and Palestine, without bias or prejudice.

Alas, this rarely happens. Even if the journalist wants to, often the corporations employing them edit out the context, details and facts. The few who have dared to voice disgust or the facts often find themselves reassigned or without jobs the next day. The gulf between reality and perception is then filled by the increasing voices of individuals and citizen journalists via social media. And they are making a difference.

News consumers around the world from New York, London, Paris, Berlin, Sydney, Delhi and Nairobi, it is time to question what you read; do not accept what you are seeing. Push, question, cross-reference. 140 characters is a start, but not the truth.

I scribble my notes as fast as I can, collect my interviews, verify with official sources and run to the laptop to type and condense my ideas before the power cuts out. The stress is always "Will I make it before the power outage so I can file the story?" On some of the best days, I have just two hours or less of electricity. I was in darkness the last nine days of the war. And yes, there is a deadline on dying too! If I am lucky, I'll catch one or two hours of sleep before I have to begin reporting again. This war is more than blood; it's psychological and emotional torture, expertly designed to strike an already marginalized group and reduce us to less than human.

There are differences between local and international journalism. The local variety needs no wider context, just the images of the human carnage and desperation is enough. We know the context and history. We live it. International media needs to answer more questions and add historical context. Accuracy and truth are vital. I see an UNRWA school used as a refugee shelter being hit, but I will ask people affected by those circumstances for their story on the American-supplied Israeli F-16s, drones, Apache helicopters, Israeli tanks, cruise missiles, naval warships and mortar shells. Yes, where the weapons come from needs to be stated. US media reports Israeli claims that Iran supplies Gaza with weapons, but never mentions who supplies Israel. In Gaza, we're still looking for those Iranian weapons that Israel says we have. What Gaza factions have are small weapons and homemade rockets. What the Israelis have is state-of-the-art American military equipment.

During 2011, I covered the Arab Spring from Cairo and the Sinai. Gaza is different. It is my home, the place where I was born, where I have my family, relatives, friends and some colleagues. This is where my grandmother lives—where my cousins and uncles also live—from far north in Jabaliya to far south in Rafah.

I am associated with many places—at different levels—in Rafah, from personal to professional and casual acquaintances. I try to listen more than talk, except to ask questions, and commit myself to serious journalism. During the last four weeks of Israel's most recent brutal attacks, it has been difficult to suppress my emotions, a tough task for any compassionate human.

Ironically, Israel's butchery at UNRWA's Abu Hussein School triggered me to be more professional because the facts speak for themselves and the images of the facts are all the world really needs to read and see in order to stand up and make things better than this ominous reality.

Writing about the school, I had to suppress the memories of my childhood—memories of being at the school, next to my grandmother's house in first grade, before fleeing to Rafah. Still, the images of my first teacher—Yasser—flash in my head when I see dead bodies. I am 30 years old now, but I was seven in that playground where the Israeli tank shell hit.

Likewise, at Islamic University, I felt the excitement of early adulthood, diving into my education to escape the memories of sadness among the ashes of Rafah refugee camp to reach the comparative beauty of Gaza City. This was huge for me. In the taller buildings of the city, I felt free after being trapped in Rafah.

But the air was sucked out of my lungs when I had to break the news live to CNN this week that Israel had bombed my wonderful university, the place of my education, the classroom where I had my linguistics exam after which I spent hours at an Israeli checkpoint returning home. This was not easy, and it's hard to see the hypocrisy and injustice of the world as CNN invites Israeli officials to present their justifications for hitting a university, a seat of learning.

I could choose to be blind to keep my sanity, but I prefer the dedication to the facts and truth, as insane as it is, seeing the ruins of homes and desperation on the faces of fishermen, farmers, doctors and teachers. I feel nothing should be left out, from the dust on a mother's face to the tears of fear in children's eyes to neighbors trying to make homes from rubble. Call me biased, but Gaza is my home, so I'll take that as a compliment and carry on.

Silent fear in Gaza

Operation Protective Edge began early on Monday. Since then at least 49 have been killed and 310 injured, with numbers still rising.

GAZA CITY—It is still early in the holy month of Ramadan, a time of reflection, of making amends and of fasting, abstaining from food and drink during daylight hours. Normally, the residents of Gaza look forward to the muezzin calls for prayer signaling the last prayer before eating can commence. The first taste inevitably that of sweet dates and sips of water. But not this Ramadan, not now.

Windows shake violently, reverberating as F-16 missiles crash into the ground, peppering surroundings with shrapnel and earth in a nearby field. Babies scream, dogs bark and pandemonium ensues. The streets are empty of traffic. Anything that moves becomes a target. Above, Israeli F-16s screech through the air accompanied by the banal hum of drones hovering overheard. Nowhere is safe and there is no way to get out.

Operation Protective Edge, as Israel has called it, began early on Monday with Israeli fighters delivering the first blow in the form of air strikes on ten sites within the Gaza Strip. Tensions remained high following weekend clashes between Israeli police and demonstrators in Jerusalem, East Jerusalem and Arab towns throughout northern Israel. Gaza's International Airport, built 14 years ago with funds from donor groups, has been targeted six times as of this writing.

In Gaza, Israeli bombs were answered with crude homemade rockets propelled into Israel by the resistance in a seemingly endless war of one-upmanship.

Caught in the crossfire are the civilians of Gaza and southern Israel.

Drones, missiles, tanks, helicopters, ground troops and night raids are near weekly events in the Gaza Strip. Calls for retaliation within and outside of Gaza are mounting. The coming days are likely to witness more violence.

The number of people killed is in steady increase—now there have been 49 killed, 310 injured and 64 houses have been demolished. Interior ministry spokesperson Iyad al-Bizm says 192 of those injured are children and women. The numbers are changing every minute. The Interior ministry says 510 air strikes were carried out on Gaza in the past two days but this is constantly rising and air strikes are heard every few minutes across the Gaza Strip.

Economically, Gaza is already suffering. With up to 42,000 employees of the former Hamas de facto authority without pay for months, living conditions have deteriorated. Even basics, like food and water, are unaffordable without a paycheck. The lack of money for government employees affects the rest of the economy—stores, farmers, suppliers, service providers and anyone who relies on the income of others for their own income. Officials estimate more than 250,000 are being affected. Likewise, the shutting down of banks has meant tens of thousands of Palestinian Authority employees are unable to get their monthly wage. With renewed air strikes and the potential for a ground invasion looming, those who still have money are stocking whatever they can find in the markets. Everything from dried milk to lentils and macaroni is being bought up in a hurry but even these simple staples are luxuries for many.

Wael Attia, Egyptian Ambassador to Ramallah, says his country is trying to mediate a cease-fire. So far, neither Israeli military nor Palestinian resistance groups seem willing to pursue a truce. Abu Obaida, spokesman for Hamas' military wing, Izz al-Din al-Qassam Brigades, explains: "We can't stay silent while watching crimes committed in Gaza and West Bank."

Hamas leader Ismail al-Ashqar also relates an aversion to a cessation of hostilities: "Resistance will not give truce, and will not stop till occupation pledge to: stop aggression, lift the siege on Gaza, and release all prisoners released in prisoner exchange deal," he says.

Ashqar insists the resistance is "able to hit beyond Tel Aviv."

At Gaza's Shifa Hospital there lies a Palestinian child named Kenan Hamad that was the victim of a shrapnel injury. When asked what had happened to him, he said: "My cousin brought me to this hospital when a bomb hit the house."

When asked where his mom and dad were, he replied, "They are home." He is still living with the impression that his mom and dad are still there, but in fact his family were buried today.

The Israeli Military has suggested a ground operation may be imminent and troops as well as weapons have been seen assembling on the border of the Strip. On Wednesday morning, Israel's navy joined the battle and began shelling Gaza from the sea.

The Health Ministry in Gaza announced that Gaza hospitals have a shortage of medicines and 25 percent of medical supplies are currently not in stock. Dr. Ashraf al-Qidra, a spokesman for the Health Ministry, urged the international community to respond to the needs of Gaza.

The ministry called on Egypt to open Rafah crossing in order to allow urgent medical cases access to outside hospitals. Rafah crossing has been largely closed over the past months.

Rafah open, but crossings slow, selective

Egypt has opened the Rafah crossing, but local officials say the process is slow, unsatisfactory as some of those wounded wait for over 24 hours

GAZA CITY—The hostile relationship between Egypt and Hamas is unlikely to make Egypt broker a cease-fire or offer much in terms of facilitation. Egypt opened the Rafah border crossing, largely closed since Morsi was ousted, to allow injured civilians through from Gaza. Egyptian President Abdel Fattah al-Sisi made the decision after the United Nations asked Egypt to reopen the border.

However, there are caveats: the crossing is only open for Egyptian nationals—meaning those whose parents are both Egyptian citizens—living in Gaza, injured Palestinians and medical supplies, according to Palestinian Border Control officials and Egyptian authorities.

It seems that even the injured are having trouble getting through: on Thursday, Egyptian authorities only allowed in "a few" injured people and three buses of Egyptian nationals, according to Maher Abu Sabha, Director General of Gaza crossings.

Late Thursday, a group of ten Gazans, injured Wednesday evening in a Khan Younis beachfront café while watching the Netherlands vs. Argentina World Cup game, still waited for ambulances to transport them through the crossing. Not all ambulances with injured people went through on Thursday, said an official at the Rafah crossing Operation Room who preferred to remain anonymous.

Meanwhile, the Palestinian Interior Ministry says thousands of others are registered to travel, but are not being allowed through the supposedly "open" border.

On Wednesday, despite uneasy relationships between Hamas and Egypt, Foreign Ministry Spokesman Badr Abdel Aaty expressed Egypt's concern over the escalation of violence in Gaza.

In a press release, Abdel Aaty called on both sides to show more restraint and refrain from further violence. He warned against complicating the situation, which he said would make a return to negotiations difficult.

In previous wars, Egypt played an important role in mediating cease-fires between Israel and the Palestinian resistance, an influence that has seemed to taper since al-Sisi came to power.

According to a source within Hamas, Abdel Aaty's message was received as "a warning that Israel would wipe parts of Gaza off the map."

"This is not the message that Hamas was waiting for," the source said. "Egypt has been brokering previous cease-fires—they should have made sure to pressure Israel to release all prisoners in the October 2012 prisoner exchange deal."

The Egyptian government has accused Hamas of aiding militants to cause riots in Sinai, an allegation that Hamas has refused. Many of the tunnels, which were once a main source of revenue for the de facto government, have been destroyed.

In 2011, Egypt took credit for brokering the prisoner exchange in which 1,027 Palestinian prisoners were released in return for Israeli soldier Gilad Shalit, who had spent five years as a captive.

During the recent Israeli bombing of Gaza, the border crossing at Rafah has been mostly void of any security personnel or staff members. At night, the Rafah border is a no-reach area.

Even in the daytime, the crossing can be a foreboding place for those trying to cross, said Abed Afifi, a cameraman shooting footage at the Rafah crossing said on Thursday.

"Israeli drones are hovering overhead and Israeli tanks continuously shell nearby," Afifi said.

Hundreds of foreign passport holders with Palestinian origins stood at the gate of Rafah in hopes that they could evacuate Gaza. They left when Egypt announced the border was closed again. Thousands of students and workers from abroad with nearly expired residence permits are also stuck in Gaza.

Usually, Rafah is open once every two weeks to allow people to travel through for Umrah (pilgrimage) into Saudi Arabia. This came after the Saudi government put pressure on Egypt not to ban those doing Umrah or Hajj.

Among those transferred Thursday morning was Mohsen Kaware, who sustained critical spinal injuries after an Israeli missile hit his house in Khan Younis, one of the first attacks since the escalation of violence that started on Monday. The air strike killed at least seven people and injured 20 more civilians.

Hamas political chief Khaled Meshaal appeared on Al Jazeera on Wednesday saying that he is seeking help from Arab nations, most importantly the Egyptian armed forces.

"We are waiting for Egypt's great army [to respond]," Meshaal said.

Meanwhile, Abu Sabha of the border crossings said that he has not been informed by Egypt if the border will be open again Friday for the thousands stuck in the coastal enclave.

As civilian death toll rises in Gaza, Hamas sees growing local support

The more Israel strikes Gaza, the more Hamas regains popularity amongst locals despite increasing attacks that they say target civilians

GAZA CITY—Deep below the ground, scattered in hideouts and out of sight, most of Hamas' leadership is in a familiar survival mode, trying to make it difficult for Israeli air strikes to target them.

Aboveground, however, Israeli forces have continued to target their homes and families with F-16 missiles—and regularly, locals say, hit the wrong targets and instead hit entire families that have nothing to do with the group.

Yet despite the rising death toll and destruction across Gaza, there was a general feeling here on Friday that the more Israel pounds the Strip, the more popular Hamas becomes, a turnaround for the organization whose popularity has taken a nosedive during its seven-year governance of Gaza.

"In the past, we used to put the responsibility of the siege that we are suffering from on Hamas due to their policies in governing Gaza," said Mofeed Abu Shamala, editor in chief of Gaza's *Al Mujtama* newspaper. "But during the Israeli aggression, we think highly of Hamas and I feel they start to get more popular among the population."

On Friday, Israeli F-16s and rockets continued to torment the Gaza Strip, killing 105 Palestinians, injuring at least 750 and turning more than

200 homes to rubble, leaving thousands of men, women and children homeless, their possessions destroyed and lives in tatters.

Israeli authorities say they have launched 1,100 air strikes—or one air strike every 4.5 minutes—since Israel's most recent offensive began on Tuesday. Meanwhile, an estimated 460 retaliatory rockets and mortars have been fired from Gaza in the last four days, with dozens intercepted by Israel's Iron Dome defense system.

In Gaza, locals are apprehensive about a potential ground invasion, an option Israeli leaders have said they are considering, and one which has seen 33,000 army reservists called up in preparation.

Across the electrified segregation fence separating Israel and Gaza, Israeli tanks have been gathering at the border for days.

Targeting civilians

The majority of Gazans expressed shock on Friday at the intensity of Israeli air strikes and the frequency of attacks carried out on family homes. Israeli forces, they say, are intentionally targeting civilians.

As of 2 pm GMT on Thursday, when the death toll was 94, the UN Office for Coordination of Humanitarian Affairs said 77 percent of those killed in Gaza were civilians, including 11 women and 21 children.

Early Friday morning, Palestinian physician Anas Abuelkas was killed when his home was targeted around 3:30 am (1:30 am GMT) by three Israeli F-16 missiles. While he slept, his body was split into small, scattered pieces around his apartment.

The doctor's killing triggered anger in his Tal el Hawa area in Gaza City. Neighbors say he was not affiliated with any political party and was a dedicated, serious medical practitioner. The location of his home provided no further clues for residents: his apartment was next to Farha, an association that provides loans to young Gazan couples who are struggling financially to marry.

Mahmoud al-Najjar, a resident in Khan Younis, was in shock as he and others collected the remains of eight members of the al-Hajj family who were killed in an air strike late Thursday that also took the lives of several neighbors.

"How can Israelis claim they are not targeting civilians?" Al-Najjar said. "If Israel means to stop rockets attacks, why are they attacking people sleeping in their homes?"

"It haunts me"

Sharif Mustafa, a 36-year-old civil servant and father of three, says his neighbors in Rafah, the Ghannam family, were surely the wrong target.

Israeli forces must have meant to hit the house of Jihad Ghannam—a member of Islamic Jihad—but instead hit his cousins while they were asleep, Mustafa said.

"[They are] a very poor and peaceful family, who don't interfere in the life of others," he said.

"But did Israel really care who was targeted or killed?" he wondered aloud.

The entire neighborhood of Yebna, an area in Rafah that was one of the hardest hit locations this week, reeled in shock on Friday at the damage done to the Ghannam family's home.

An impromptu rescue team of residents searched through the family's four-story home, now a pile of rubble, looking for the bodies of their neighbors.

As 20-year-old Kifah Shihada Dib Ghannam's burned body was carried from the debris, neighbors standing behind Mustafa wept when they saw the young mother with whom they had been praying on Thursday evening.

The body of seven-year-old Ghalia Ghannam was also discovered in the rubble as Mustafa looked on.

"I would never imagine that my children would be among those children," he said.

"I just feel that this is one of my children and it haunts me."

An unidentified older woman, also killed in the attack, took the worst hit, neighbors said. Her body was taken to the hospital completely burned, triggering a call from a local human rights group for an investigation into the weapons that Israel is using.

During Operation Cast Lead, Israel's attack on Gaza in late 2008 and early 2009, international doctors in Gaza's hospitals noted that the bodies showed signs of unusual symptoms, attributed to Israel's use of experimental DIME (Dense Inert Metal Explosives), flechette weapons and white phosphorous.

"Rockets have chemicals and poisonous materials, and it's vital for international groups to come and examine the evidence," said Mohammed al-Jamal of the Palestinian Human Rights Defenders network.

One major difference between Israel's current offensive on Gaza and others in 2008 and 2012, al-Jamal said, are this week's timing of Israel's bombings at night, which he said are meant to maximize the number of casualties.

Several Gazans have told the *Middle East Eye* that air strikes this week have seemed to increase in frequency during *iftar*, the evening meal during Ramadan that breaks one's fast. With electricity often cut off across most of Gaza after 10 pm, it means that many of the worst strikes come while Gazans are in darkness.

"Targeting civilians merits war crimes, where all signatories to the Geneva Conventions must take action immediately," al-Jamal told *MEE*.

Cease-fire talks

On Thursday, US President Obama and Israeli Prime Minister Netanyahu talked by phone for the first time since the offensive began on Tuesday. Obama offered to facilitate cease-fire negotiations between Israel and Hamas.

Whether the US will have direct contact with Hamas remains to be seen. Qatar and Turkey are likely to mediate, analysts say.

Hamas has accused Israel of reneging on the terms of the 2012 cease-fire, which was brokered by President Morsi of Egypt.

Speaking for the first time since the offensive started, Mahmoud Zahar, Hamas' senior political leader, said in a recorded statement on Friday that was broadcast by Hamas' Al-Aqsa Satellite Channel that Hamas is not afraid of Israel's threats and its aggression will fail. Zahar alluded to the fact that Israel would have to make amends for the broken cease-fire agreement:

"Israel started the war, and we will be the one preparing the document which Israel will have to sign," Zahar said.

Although a White House statement released earlier this week expressed concern about the escalating attacks, many Gazans say they believe the American position is biased and will be watching closely to see how serious the US is about brokering an end to violence in the blockaded Strip.

Palestinian children killed in Israel strikes

At least 13 Palestinian children have been killed in Israeli air strikes so far

RAFAH, GAZA STRIP—Umm Fadi, the mother of three daughters and a son, is trying the best she can to comfort her children. But her nine-year-old, Raghd, is in tears all night, an Israeli air strikes continue to hit the besieged Gaza Strip.

"It's hard to explain politics to children—they hear from other neighborhood children that it's Israel bombing Gaza again, but still I can't give them an answer as to why," Umm Fadi, who lives in Tal al-Sultan with her husband and children, told Al Jazeera.

On Thursday, an Israeli air strike killed seven Palestinian civilians, including five children, in the largest death toll from a single attack since the start of the three-day offensive, the Palestinian Health Ministry said.

The Gaza Health Ministry estimates that 32 Palestinians have been killed and more than 230 others injured in several hundred Israeli air strikes on the Gaza Strip since Israel's latest military offensive began. An additional 64 Palestinian houses have been completely destroyed.

"I am afraid myself, and my children come to hide in my bedroom. How can I possibly show them that I am not afraid?" Umm Fadi said, explaining that she doesn't leave her home, not even to run daily errands, for fear of being injured or killed.

According to Defence for Children International Palestine, at least eight Palestinian children have been killed in Israeli bombings, and dozens of others have been wounded as of Wednesday. Six children were killed in a single air strike alone, the group reported, when an Israeli bomb landed on the home of Odeh Ahmad Mohammad Kaware, an alleged Hamas activist, in Khan Younis in southern Gaza.

"Yesterday, in order to destroy a house which is not a military target, six children died," said Eyad Abu Eqtaish, DCI Palestine's accountability program director. "It's the role of the international community to apply pressure on Israel to meet its obligations under the Geneva Conventions."

"It's clear that Israel is indiscriminately targeting the Gaza Strip and this is clear by the big numbers of Palestinian civilians, among them children, who were affected," Abu Eqtaish told Al Jazeera.

In a statement released on Tuesday, Israeli Prime Minister Benjamin Netanyahu denied allegations that Israel is targeting Palestinian civilians. "Israel targets Hamas terrorists and not innocent civilians. By contrast, Hamas targets Israeli civilians while hiding behind Palestinian civilians. Hamas, therefore, bears full responsibility for any harm that comes to Israeli and Palestinian civilians alike."

According to Palestinian doctor Ahmed Abu Tawahinah, Palestinian children in Gaza suffer from extreme stress as a result of the violence, and often need a lot of support to deal with post-traumatic stress disorder.

"Trauma is a term which they have used in the West when they were talking about normal situations and there is a breakdown. This breakdown is the trauma, but for us Palestinians, trauma is the daily life," Abu Tawahinah told Al Jazeera.

"The term trauma itself is not enough to describe what is going on in Gaza. I am not convinced we expressed the horror."

Thirty-three Palestinian children were killed during Israel's last major military offensive in Gaza, DCI Palestine reported, while 353 children were killed and another 860 were injured during Israel's three-week operation in 2008–09, dubbed Operation Cast Lead.

Two months after the November 2012 campaign, the United Nations' agency for Palestinian refugees (UNRWA) found that the PTSD rate rose by 100 percent, and that 42 percent of patients were under the age of nine. UNICEF also reported that 91 percent of children surveyed in Gaza had trouble sleeping, 85 percent couldn't concentrate and 82 percent reported feelings of anger and symptoms of mental strain.

"Children do not have the capacity to cope with these difficult circumstances. Parents and family members provide as much support as possible for their children, to calm them down and to decrease their fear," said Hussam Elnounou of the Gaza Community Mental Health Programme, which is operating a 24-hour psychological support hotline for Palestinians in Gaza.

Elnounou told Al Jazeera that traumatized children often develop psychological problems, which can include clinging to their parents, wetting their beds and fear of loud noises, as a result of the Israeli bombings.

"Gaza is under continuous siege. . . . The situation is already very bad, politically, economically and socially. This war is adding oil to the fire."

In Rafah, Umm Fadi told Al Jazeera that her daughters have started to wet their beds, something that also happened during the Israeli military operation in November 2012. "Now trauma is living in us again. Even closing the door of the fridge can scare my daughters."

Food and water shortages hit Gaza hard as prices spiral

Anticipating harder days ahead, Gazans rack up credit on what little food they can find, shopkeepers lament that their limited resources are rotting on the shelves

As the war on Gaza continues, various aspects of life are becoming deeply impacted. People's freedom of mobility is seriously reduced and everyday necessities, including water, basic food stuffs and fresh fruits and vegetables, are becoming more inaccessible and unaffordable.

"The streets of Gaza remain mostly empty and almost all shops are closed," the UN's Office for Humanitarian affairs warned in an emergency report released Friday.

Osama al-Jarwsha, a noticeably slim 21-year-old, is one of the very last shop owners to have kept his doors open in the face of the Israeli aerial onslaught. His vegetable shop lies on a street that was until recently one of the busiest parts of Gaza City, where he caters to at least 30 residential towers housing hundreds of families.

On an average day, he sells hundreds of shekels worth of vegetables, but in the last few days, his shop has been all but deserted, despite the fact that Jarwsha is the only vegetable vendor on the street.

"We are in a war—people are frightened to step outside to do grocery shopping," Jarwsha told the *Middle East Eye*.

Abu Fouad, a 51-year-old working as taxi driver, is one of the few brave shoppers to come in to Jarwsha's store. But, as father of six sons, he says that sitting at home with so many hungry mouths is just not an option.

"I want to get anything I can get from lentils to whatever is left so that we can have a meal," says Fouad.

He says he's lucky it's Ramadan as this means he only needs to get enough for one family meal. At other times he would need the usual three meals.

"Whatever it is, the prices are now outrageous, and I no longer get the fresh cucumbers that are planted a few hundred meters from here," he told *MEE*.

Behind him there are several agricultural houses, but with Israeli drones and jets it requires an iron will to go out into the open and pick what might be right in front of your nose.

Infecting the whole chain

And it is not just shoppers and shopkeepers who are feeling the pain. Almost the whole agricultural industry and supply chain have been broken by the ongoing hostilities. From the farmers whose land and produce is being bombed by Israel, to the customers who hesitate to shop, and the tens of thousands of Hamas/Palestinian Authority employees who are still waiting to be paid for months of work, everyone is having a hard time paying their bills and buying food and gas.

As the constant barrage of Israeli F-16 cruise missiles continues, the banks remain closed.

During Israeli wars against Palestinians, most Palestinian banks and official organizations remain shut, which means a total halt to family activities. This is what Gaza economists see as a deliberate obstacle laid down to sabotage Gaza's economy and public services, and to disrupt family routines.

"The Ramadan and Eid season is already dying, as our market usually relies on seasonal goods that are needed by the population," says Maher Tabaa, a Gaza economist and public affairs officer at the Palestinian Chamber of Commerce.

Tabaa believes that even if the border crossings into Israel or Egypt are opened soon, many perishable foodstuffs, such as dairy products, will be expired by the time they arrive at the markets.

Another vital product that relies on daily bank transfers is fuel. "If there is no transfer, then no fuel will come," says Tabaa. "If that leads to something, then it leads to a further recession of the Palestinian economy."

A businessman dealing with Israeli merchants who wished to remain anonymous said: "We are not in the luxurious position to order from Israeli merchants without payments."

"Without payment, there are no supplies coming through, meaning that my ability to import basic products, like milk, is jeopardized."

"Israeli service providers don't care about wars. They want payment in advance before they deliver. If milk for our children runs out in the coming days, we will have more of a crisis," he adds.

Runaway inflation

After days of bombardment, all products are now scarce in Gaza. Farmers dare not harvest their crops for fear of being targeted by Israeli missiles, which are ravaging large swaths of agricultural land as well as urban residential areas.

The Interior Ministry announced that damage was estimated at around $2.5m in Gaza's agricultural sector alone, but the worst may be yet to come. Back in 2012, when Israel launched what by all accounts was a smaller action than the current Operation Protective Edge, some $20m worth of damage was inflicted on Gaza's farmland, according to the Palestinian Agricultural Relief Committees.

Jarwsha says scarcity has pushed up prices in just a few days, wreaking havoc on a civilian population that was already hard-hit by unemployment, which creeped up toward 40 percent in February.

"Even those who can afford something find the price increase expensive," says Jarwsha.

"Prior to the war, seven kilos of potatoes cost 10 shekels ($3). Now it's four kilos for the same price. Onions were eight kilos for 10 shekels ($3), now it's down to five kilos," he says.

After power outages and being forced to close for a few days, the produce on Jarwsha's shelves is now starting to go bad. He had stockpiled before the crisis, but with few customers and limited refrigeration capacity, not to mention long power outages that make refrigeration even harder, his extra supplies are also on the verge of spoiling.

Some of his customers are willing to risk their lives by coming to the shop, but many have to ask for credit due to lack of funds. His debt book is now full of the names of customers who have promised to pay him back. Jarwsha estimates he is owed tens of thousands of shekels (thousands of US dollars), and is unsure how much of it he will receive.

Other sellers, however, are taking a different approach. 25-year-old Hamza al-Baba, who runs a butcher's shop in Gaza, says he is trying to sell everything as fast as he can, even if many of his customers are unable to pay.

"Selling meat now, even on credit, is better than having it rot when refrigerators are off," says Baba, while explaining that he's scared of working and opening up his shop.

All shopkeepers are worried that they too may become a target for Israeli strikes, which have so far killed more than 120 Palestinians in Gaza since Monday and show no sign of abating.

But Baba says his troubles started long before Israel decided to start its latest aerial attacks early on Monday.

"This recession has affected us. After all, not many people are buying meat anymore. They use chicken-flavored stock instead," he says.

Some in Gaza have developed the habit of walking around during the last bit of daylight—just an hour before *iftar*—to buy whatever fresh fruit and vegetables they can. With Israel's F-16's targeting private and public transport, however, most of those who don't live within walking distance are choosing to stay at home rather than take their chances.

Baba believes that this has left most people using canned foods and preserves to survive. The lucky few who have money are holding on to it, and relying on credit as best they can, in case the situation gets even worse and Israel's collective punishment of Gaza intensifies further.

"There are worse days ahead, and they're saving whatever they can for that," Baba says.

Israeli jets destroying Gaza water and sewage systems: officials

Health crisis looming an Israeli attacks accused of targeting already fragile water and sewage infrastructure

Israel's Gaza offensive, which by its sixth day has claimed at least 145 lives, including 28 children and has injured as many as 1,000 people, threatens to bring an even deeper humanitarian disaster to the area, with vital water and sewage systems being destroyed by Israeli air strikes.

Palestinian officials on Saturday claimed that the Israelis had targeted water wells in different parts of Gaza City, leaving thousands of families without access to clean drinking water. An Oxfam official said going into the weekend that 90 percent of the water in Gaza was already unsafe to drink.

The sewage system is also a target, with Israeli warplanes targeting sewage treatment stations in West Gaza City early on Saturday. The areas most affected are Shati refugee camp, Tal al-Hawa, Sheikh Ejleen and most western districts, according to Saed al-Din Atbash, head of water facilities at Gaza Municipality.

Atbash told reporters in Gaza City that Israel is deliberately targeting the wells.

"Warplanes have targeted two wells directly, one near al-Maqwsi area [a densely populated area with residential tower blocks] and another in al-Zaytoun, both used by 7,000 inhabitants," he said.

Israeli warplanes have also targeted five water pipelines that supply large numbers of Gazans. With each line providing water to 20,000 inhabitants, as many as 100,000 people could be affected by the attacks.

The latest damage to vital infrastructure is further straining the Palestinian health system, and the World Health Organization has already appealed for $60m to help prevent its collapse. Gaza Municipality estimates the damage to each of the water wells at $150,000. The cost to the civilian population could well be higher, forcing families to try and stockpile expensive and scarce drinking water.

"Services are now struggling to cope and the insecurity is making it difficult to deliver aid," Oxfam country director Nishant Pandey said last week, as *Christian Today* reported on Friday.

Oxfam's partners have had to suspend efforts to chlorinate water supplies in Gaza because of the ongoing violence, despite 90 percent of water in Gaza already considered unsafe to drink. Surviving infrastructure faces another threat: Oxfam fears that water pumps and sewage plants could stop functioning within days because of severe shortages of fuel.

Shati refugee camp, in northern Gaza, is among the worst affected areas. Home to Ismail Haniyeh, who until last month exercised prime ministerial authority in Gaza, the camp is seen as a valuable target and has been hit at least once by Israeli F-16s, local eyewitnesses said.

Atbash said repairs to the water line will require a period of calm, and until then about 70,000 residents will be deprived of water in the refugee camp.

Gaza Municipality sees the Israeli attacks on the water and sewage systems as "collective punishment" of the Palestinian people.

"Under international law, the targeting of civilian water supplies is classified as a war crime," Atbash said. "The Israeli occupation's fighter jets targeted a sewage station holding 25,000 cubic meters of untreated sewage, pumped in from four areas daily."

The latest attacks are exacerbating an already critical sewage situation. The *New York Times* reported last year that 13 sewage stations in the Gaza Strip were either overflowing or were close to overflowing, and 3.5 million cubic feet of raw sewage was finding its way to the Mediterranean Sea on a daily basis.

Atbash appealed to the international community to urge Israel to stop targeting water and sewage facilities, saying that all occupied civilians have a legal and human right to clean water, sanitation and hygiene.

"We are constantly working to improve municipal water facilities for citizens in Gaza. The Israeli occupation is deliberately destroying the water wells in order to increase the human suffering during the hot summer season," he said.

As anywhere else, consumption of water in Gaza increases in the summer, but power outages due to Israel's destruction of electrical systems have forced water pumps used by families to be shut down.

"We often don't have access to both water and electricity in the same hour," said Umm Ramzy, a mother of seven children who daily has to confront the fact that occasional drips from the water tap will not take care of family needs or domestic chores.

The Gaza Strip needs on average 180 million cubic meters of water annually, while the capacity of the local aquifers is no more than 80 cubic meters per year. To handle the shortage, the municipal water supply is cut at certain times and distributed to different areas according to population density, which Umm Ramzy finds difficult to live with.

"When I wash I need water, when I cook I need water, when we are thirsty we need water, when my children use the toilet they need water," she said.

One of her children announces that there is no water to flush the toilet for the second day. If this situation continues, Gaza residents will be subjected to a humanitarian crisis worse than the immediate one of trying to survive under Israel's air strikes. In some areas, a few trucks are distributing limited water to families, but for drinking only, not for anything else, said residents of Shati refugee camp.

"We never think of taking a shower," Umm Ramzy told the *Middle East Eye*. "That's a luxury right now." Gaza's summer can be unbearably hot, where families find it difficult to cope with daily life. With war, it certainly makes it worse than before.

The World Bank has plans to improve the situation through the proposed $43m North Gaza Emergency Sewage Treatment Project, which according to the World Bank "aims to (a) mitigate the immediate and impending health, environmental and safety threats to the communities surrounding the poorly treated and rapidly growing sewage lake in the Beit Lahia area of northern Gaza; and to (b) contribute to the provision of a satisfactory long-term solution for the treatment of wastewater in the Northern Gaza Governorate."

However, no funding has yet been committed to the project, and with everything in Gaza on hold while the Israeli military operation continues, it looks as though things are set to get worse, before they get better.

A family struggles to keep hope alive in Gaza

The Zurik family, like many others in Gaza, has not slept for days as bombs and missiles fly past their home

GAZA CITY—"I am so scared that this bombing is going to hit me," says 11-year-old Deena Zurik, who can no longer bear to stay in her own bed and runs over to her mom and dad.

It is 4 am here, on the sixth day of Israel's war, and Deena Zurik is supposed to be asleep. But Israeli F-16s have just bombed the police headquarters with seven missiles, which were followed by four missiles fired at the Ansar security compound, and the noise has shaken the 11-story building where she lives with her parents and five brothers and sisters.

She hasn't gone to bed before sunrise for the last few days, as the bombing is always worse at night.

"I am always afraid to sleep alone. The missile shakes the room," says Deena as she tugs at her pink and orange dress.

Even when she does sleep, Deena says, "I dream of them bombing and I am back from school, with nowhere to hide."

It's not only the shaking and rattling that reminds her of the bombs. Looking outside at what was once her neighborhood brings traumatic memories. More than once in recent days, Deena has seen a house on her street bombed and people with severe injuries being pulled from the rubble.

Deena and her brothers and sisters cannot go outside to play anymore and even the television does not provide reprieve from the conflict. While not long ago she watched Touor al-Jannah, a popular children's channel in the Middle East, the television now only shows the news, where she sees images of children like her being brought to hospitals bleeding, injured or worse.

Her parents, just like countless others across Gaza, cannot bear to switch off the news as they desperately try and find out what is going on around them.

"All my friends in the building and school only talk about the bombing and what they see on TV," says Deena.

Nor is there any indication that Deena will sleep any better tonight. Gaza is about to enter the seventh day of air strikes, which have already killed more than 167 people in Gaza and left some 1,200 injured. According to the United Nations, the majority of these have been civilians, with women and children also getting caught in the fire.

Bomb strike

When an air strike hits nearby, Deena immediately runs into her mom and dad's arms. She and her younger sister, Ala, who both like pink and wear the same dresses, cling to their mother, hugging her legs tight. But while their mother Lina puts on a brave face, she, too, is terrified of the bombs.

"I am afraid myself, but I have to pretend I am not and try to comfort them," says Lina. "It's more shocking when I wake up to missiles shaking the building."

Since Israel withdrew its troops from Gaza in 2005, Lina has seen her fair share of Israeli military operations against the Strip. She's lived through Summer Rains, Autumn Clouds, Hot Winter, Cast Lead, Returning Echo, Pillar of Defence and now Protective Edge, and while she says that the sense of community these campaigns of collective punishment create has helped her deal with the stress, she can never fully desensitize herself.

As a school teacher, she is also accustomed to dealing with children's trauma on a daily basis, but when it's her own children, she admits to feeling helpless, especially when she sees her children climb under beds for protection or hide under blankets.

Lina and her husband, Loai, know that none of these methods will save them from the Israeli missiles if they strike, but they say they feel the need to keep the illusion of security alive for their children. Loai says that he finds the whole situation extremely hard, and says that it is only getting harder as his children grow up and start asking more and more questions about why the bombs are falling and when they will stop.

The younger children may forget this conflict, like Deena has largely forgotten the 2008 Cast Lead operation, but the older ones are bound to remember. Deena says she keeps having flashbacks of seeing a neighboring house collapse and seeing one of her neighbors killed.

Palestinian psychiatrist Yasser Abu Jamie explains that this is a common problem among Palestinian children and adults.

"After all, there is only so much that human beings can take," Abu Jamie said. "Constant bombing is damaging to human beings."

Gaza is home to 1.8 million people who are exposed to traumatizing situations, whether direct or indirect, on a regular basis. Even for those children in relatively peaceful neighborhoods, they tend to eventually see gruesome images on TV.

"In Gaza there is no pre-trauma or post-trauma: it is continuous trauma," says Abu Jamie.

The cycle of trauma also becomes self-perpetuating. The trauma of the children intensifies the trauma felt by the parents who feel helpless at their inability to sooth and protect their children.

With drones hovering over Gaza at all hours, it can be hard to escape from this almost paralyzing fear, says Loai.

"Drones make me afraid," Deena said. "I always dream of the noises they make."

Family separation

Family gatherings and religions occasions, like Ramadan, often serve as a welcome distraction from the otherwise harsh security and economic conditions experienced in Gaza. But this year, even the Holy Month that Deena has been looking forward to has been destroyed.

During Ramadan, Palestinian families often exchange family visits with all their relatives. It's seen as part of their Islamic duty, although Deena has always viewed it as a fun occasion to see all her cousins.

"I like to be with my cousins who are the same age as me, but now because of the bombing, we can't do it," she says.

Her father used to bring all of the family in the car and drive to see relatives in Gaza three or four times a week. Even this small luxury is out of reach for many in Gaza, but for Lina and Loai, two middle-class teachers, it was a welcome routine.

The recent confinement and inability to get out and move around has left the Zurik family feeling trapped and claustrophobic. Mother and daughters alike are itching to go outside, but know the tales of so many who have been killed in the last few days that they dread stepping out of the front door.

"This wouldn't be so bad if we knew we were safe inside," explains Lina. "But the worst part is that we all really know that we are not."

Deena compensates for her elective confinement by staring at the city from her large window.

The view gives little comfort: the scars of war are everywhere to be seen. Even as the bombs stop falling, their hiss is replaced by the wailing of ambulance sirens, which eventually give way to the sounds of bombs and drones once again. They prevent her from sleeping and thinking of happier times.

Psychological warfare intensifies in Israel–Hamas conflict

Israeli psy-ops tactics, such as false air strike warnings and leaflet campaigns, have in this conflict been met by Hamas' own efforts in satellite TV and social media

NUSEIRAT CAMP, GAZA—When the neighbors of Khaled Abu Zayed received a phone call from an Israeli automated machine saying that their home in Nuseirat refugee camp in central Gaza was to be bombed and they must evacuate, he ran outside in his underwear, screaming that Israeli F-16s were about to strike their home.

Abu Zayed, a father of five, says that five minutes after the call no one was left in the whole neighborhood. Women, children and the elderly all just ran with whatever they were wearing or could grab in a hurry.

Usually, houses are bombed within one to three minutes after an automated call, but in this case, 38-year-old Abu Zayed spent all night outside. His house was not attacked and, after hours of waiting, his family and neighbors decided to take their chances and return home.

Despite the anxiety and fear that sent him running into the night, Abu Zayed does not count himself lucky. His neighborhood was not spared by some kind of glitch in the Israeli operations, he says. Instead, he believes the call was a tactic intentionally meant to cause maximum impact without firing a single shot.

"This is psychological war, meant to terrorize and cause maximum 'collective fear' by calling us at night," Abu Zayed told *MEE*.

These kinds of calls often impact entire cities at one time, causing residents to flee for fear that their homes will be leveled. Just this weekend, leaflets dropped by Israeli forces over northern Gaza informed residents to flee south or put their family at risk. "Beware," the leaflet said.

Gaza's Interior Ministry urged residents in northern Gaza to ignore the leaflets and stay put, even sending field workers to reassure civilians after such warnings. But many residents were too scared to stay and an estimated 17,000 fled in less than 24 hours.

Mohammed Tabsh, a political analyst who writes widely on Gaza, said Israel pursues these tactics to "dismantle the Palestinian front by creating public opinion against the resistance."

Abu Zayed says the 08 number, an Ashkelon-based phone number thought to belong to Israeli intelligence, calls Gazan phone numbers at random, sending a variety of threatening, pre-recorded messages, from requesting an evacuation to asking people to inform on Hamas operatives or disclose their whereabouts.

Abu Zayed says some calls have even issued ultimatums, telling residents to cooperate with Israeli security services or face having their homes bombed.

Bombing attacks rarely follow, but the calls create fear and panic nonetheless.

Not everyone gives in to these calls, but almost all are subjected to and somehow affected by this kind of psychological warfare.

Mohammed Akila, a 45-year-old father of nine who works with ambulance crews in Gaza, says that his children are constantly horrified by what they hear or see in the media.

"Psychological warfare has a greater effect on my family than physical attacks," Akila says. "The constant humming of drones is a psychological war affecting children and adults alike."

Hamas hits back

Phone calls and leaflets aren't the only Israeli tactics. Last year, Israeli Prime Minister Benjamin Netanyahu's office reportedly offered students scholarships to Israeli universities if they would post pro-Israel messages on social media networks.

This followed a "media bunker" set up during Israel's offensive on Gaza in 2012, with hundreds of young Israeli volunteers posting updates to social media sites with Israeli points of view. The student union at the Interdisciplinary Center Herzliya, a private Israeli university, has organized a similar initiative during the past week, *Electronic Intifada* reported.

Over the years, Hamas—much like the civilians it rules over—has been subjected to this form of Israeli warfare. But Hamas is learning. In what analysts call an "unprecedented" move, over the course of Operation Protective Edge, Hamas has adopted Israeli tactics, including using its satellite channel, Al-Aqsa, to broadcast messages in Hebrew to warn Israelis that they will be attacked.

Normally busy Tel Aviv stood still on Saturday night after Hamas warned that rockets would be heading that way.

Fathi Sabbah, a Gaza analyst and columnist for London-based *al-Hayat* newspaper, told *Middle East Eye* that Hamas has focused on promoting its military power in order to replicate the kind of psychological warfare seen in Gaza over the years. The group has also reportedly set up a Hebrew-language website that provides news, videos and pictures of its activity and what is happening in Gaza.

Hamas' military wing, the Izz al-Din al-Qassam Brigades, has hijacked phone numbers to send text messages to half a million Israelis, including army officers.

The beginnings of a tit-for-tat propaganda war have started to emerge. Last week, after the Israeli military penetrated the airwaves of Al-Aqsa and started broadcasting its own news in the middle of news coverage, Hamas' military wing responded by hijacking the scheduled Channel 10 coverage and broadcasting their own message in Hebrew.

"Hamas is conducting the war on two fronts: operational fighting on the ground and psychological war," Sabbah said.

The case of Hamas announcing it would hit Tel Aviv was the biggest psychological tactic so far, drawing attention from around the world.

"This was not just armed warfare," Sabbah said. "Hamas surprised us by making it psychological, using videos to show Israeli's fear of resistance rockets falling in Israel."

Authorities and activists have also increasingly turned to social media to try and stop the spread of misinformation and to reassure people, as well as bring more international attention. Still, these tools cannot reach everybody, especially the elderly who remain the most at risk.

Gazan authorities arrested several Palestinians believed to be collaborating with Israel by allegedly making threatening phone calls to spread rumors and stir panic.

While Sabbah said Hamas' psychological retaliation is slowly starting to alleviate the pressures that Palestinians feel, he explains that the civilian population in Gaza is slowly getting more experienced in dealing with tactical mind games.

"Two previous Israeli military assaults on Gaza and hundreds of random Israeli attacks have weakened the overall impact of Israel's psychological war on Gaza," he adds.

But while the population may be gradually getting used to these kind of tactics, they can still inflict significant damage.

"Because no one wants to die in their house, they leave their homes," Sabbah explains.

Palestinian journalists under Israeli fire

The death of Hamed Shehab on Wednesday in an Israeli air strike has triggered fear and anger among journalists in Gaza

GAZA CITY—With tearful eyes, the Al-Aqsa TV anchorman announced the death of Palestinian journalist Hamed Shehab on Wednesday evening, hit by an Israeli air strike while driving home on Omar al-Mukhtar street.

Shehab, 27, was working for local press company Media 24. He was driving a car that had the letters "TV" affixed to it in large, red stickers when it was struck by an Israeli missile. The bombing, carried out on one of Gaza City's busiest streets, has triggered fear and rage among journalists in Gaza.

"Such [an] attack is meant to intimidate us. Israel has no bank of targets anymore, except civilians and journalists," Abed Afifi, a cameraman for the Beirut-based Al Mayadeen TV channel, told Al Jazeera.

Afifi said Shehab was an independent media professional and was not affiliated with any political party.

Shehab's body arrived at Gaza's Shifa Hospital in pieces, burned and unidentifiable. His silver-colored Skoda car was riddled with shrapnel and covered in blood. Another eight Palestinians were injured in the same attack.

The Palestinian death toll sat at nearly 100 Palestinians as of Friday morning, while hundreds of others have been injured over the past four days of Israeli air strikes. The UN estimated on Thursday that at least 342 housing units had been destroyed and at least 2,000 Palestinians displaced in the bombardment.

Ihab al-Ghussein, from Gaza's Interior Ministry, commented on Shehab's death from Shifa Hospital: "This crime is meant to break the will of Palestinian media professionals who are working day and night . . . to show the brutality of the occupation."

Ghussein held the international community responsible. "No doubt this is a crime, but journalists will not stop their mission," he added.

Meanwhile, the Israeli government said it had no initial information about the incident, while an Israeli army spokeswoman told Reuters news agency that the military was checking for more details.

The Palestinian Journalists Syndicate condemned Shehab's killing as a war against press freedom. "This is a deliberate and planned crime to discourage Palestinian journalists from showing occupation crimes and horrors of collective punishment against the Gaza Strip," a statement from the group read.

The Syndicate said it would appeal to all international media groups to withhold membership from the Israeli Journalists Syndicate in response to Shehab's killing.

This isn't the first time Israel has allegedly targeted journalists in Gaza. In November 2012, the Israeli army carried out four separate strikes on Gaza-based media, killing two cameramen, injuring at least 10 other media workers and damaging four media offices.

Israeli government spokesperson Mark Regev justified the bombings at the time, saying that the people targeted were not "legitimate journalists."

But Human Rights Watch said that the Israel air strikes had violated the laws of war. "Journalists who praise Hamas and TV stations that applaud attacks on Israel may be propagandists, but that does not make them legitimate targets under the laws of war," said Sarah Leah Whitson, Middle East director at HRW.

Most recently, on July 8, Reporters Without Borders accused Israel of preventing journalists from reporting on the upsurge of violence and arrests in the occupied West Bank, East Jerusalem and inside Israel.

Mousa Rimawi, head of the Ramallah-based Palestinian Center for Development and Media Freedoms (MADA), said that Israel has frequently targeted Palestinian and international journalists during major military campaigns.

"The purpose," Rimawi told Al Jazeera, "is to silence media and to prevent the journalists from covering the crimes that are committed by Israel against [the] Palestinian people."

"Without pressure from international civil society, Israel will continue to target journalists because they are behaving like a state above international law," Rimawi added. "There is no pressure and nothing that can stop them [from continuing] this policy."

But for journalists like Afifi, who has only had a few hours of sleep over the past four days outside the morgue at Shifa Hospital, the job is not something they are willing to compromise

"All these attacks on civilians should not stop us from working—the world has to see what Israel is doing in Gaza," he said.

"I never like the night"

Palestinian families fear Israel's night-time air strikes, as the civilian death toll soars in the Gaza Strip

GAZA CITY—For Ala al-Jarwsha, his wife and their two children, the most difficult moment of the day comes when night falls. Huddled together in the darkness, the parents struggle to comfort their children, who constantly ask about the loud explosions heard outside.

The family moves from one corner of their apartment to the next, as this is where they feel most safe. Other families living nearby sleep under their beds to try to protect themselves.

"It is a heated night, where we don't know who will be in the news. It could be all of us," the 31-year-old father told Al Jazeera, as his eldest child, three-year-old Mohammed, grabbed at his leg and didn't let go.

It is just one hour after midnight, and no one is asleep in the family's home—not even Jarwsha's two children, Mohammed and Ahmed, aged one-and-a-half. This has been the case for the past five days, since Israel's military offensive on Gaza began.

"Dad, we are going to die," one of the children said, with tears in his eyes.

The Jarwsha's home is just a few hundred meters from the house of a Hamas leader in Gaza, making the family more fearful than most that their home may be hit by an Israeli bomb.

In the early morning hours on Friday, the house shook three separate times as a result of nearby explosions. "We only have faith in [God] to protect us," Jarwsha told Al Jazeera.

The Jarwshas' fears are widespread among many in Gaza. At least 121 Palestinians have been killed as the violence entered a fifth day on Saturday. Nearly 1,000 others have been injured. According to the United Nations, Israel has fired more than 1,100 missiles and 100 tank shells, and carried out about 330 naval shellings.

The UN also reported that the destruction of residential buildings is the main cause of civilian casualties in the current violence engulfing Gaza: an estimated 342 housing units were destroyed as of midday on Thursday, forcing 2,000 Palestinians to seek refuge with relatives.

The Israeli government has denied allegations that it is targeting civilians in Gaza, and insists that it is only going after members of Hamas. The Israeli military also implied that civilian homes in Gaza serve "military purposes," and wrote on social media that its soldiers "target them for a reason."

"Israel targets Hamas terrorists and not innocent civilians," Benjamin Netanyahu, Israel's prime minister, said on Tuesday. "Hamas . . . bears full responsibility for any harm that comes to Israeli and Palestinian civilians alike."

But the UN estimates that 77 percent of all deaths so far in Gaza have been civilian casualties. Navi Pillay, the UN human rights chief, expressed concern on Friday over the mounting civilian death toll.

"We have received deeply disturbing reports that many of the civilian casualties, including of children, occurred as a result of strikes on homes," Pillay said in a statement.

"Such reports raise serious doubt about whether the Israeli strikes have been in accordance with international humanitarian law and international human rights law."

With electricity outages usually lasting between 12 and 16 hours each day, families don't have access to much information about where the air strikes are taking place. The power outages also impact peoples' ability to share Ramadan meals, with many forced to eat whatever they can find, often in the dark.

"It is only [in the] daylight that we can live. I've never liked nights during Israeli wars. Whether we are being bombed by F-16s or [Palestinian] rockets are fired from nearby, we are afraid, as the noise is too loud," Jarwsha told Al Jazeera.

This has left families in Gaza spending every night fearing where and when the next air strike will hit. "Israeli shrapnel never discriminates," said Jarwsha, as his wife and children cried.

"For this reason, I've never liked the night. It [reminds] me of how vulnerable we are in this unprotected home."

Hamas and the cease-fire that wasn't

Hamas almost immediately distanced itself from a cease-fire proposal that didn't meet any of its aims—or come through the right channels

When rumors began spreading late on Monday about a possible Hamas–Israel cease-fire brokered by Egypt, Ismail Haniyeh—the top Hamas leader in Gaza—appeared in a pre-recorded TV interview from an unknown location to address Palestinians.

In the video, Haniyeh's message was clear—he wanted to reassure Gazans that he and Hamas were unwilling to compromise on the innocent blood spilled in Gaza during the previous nine days.

"It is not possible for any party to bypass the conditions set by the Palestinian resistance to implement a period of calm," he said in the clip.

Hamas has since said that it didn't see the cease-fire draft until after it was made public. This suggested to Hamas that the cease-fire proposal was more a media ploy than a true political initiative to end the conflict.

"We want to stop the aggression on our people, but the problem is the realities of Gaza such as the starvation siege, the closure of borders, the humiliation of people," Haniyeh said.

There appears to have been a consensus between Hamas and the Qassam Brigades, its military wing, on the Egyptian proposal. The Qassam Brigades gave a press statement on Tuesday at 4 am saying it "was not worth the ink it was written with."

The Qassam Brigades dismissed any talk of a cease-fire, saying its battle with "the enemy" will "increase in ferocity and intensity."

A way forward?

All Palestinian factions appear to agree on the cease-fire conditions they would accept: a lifting of the siege on Gaza, prisoner releases, an end to Israeli attacks and a halt to any Israeli disruption of plans for a Palestinian unity government.

On Tuesday, Khaled al-Batsh, the senior leader of Islamic Jihad, told reporters in Gaza City that there was nothing new in his group's position, although he added that his movement appreciates the role Egypt plays.

"As far as calming down, there has been communications, but it has not reached the desired level. Initiatives should not come through the media, but through the known channels of communications of the factions and resistance leaders."

The Palestinian Resistance Committee's position is the same as that of Hamas, with spokesman Abu Mujahed telling journalists, "We have not received any initiative, and for us there is no cease-fire or calming measures."

Under the Egyptian proposal, hostilities would "de-escalate" at 9 am (6 am GMT) before a full cease-fire 12 hours later if all parties agreed.

However, Israeli air strikes continued in different parts of Gaza. The first targeted a residential tower in Sheikh Zayed, leaving four people injured, according to medical sources. Later at noon on Tuesday, several air strikes continued in different parts of Gaza. The heaviest strikes were in west Gaza City and Asda entertainment city in Khan Younis.

At press time the death toll stood at 193 killed and 1,400 injured over the past nine days of attacks—the UN has estimated that 77 percent of these are civilians.

It is likely that communication channels have established between Palestinian resistance leaders and Egyptian intelligence. It is only through these channels that Hamas could convince Islamic Jihad and the Palestinian Resistance Committee to accept an offer.

However, it does not appear that any of the three parties is willing to compromise on the conditions agreed upon by the Palestinian resistance factions.

Israeli intelligence on Tuesday started to call hundreds of Gaza land phones, using pre-recorded messages to ask Palestinians in Gaza to pressure Hamas to accept a cease-fire, said locals to *MEE* in Gaza City.

Still, political analyst Dr. Mukhair Abu Sada of Al-Azhar University is optimistic that the coming hours will see some form of a cease-fire.

"I don't think Hamas can say no to an Egyptian initiative," he says, adding, "I estimate that they will have some reservations concerning ending the siege and releasing prisoners."

"Saying no to Egypt will isolate Hamas politically. It's true they feel ignored and humiliated because no one has talked to them," he said to *MEE*.

Dr. Mussa Abu Marzouq, deputy chief of Hamas, wrote on his Facebook page this afternoon that the proposal was still being studied. It seems that he has been approached as the entry point for Hamas leadership, which is based in Cairo.

Yet, some Palestinians reject the proposal. London-based political analyst Dr. Ibrahim Hamami condemned the statement by Dr. Abu Marzouq.

"There are those who say that Dr. Abu Marzouq is forced to make such statements. That's politics, they say. No sir. It's better that he keeps silent. Politics that offers compliments on blood is not needed," he says.

The coming hours will be critical. They will determine whether a cease-fire kicks in with the conditions set by Hamas and the other Palestinian resistance factions, or whether the deadly war will continue.

Israeli threats of a ground invasion are dominating talk on Gaza's streets. However, the Qassam Brigades remain defiant in the face of the prospect: "We can't wait for that, as this is the only option to liberate our Palestinian prisoners," the group said in a statement.

Palestinians fear "no place is safe" in Gaza

Locals furious over bombing of residential homes that Israel insists are military targets

GAZA CITY—Khader Khader had less than one minute to evacuate his home.

At 7 am on Friday, the 55-year-old was sleeping under the staircase with his five children when he heard his neighbor scream, "Dr. Khader, evacuate! They are going to bomb my house!"

At that moment, Khader's seven-year-old son, Mohammed, tucked his tiny fingers into his father's trousers and froze, unable to move. Quickly getting everyone out of bed, the family ran out of the yellow villa—which Khader spent years saving money to build and only moved into two years ago—just as the first Israeli missile, a warning shot, screeched by.

"We ran anywhere we could, away from the house so as not to get hurt or killed," Khader recalled, his voice shaking.

They crammed into the car and reached the top of the street before the second missile, fired from an Israeli F-16, hit the neighborhood. Khader's home was not the target, but his neighbor's house was. "My children are traumatized from the bombing—what did they do to deserve this?" asked Khader, a respected university professor of linguistics.

His children, aged between seven and 16, have yet to return to see the damage. "The trauma is so immense that they fear coming back to their home, where we escaped by a miracle," he told Al Jazeera.

At the same time the Khader family's home was bombed, another house in Rafah, in southern Gaza, was hit by Israeli missiles. The Ghannam family received no warning and five people were killed in their sleep, while another 16 were injured.

At least 154 Palestinians have been killed and almost 1,000 others injured as Israel's military operation continued into its sixth day on Sunday. At least 70 Palestinian homes have been completely destroyed, according to the United Nations, while another 2,500 housing units have sustained minor damage.

Israeli Prime Minister Benjamin Netanyahu said on Wednesday: "Hamas will pay a heavy price for firing at Israel's citizens."

On Twitter, the Israeli army has defended its operation, accusing Hamas of hiding rockets and other weapons in "houses, mosques, hospitals [and] schools," and of operating "deep within residential areas." The military has argued that it has made efforts to minimize civilian casualties, but said that houses can be considered lawful military targets.

But the UN has said that even if a home is being used for military purposes, "any attack must be proportionate, offer a definite military advantage in the prevailing circumstances at the time, and precautions must be taken."

Jaber Wishah, deputy director of the Palestinian Center for Human Rights (PCHR) in Gaza City, said that Israel has engaged in the "punitive destruction" of Palestinian homes in Gaza. "Those houses—even if they belong to a Hamas [member] or an Islamic Jihad [member]—they should be considered civilian objects. They did not participate in the military operations," he said.

Wishah told Al Jazeera that there are three scenarios that usually occur before Israel bombs a home in Gaza. The army may carry out an air strike without any prior warning; it may fire a warning shot—known as "roof-knocking," where a dud missile will land on the roof of a house to alert the inhabitants that the real missile is on its way; or it may call Palestinian families to tell them to evacuate before their home is bombed.

"Every single home in Gaza is within the target circle," Wishah said. "No place is safe in Gaza now. Each home could be a target, either directly or indirectly affected."

Back in Gaza City early Friday morning, Khader returned to his home to survey the damage. His neighbors were also out to examine the rubble. "It's like after a tsunami," said a reporter on the scene.

Only the frame of the house was still standing; the family's personal possessions were destroyed, furniture was broken, shrapnel littered the floors of every room, and not a single door or window was intact. His personal collection of books, photographs and letters was also gone.

Khader didn't manage to save anything from his home, not even identification papers. As he inspected the destruction, still in a state of shock, another Israeli bomb struck nearby. Children ran screaming from the next house, where they were collecting clothes and toys.

"Out of all this, there is nothing that I can use," Khader said, as he stumbled around his home. "The loss is too great."

Gaza's school exam joy replaced by fear and loss

As Israel continues to pound the Gaza Strip, Palestinian children try to maintain a semblance of normalcy as they receive their exam results

Today, Palestinian headlines, news wires, tweets and emails should have been dominated by the outpouring of cheer and good will about the successful completion of secondary school graduation exams in Gaza.

Even though these celebrations take place under the very difficult conditions created by the Israeli blockade and Israel's policy of collective punishment, great effort is usually devoted to making this day special. Families get together and photos are taken, as balloons and confetti line schools and homes alike.

This year, however, the festivities and headlines are nowhere to be seen. When the secondary school results, known as the *tawjihi,* were announced on Monday, the reception was tepid at best.

Instead of the celebratory gunfire into the air with which some people used to welcome the test results, today people are taking cover from Israeli drones and missiles.

There were no fireworks or smiles. Instead, most of Gaza's 1.8 million inhabitants were busy bracing for further Israeli bombardment—the streets filled with sad faces and running feat as people sought shelter from the planes and drones above. The cries of joy were drowned out by screams of pain as funeral marches took over the otherwise quiet streets.

"I received my exam results silently, except for the noise of bombing outside," says Ismail. "But I am happy with my success after the hard work."

But while a part of him feels proud on the inside, Ismail is refusing to celebrate his results out of solidarity with those killed and injured in the Israeli attacks.

All over Gaza this week, the customary sense of academic pride has been replaced by fear and anxiety as Operation Protective Edge unleashes carnage and destruction. More than 210 Palestinians have been killed and at least 1,500 injured in the eight days since Israeli's latest campaign of collective punishment got under way.

Twenty students who would have received their results have now been confirmed dead, Gaza's Education Ministry has said.

This includes four students who were all members of the al-Batsh family. Mohammed, Yahya, Ibrahim and Qusai Batsh were all killed when an Israeli strike hit their home, killing 18 family members in one of the bloodiest strikes so far.

Sixty-three-year-old Numan Batsh, who survived the strike, can't help but think how his family was supposed to be honoring the success of its young academics. Instead, the family is left honoring their memories.

"The occupation has destroyed everything: the ground we walk on, the air we breathe, our family joy, our sleep and our children's lives," says Batsh, who dons a white *jalabiya* that sharply contrasts with his red bloodstains, his blue bruises and the black stitches on his left eye where he was hit during the Israeli attack.

"The Israelis turn all joy into tragedy. Human beings have been left with no chance to enjoy their children's success after years of hard study for a better life."

While so much of his family has perished, the elderly man is not alone in his pain and suffering, a fact that still manages to bring a smile to his face despite his great loss. Many of his neighbors are mourning his loss alongside him. There is a universal feeling among those who have passed the exams, and those who have relatives who have passed the exams, that they will not celebrate out of solidarity with the bereaved.

Ahmed al-Qanou scored 99.3 percent on his exams, but after getting his marks he refused to speak with the local media, which usually flocks to the homes of high-scoring student to cover their happy reactions.

But while he has worked extremely hard, Qanou says he doesn't want to discuss his scores as long as Israel continues to drop missiles on an already besieged Gaza, massacring whole families in their homes. The joy he waited so long for can wait some more, he explains.

"In every home, family and neighborhood, there are injured, sick and martyred," he says. "How can we celebrate amid such pain? For now we must silence the joy in our hearts."

Palestine's Education Minister, Khawla Skakshir, told reporters yesterday that 84,211 students completed their exams, with a pass rate average of 60.4 in the West Bank and Gaza.

Meanwhile, Zakaria al-Hur, the Director General of Gaza's Education Ministry, explained that Gaza will postpone announcing results properly until the end of the crisis.

"In Gaza, we decided not to publish results under these dreadful circumstances, although Ramallah decided to release the results," he told the *Middle East Eye*.

"I have taken calls from journalists, parents and respected figures urging us to postpone announcements," he added.

The exam results are online for students lucky enough to have electricity and an internet connection, but they are unable to do much with them.

"Some of our Gaza students who were killed scored top grades, but they were killed before knowing the result of their hard work."

These results, however, do appear to have been removed by the Education Ministry and the names and grades of students killed last week have not been published on the website.

So, when tens of thousands of students would usually be running to Gaza's universities like al-Azhar University, Islamic University and Al-Aqsa University to sign up for courses that matched their grades, Gaza is a ghost town as people hide from ever-present drones and bombs. This year, there will be no colored ribbons, balloons or sweets to congratulate *tawjihi* students.

"It's a Palestinian wedding, which Israel killed," Hur adds.

Hamas growing in military stature, say analysts

An expert in Hamas affairs says the group's use of tunnels to launch incursions, its ability to repulse commando raids and its use of powerful Gaza-manufactured rockets are signs of a growing military maturity

GAZA CITY—The strength projected by Hamas is based on the military potential of the movement—its capacity to employ force against the enemy. Both engineers and fighters from Hamas' military wing, the Izz al-Din al-Qassam Brigades, have died over the years so the group could achieve its current military capacity.

It has been a painful process of trial and error, analysts say. When Hamas was established in 1987, it planned to simply copy Israel's iconic submachine gun, the Uzi. Now it has M-75 missiles with a range of about 80 kilometers that can reach further than Tel Aviv.

Hamas' ability to repulse two Israeli special forces beach landings with air cover in the last week has not gone unnoticed internationally. Hamas also immobilized Israeli tanks and launched tunnel incursions, raising questions as to what capacity the military wing has developed since its defeat in Operation Cast Lead in 2008–09.

"The wars of 2008–09 and 2012 caused Hamas to mature. Now we see the introduction of newer rockets," said Ibrahim Al-Madhoun, an expert in Hamas affairs. "Its military capacity has improved in both quality and quantity," he told *MEE*.

Madhoun says the progress stems from painful experiences during Operation Cast Lead. For instance, the Qassam Brigades has introduced new anti-tank missiles that are able to hit tanks from a further distance. The Russian Tandem warhead can penetrate up to 900 mm of armor. This is unlike 2008 when P7 and RPG-7 missiles failed from a shorter distance.

Although there is no information on how many Tandem warheads Hamas has, Madhoun says Hamas is keeping other weapons as a "surprise" for ground invasions in Gaza.

"Inter-city tunnels are another factor providing Hamas with defensive tactics and an ability to surprise Israel," he adds. Israel's military said on Thursday that it had fought back an incursion by Hamas under a heavily fortified border near Sufa kibbutz—but the Qassam Brigades said it had successfully completed a "mission" during the underground raid.

Military mastermind

Ahmed Jabari, a chief commander of the Qassam Brigades who was assassinated in an Israeli air strike in November 2012, is widely seen as responsible for planning a domestic missile manufacturing capability that has developed in defiance of an Israeli–Egyptian blockade on the strip. In Jabari's honor, Hamas introduced two new missiles, the J80 and J160.

The group also saw improvements in training and specialization. It organized itself into different divisions, including explosives, engineering, rocket launching, snipers, naval defense, air defense and manufacturing, according to analysts.

Since 1987, when Hamas first emerged, the group's rocket variety and range—both closely guarded secrets—have steadily improved.

Manufacturing by the Hamas military is an evolving process which, according to Al-Madhoun, has developed as a result of the determination of the military wing.

Compared to 2008 and 2012, when experts in Gaza say that Israel took Hamas by surprise, Hamas' response in the current conflict suggests that it is more aware of its strengths and weaknesses.

The patterns of rocket fire from Gaza have seemed consistent over the last 10 days of war. There are estimates that Hamas' military is only using less than 20 percent of its weapons capacity, Madhoun said.

Indeed, Madhoun says that other divisions have also not used their full military capacity yet, predicting months more of rocket firepower.

"There are also more human resources not yet used or exhausted," he says, indicating that the response so far has concentrated on rocket attacks and the number of rockets is "neither increasing, nor decreasing."

"I believe that—in general—the Gaza resistance is not yet moving at full speed," he told *MEE.*

During the past 10 days, Israel strikes have killed 230 Palestinians and injured 1,700 Palestinians, the vast majority of them being civilians, mainly children and women according to the United Nations.

One Qassam navy commander, Mohammed Shaban, was killed—but Madhoun says Shaban was not a leader but a field operative and that a few hundred more remain in the navy unit. In the past, members of the Qassam Brigades were killed either on the way to launch rockets or on the way back.

Potential Israeli plans for a ground invasion in the coming days have been met with defiant statements from the Qassam Brigades, which has said they favor this as the "only option to liberate our Palestinian prisoners."

In 2003, Hamas leaders estimated the number of troops in the Qassam Brigades at around 20,000. However, some observers believe it is closer to 40,000.

One reason for this is that after Hamas won elections in Gaza in 2006, the limit on military recruitment was extended by the Hamas-led government. The group is also aligned with other factions that each have a few thousand fighters.

Despite its monitoring technologies, Israel has little idea of the exact size of Qassam's arsenal. "This [arsenal] is mostly manufactured locally—but yes, Hamas has also benefited from the chaos in Libya, which has seen missiles brought in."

An analyst from Jane's Intelligence—a London-based consultancy—told Reuters this week that in this offensive the brigade has unveiled new rockets and launchers that they made themselves—so the fighters are less dependent on smuggled weapons.

While Iran has traditionally been seen as the main patron behind Qassam's military capacity, Madhoun says that the relationship has suffered lately after Hamas did not follow Tehran in backing President Bashar al-Assad in Syria.

Another sign of Hamas' improving military capacity is in its drone technology. On Monday, the Israeli military announced it had shot down a drone that Hamas had named the Ababeel, describing it as its first bomb-carrying unmanned aerial vehicle.

Wary of invasion

Madhoun says that the use of the Kornet, a Russian anti-tank guided missile, four times by Hamas and Islamic Jihad has made Israel think twice before launching a ground invasion that would lead to many casualties among Israeli troops.

He adds that it would be wrong to underestimate Hamas' capacity to face Israel's troops.

"One useful tactic for Hamas is capturing Israeli soldiers and it has proved itself more than capable of doing this," he adds.

If it launches a ground invasion, Israel is likely to face not only Hamas' renewed military strength and camouflage capabilities, but also the potential for mass troop casualties and international criticism of its "scorched-earth" tactics, said Madhoun.

Ambulance workers brave Gaza dangers

Paramedics, emergency responders and ambulance drivers in Gaza City face great risks as they tend to the injured

GAZA CITY—Ibrahim Abuelkas is eight hours into his 24-hour shift, and every minute is filled with new risks. Suddenly, the 35-year-old gets a signal from his colleague Saed Zaineddin, the emergency operator, and the red and white ambulance is off again.

There is not much talking on the way to the location, as Abuelkas says he is "entering the unknown." Abuelkas and his driver use body language and gestures more than words. Within a few minutes, they are driving side-by-side with another ambulance, also headed to the city's al-Zaytoun neighborhood.

Abuelkas does not know what exactly to expect when he steps out of the van. The moment he arrives, people run toward him, screaming, "Ambulance, come here, come here!" The people here expect another Israeli air strike any minute, and they are frantically trying to evacuate the women and children.

The ambulance driver quickly navigates through the crowd, lights flashing, to assist a number of residents that have been injured by an Israeli bomb. "Usually we travel in ambulance pairs to the same location to assist as much as possible," says Abuelkas as the ambulance sirens wail.

The injured are helped into the back of the ambulance, which then rushes toward Shifa Hospital. The moment it arrives, the Operational Rescue Team opens the ambulance doors to off-load the patients, who are taken on stretchers to reception and triage.

The workers clean the ambulance, check that supplies are stocked and take a brief rest with other ambulance crews until the next call comes in. Then, it's time to move again, this time to another part of Gaza.

The Israeli cabinet accepted an Egyptian proposal on Tuesday morning for a cease-fire to end the fighting in Gaza, which began on July 8 and has killed 189 Palestinians and injured more than 1,400 others. While Palestinian Authority President Mahmoud Abbas welcomed the cease-fire, Hamas leaders have yet to officially comment.

Meanwhile, Hamas' armed wing, the Qassam Brigades, said the proposal "was not worth the ink it was written with."

Ambulance drivers in Gaza have been working non-stop in extremely difficult conditions throughout the Israeli military offensive. According to the United Nations, one doctor has been killed and 19 medical staff have been injured in Gaza since July 7, while two hospitals, four clinics, one treatment center and four ambulances have sustained damage in Israeli air strikes.

The emotional impact has also taken a toll on medical workers in the besieged coastal enclave. Abuelkas told Al Jazeera that one of the worst calls he responded to was to help the al-Batsh family: eighteen members of the same family were killed by an Israeli missile in Gaza City on Saturday.

When he got to the site of the bombing, he didn't know what he would find. At the house, he met women, children and old men; everyone was either screaming, crying or silent, in shock. He said the most difficult part was collecting dismembered body parts to identify the dead and prepare them for burial.

"This was a terrible, emotional mission—we found all types of injuries: light [and] medium to critical, body parts blown off, amputated limbs and other dead bodies," he said.

For many days during the Israeli assault, the roads in Gaza City were empty as residents hid indoors. "I have been afraid of bombing, but the fear of the unknown haunts me," Abuelkas says, while holding a Quran and reciting prayers in the lulls between calls.

Abuelkas started this job in 2008. While he says his first months on the job were challenging, his colleagues now say he has become more experienced, and he is able to deal with more. He has witnessed three major Israeli operations in the Gaza Strip: Operation Cast Lead in 2008–09, Operation Pillar of Defence in 2012 and the current escalation in July 2014.

He says he has noticed a difference between the three wars: "In 2008, we saw missiles split flesh into chunks, missiles that burned the whole body and amputated limbs clean off, like a surgeon. In today's attacks, we mostly find missiles that dissolve flesh into even smaller scraps. It's more violent, if that's possible."

Attending to Gaza's injured isn't the only thing on Abuelkas' mind, however. When he's working, his thoughts inevitably turn to his own family and his five children—the eldest is 12, and the youngest is only one. His family lives in al-Zaytoun, one of the worst-hit areas in the recent Israeli bombing.

As much as he worries about his wife and children, they also worry about him. "When they see me on live TV carrying bodies, at least they know I'm alive," he says, as his operator informs him of another air strike and more casualties.

Finally, after 24 hours rushing between tragedies, Abuelkas' shift ends. "At least then, I know [that] whatever happens, I'm with my family."

The cautious silence in Gaza between the noises of war

Gaza families scramble to bury their dead, console victims' families and prepare for next round of Israeli attacks

GAZA CITY—The cautious silence between the noises of war in Gaza was broken by car horns; within a span of five hours, everyone rushed to shops, markets, and ATM machines for money, food, water and other supplies. They also quickly checked on relatives and neighbors to get news.

The five-hour humanitarian pause between Israel and Hamas started in the Gaza Strip after 10 days of constant war.

Israeli air strikes and rocket attacks from Gaza continued until the short truce started at 10 am local time (7 am GMT).

Several Gaza journalists have taken this chance to check on their families. Some of the journalists have not seen their families at all over the past 10 days.

The death toll is now 249 Palestinians killed and approximately 1,880 injured, says health official Dr. Ashraf al-Qidra. The UN states that most of the casualties have been civilians. Hamas rockets have killed one Israeli and lightly injured others.

Usually, during a period of calm, Gaza's population first inspects the damage done, then tries to find injured people in the rubble and bury their dead before visiting the mourning tents to give condolences.

A few minutes before the cease-fire began, an Israeli tank shell hit a house in southern Gaza, killing three people, said medical sources.

"A five-hour cease-fire is not enough time for everyone to bury the dead, pay respects and prepare for the next attacks," says 32-year-old Ashraf al-Helow. Food and water supplies have become a top priority for families, and they are growing scarce as the attacks carry on.

"It's true, we are tired of this war, but we don't want to go back to the situation before this war either," he adds. Everyone is anxiously awaiting the man who sells chicken so they can buy some and then get back home and take cover before the 5-hour truce ends.

The truce has largely been respected by both sides. It was a moment when a "thirsty population could get some water into their mouths," says Abu Zyad Hajj, a 61-year-old man, while standing in line wearing his white *Jabaliya*.

"Gaza has experienced an immensely difficult eight years under Israeli siege—that can't and shouldn't continue forever," he told *MEE*.

He says that Israel is aware that its occupation and blockade are turning a whole population against it, fostering support for the growing Palestinian resistance. This was not the case a few years ago, as tens of thousands of Palestinian workers in Israel—of which he was one—were against harming Israeli nationals.

"Until this moment, I was against the idea, but when I am about to die and our appeals to the world fall on deaf ears, then I don't know what to do," he laments.

Just then, the meat seller announces that his stocks are out and his supplier can't come because of the Israeli drones hovering over his chicken farm. Everyone in line must go home empty-handed.

The cease-fire—to last until 3 pm local time—was requested by the United Nations, with the intent to distribute supplies and aid to people seeking shelter, food, water and hygiene kits. Over 22,000 Palestinians are using UN schools as shelters, after the Israeli army warned that their homes could be targeted by the military.

Abu Zyad wishes the five-hour window of calm could be lengthened so he could get all he needs for his family—he feels that much worse attacks are to come after the pause.

Ground invasion

Benjamin Netanyahu, the Israeli Prime Minister and Defense Minister, has ordered Israel's military to begin a ground offensive on Gaza late Thursday, just before the Muslim sabbath on Friday.

A statement from Israel's military said that the offensive will include "infantry, armored corps, engineer corps, artillery and intelligence, combined with aerial and naval support."

Israel transferred tens of thousands of troops to the Gaza border to begin the ground offensive on Gaza.

The operation, which started late Thursday, killed several people, the first victim being a three-month-old baby boy, Fares Al-Tarabeen. His body arrived at Shifa Hospital. He was still wearing his diapers.

Doctors at Abu Yousef al-Najjar hospital told *MEE* that scores of people were brought to the hospital after breathing poisonous white gas. The patients were unable to breathe and doctors were unable to treat them, not knowing what kind of gas was used. People who breathed the gas screamed uncontrollable and were difficult to restrain. The Palestinian Health Ministry appealed to international groups to help deal with the crisis and help in identifying the kind of gas that was used in the first hour of the ground invasion.

The United Nations says at least 1,370 homes have been destroyed in Gaza and more than 22,000 people have been displaced in the recent hostilities.

The ground invasion is expected to increase the number of displaced families in the days to come.

No respite in Gaza as casualties rise

At least 55 Palestinian civilians, including children, have been killed since Israel began its Gaza ground invasion

BEIT LAHIYA, GAZA STRIP—The Kamal Adwan hospital in northern Gaza buzzes with activity, as dozens of Palestinians rush in with injuries from artillery fire. Usually, patients feel protected in the hospital, but not on Friday morning, after news spread that an Israeli tank shell hit a hospital in Beit Hanoun.

"The moment I see Israeli missiles shelling hospitals, I get more concerned that we are not safe either," says 57-year-old Abu Iyad, who lives less than one kilometer from the Israeli tanks positioned along the border in Beit Lahiya.

Israel's military dropped leaflets asking residents to leave their homes on Thursday. The leaflets arrived as Israel launched a ground operation into the besieged Gaza Strip, pushing deeper into the territory at five separate entry points. Israel said the aim of the operation was to destroy tunnels and rocket-launching sites in Gaza.

Israel struck more than 100 separate sites in Gaza overnight on Thursday in the first hours of its ground operation. It also reported destroying nine underground tunnels and 20 concealed rocket launchers.

So far, Israeli forces have not gone further than two kilometers inside Gaza. But the number of Palestinian civilian casualties has risen, as more than 280 Palestinians have now been killed in 11 days of violence. Another

1,900 Palestinians have been injured, as civilians have borne the brunt of the violence so far.

"It seems neither [Israeli Prime Minister Benjamin] Netanyahu nor [US President Barack] Obama want to know that it's we civilians who are the targets—resistance is our last resort to gain freedom and breathe some air into our lungs," Abu Iyad told Al Jazeera.

Late on Friday, constant shelling could be heard across the Gaza Strip, an Israeli F-16s struck buildings throughout the territory and warships fired missiles from their positions just offshore.

"The [Israeli army] is operating against Hamas and the other terrorist organizations in the Gaza Strip from the sea and air, and now on land as well," Netanyahu said on Friday afternoon before a special cabinet meeting. "Because it is not possible to deal with the tunnels only from the air, our soldiers are now doing so on the ground," he said.

Meanwhile, Obama has reaffirmed his support for the Israeli operation, but urged restraint. "No nation should accept rockets being fired into its borders or terrorists tunneling into its territory," Obama said, according to the Associated Press news agency.

Dr. Ashraf al-Qidra of Shifa Hospital in Gaza City told Al Jazeera that 55 Palestinians had been killed in the first 24 hours of Israel's ground operation, including three children from the Abu Musallam family—Ahmed, Walaa and Mohammed.

Eleven-year-old Ahmed's face was blackened with burns and smoke exposure. Next to him at the Kamal Adwan hospital morgue laid his sister Walaa, 12, and brother Mohammed, 14; they were all wrapped in white burial shrouds.

Ismail Musallam, the children's father, said they were asleep when an artillery shell hit the family's apartment in the al-Nahda residential tower. The father started digging the children out from under the rubble alone, before local ambulance crews arrived.

The family's home was inaccessible for relatives trying to visit the children before their burial, as is the norm, and their funeral was also delayed because the family was unable to move for several hours under heavy Israeli fire.

In Khan Younis in southern Gaza, nine people were killed overnight on Thursday, including four members of the Radwan family. Israeli bulldozers were spotted levelling agricultural land in the so-called buffer zone between Gaza and Israel.

Al-Wafa Hospital has also been under attack, according to Attia al-Wadia, head of public relations at the rehabilitation hospital. "Israel continues to bomb, to force doctors to evacuate," al-Wadia told Al Jazeera, explaining that hospital staff moved 18 seriously wounded patients to another facility, fearing that they would be hit by an Israeli strike.

Finally, after hours of delays, the three children from the Musallam family were buried in a haze-filled cemetery, as black smoke poured out of a nearby building.

The bodies were carried on stretchers by a group of men. Ahmed's face was covered in black burns, while his brother and sister's bodies were riddled with shrapnel injuries. Tension was palpable amid the mourners, as they feared another Israeli bombardment.

"They were just asleep in warm beds a few hours ago. Now they are all cold in a morgue, dead," a family member who did not give her name told Al Jazeera earlier in the day at Kamal Adwan hospital.

"Look, she was just at the age of blooming roses. What threat was she? What did she do to Israel to deserve this?"

Gazans support resistance despite heavy toll

"For decades Israel has never offered anything free of charge. You have to fight to get what's yours," says Mohammed Joudeh, a resident of Gaza.

RAFAH, GAZA—The price of resistance may be high, and getting higher by the day. On Friday alone, 55 Gazans were killed, as shelling decimated two entire families. The paradox of Gaza is that as the death toll increases, so does the defiance of its people.

"We have to make a choice: either they finish us or we finish them," 66-year-old Amnah Odah told *MEE*. "This situation cannot continue, or return to what it was 11 days ago—under Israel's eight-year siege—where life was equally bad, if not worse."

When asked what she would say to Prime Minister Benjamin Netanyahu if she had 30 seconds, she replies, "You brought this on—there is a limit to Palestinian and human patience after all."

"Putting Gaza on a diet of malnutrition and collective punishment, cutting off water, interfering with salaries, blocking other basic human rights and not letting basic construction supplies come through the Rafah crossing is unbearable," says Odah. "Of course this is causing people to revolt and stand up for their rights.

"Oppressed Arabs revolted against previous tyrannical regimes. The Israeli occupation is just a continuance of that: stealing our land, wrecking our economy, insulting our identity for 66 years of occupation and blockade," Odah adds, as she lies on a simple mattress in a modest house in the Rafah refugee camp.

Odah is not alone in her feelings, despite knowing there will be more losses and many more casualties on the Palestinian side if fighting continues.

"If we knew those killed were adults fighting on the front, I would be proud, but when I see so many children dying, I am heartbroken," she says.

"We wonder if Israel is killing children to send a message that no one is safe. I think Netanyahu made it clear that nobody is immune in Gaza—I think targeting civilians is meant to disrupt and terrorize people collectively."

Mohammed Joudeh, a 45-year-old father of four, also thinks Israel's goal is to intimidate people in order for them to turn against the resistance and give Israel the chance to continue its unreasonable demands and blockade. However, reality on the ground seems to indicate that the Israeli offensive which began on July 8 is having the opposite effect.

"People here are supporting the resistance. It's obvious in all areas, despite our suffering," says Joudeh.

Joudeh does not think that Israel will succeed in its latest attempt at intimidation. He says that as hard as it may be, attacking civilians is losing its impact. After so many years of these attacks, Palestinians feel that the only way to gain national rights and improve living conditions is to resist, he explains.

"For decades Israel has never offered anything free of charge. You have to fight to get what's yours," he says.

But despite their perseverance, civilians caught on the front line of Israel's military attacks for the past 14 years also say it's time to end the bombing. They insist that they are tired of living in perpetual fear. Forty-five-year-old Mohammed Abu Shalob is one of the many who says he has had enough of Israel's shelling.

The latest ground attack launched late Thursday forced him and his 10 family members to flee their home, which is right next to the ruins of the Gaza International Airport in Rafah. Miraculously, the whole family is still alive, if still very shaken by the incident.

"We were indoors when six artillery shells hit our house," says Abu Shalob. "One wall collapsed around us, forcing the whole family to run in the middle of the night to find shelter from Israel's tank shells."

Four of Abu Shalob's neighbors, however, were injured.

"We had to call ambulances as we couldn't walk because the ground was covered with fragments of nail shards from the missile," says Abu Shalob.

"Nor could we breathe properly from the white gas which came out of the rockets, making our mouths dry," he adds, while lying down on the soccer field of an UNRWA school, where many of the displaced have taken shelter. While the UN is providing the most basic rations, it has been caught unprepared for the scale of the emergency, with many of the displaced complaining that there are inadequate food provisions for the *suhur* and *iftar* meals of Ramadan.

In each classroom there are usually around 50 women sleeping. Men sleep scattered across the soccer field, while others sleep out on the street corners, some using their sandals as pillows, others using their shirts and empty cartoons of powdered milk.

Even the UN schools, however, do not necessarily provide shelter from the shelling. During the conflict ambulances have been fired upon and forced to retreat. Abu Shalob says that he was forced to walk a few hundred kilometers to a place where ambulances could be reached.

While Israel has previously been accused of purposefully targeting civilians and civilian infrastructure, Abu Shalob says that, at least for him, this war feels different from the 2008–09 or 2012 wars. "Before, we didn't have Israel's artillery directly targeting our homes," he says.

Another disturbing development, according to Abu Shalob, is the alleged use of tall buildings by Israeli forces, who use them as sniper stations.

Joudeh has also noted this tactic and says it leaves Palestinians with little choice

"After all, this does not mean that people are willing to go to a cease-fire—it's either we live in full dignity, or have no real life," says Joudeh.

For him, technology has shaped a new Palestinian generation that is unwilling to accept the humiliation that their families endured under Israel's occupation. "We have done it for 66 years. Israel has to realize enough is enough," he adds.

But the price of resistance is high. According to Palestinian sources, the last 24 hours alone have seen Israel launch 260 missiles and rockets, while Palestinian factions have sent about 105 rockets and mortars to Israel. The Palestinian death toll in Gaza is now fast approaching 300, including many children. One Israeli civilian and one Israeli soldier have also been killed.

In Abu Yousef al-Najjar hospital in Gaza, doctors announce a state of emergency as more people are evacuated and taken to new locations.

"Since early evening, we've been targeted by Israeli artillery, with leaflets dropped, ordering us to evacuate our homes," 38-year-old Hani al-Mahmom told *MEE*.

The fear and confusion is palpable on the ground. As the shelling resumes, Rafah's population rushes around, trying to flee to six UN schools in the city, the only makeshift shelter the residents have.

Mahmom and his family were among those fleeing in the early hours.

"Two days ago I was at my home, despite the bombing, but now I am displaced. We are still resilient and supportive of Gaza's resistance—but we are also still victims of Israel's cruelty," he says.

"If we were the ones launching rockets, I would accept Israel returning to target our homes, but we are not."

The increasing number of targeted civilians is raising questions among international groups about Israel's intentions. Mahmom believes that Israel's war does not intend to break Hamas, just weaken it.

He says that his children will not forget these sleepless nights when they grow up, and he fears that this only jeopardizes the chance for peace in the region. When a seven-year-old knows that Israel is besieging him at such a tender age, there can be no peace, Mahmom explains.

Israel strikes Gaza apartment blocks

A Gaza City apartment building has been hit by repeated Israeli strikes, leaving families in fear of the next bombing

GAZA CITY—Remas Kayed can recount the attack, which both her mother and father still can't believe they escaped alive. "The Israeli F-16 bombed mommy's bedroom—look, come and see," the six-year-old told Al Jazeera, going to inspect the damage to the family's apartment on the seventh floor of Daowd Tower.

At 3 am on Thursday, Khaled Kayed's father came to invite him, his wife and his children to share a suhoor meal. As the family left their apartment, Khaled said, they "just managed to close the door and the building started to rock and sway from an Israeli air strike."

Frozen by fear, the family quickly went back inside, crammed into one room and shut the door. "We were shaken by a bomb from an Israeli drone," Khaled recalled while examining the debris from the missile, which landed in the children's bedroom.

Both Khaled and his father live in an apartment tower that is home to doctors, university professors and civil servants.

"Just three minutes separated us from definite death," said Khaled, an employee of the Ramallah-based Palestinian Authority, as his daughter Remas examined what remained of her bedroom.

The apartment's yellow curtains were ripped and burned. Clothes belonging to Kayed and his wife were full of jagged holes from the shrapnel. The bed was split into pieces and the linen was covered in dust and smelled of hot metal.

"Israel is the tomcat of bullies, just aiming to terrorize trapped civilians in their homes," Khaled said.

After 10 days of Israeli aerial bombings of the Gaza Strip, Israel launched a ground offensive into Gaza late on Thursday. Israel said the escalation was meant to destroy tunnels linking Gaza to Israel, and that its military was "prepared for an expansion of the ground action."

Israel has denied that it is targeting civilians in Gaza, instead arguing that it is going after fighters affiliated with the Palestinian faction Hamas. The Israeli army defended its military operation, accusing Hamas of hiding rockets and other weapons in "houses, mosques, hospitals [and] schools" and of operating "deep within residential areas." The military also said that houses can be considered lawful military targets.

But Israel has been criticized by international human rights groups for targeting civilian homes in Gaza in its latest offensive, as several apartment blocks have been hit by Israeli drones and missiles. About 1,780 families in Gaza have had their homes completely destroyed by Israeli air strikes, according to United Nations estimates, while about 96,400 people are now in need of shelter across Gaza.

The Gaza Health Ministry reported that more than 245 Palestinians have been killed in the violence in Gaza so far, including at least 39 children. Another 1,920 Palestinians have been injured.

The UN found that about 25,000 Palestinian children in Gaza are suffering from post-traumatic stress disorder and are in need of psychological help as a result of the ongoing Israeli military offensive. According to Khaled, his children are all traumatized. "Why is Israel bombing us?" his daughter Remas asked repeatedly.

Back at Daowd Tower, apartments seven and eight are the worst hit. The building's outer structure is heavily damaged, while broken furniture, personal belongings and toys are strewn about.

The building's owner, Suhil Abu Jebba, said all 15 apartments have suffered damage, and five cars parked outside were destroyed. One of the cars belonged to a well-known academic who estimated that the damage amounted to around $14,000.

On Thursday, Israeli F-16s fired three missiles at the apartment building again, one of which hit the building just as ambulances and fire crews were arriving. Five residents were injured, including one ambulance crew member.

"Everyone from the neighborhood managed to run outside. We were all just terrified, shaking and children crying," said Khaled, who fled his apartment using only the light from his cell phone. The scene, he said, reminded him of "an earthquake with flames in every corner, dust and smoke everywhere and sharp, shattered glass all over the floor."

90 percent darkness in Gaza

As the Israeli attacks on Gaza intensify, Gazans are only getting two hours of electricity each day, increasing their hardship considerably

GAZA CITY—Hassan Zyara is crying loudly. He wakes up his father Tahseen, his mother and four brothers too. It's after midnight, and very dark in the apartment because there is no electricity. His father asks him why he's crying, and two-year-old Hassan tells his dad he is too frightened to go to the bathroom in the darkness.

"He usually has a small light on and is never afraid, but this almost total darkness scares him and he won't move alone at night," says Tahseen to *MEE*.

Zyara blames not only the present crisis, but also Israel's occupation and long-term blockade. Access to normal levels of electricity has reduced every year since 2006 when Israeli warships hit Gaza's only power plant. Prior to that, Gaza's power plant would service the Gaza Strip at almost full capacity.

And now, under Israel's military offensive by land, sea and air, the Gaza Strip is left only with two hours of electricity at most per day. Some areas have not had electricity for the past 48 hours at all.

"There's not much we can do in two hours. How do we do the laundry, connect the water generator, charge our cell phones to contact family and friends who may be sick or worse, or check for news on TV, or do simple kitchen chores?" says Umm Mohammed, the wife of Tahseen.

She knows that 120 minutes is too short a time to get everything necessary done. But that's the reality that she has to face now.

On Friday, Gaza's Electricity Distribution Company announced that Israel refused to allow electricity already purchased from an Israeli company to be accessed by Gaza, meaning outages are up to 90 percent.

Gaza never experienced such power shortages in previous wars, say electricity company officials.

For the past 12 days, Gaza has been under Israeli attack. The death toll also increased on Saturday. In all, 334 people have been killed and 2,391 injured. Israel carried out 2,450 air strikes and shot approximately 850 artillery shells and 775 shells from warships. Palestinian resistance groups fired around 1,500 rockets and missiles, which Israel announced killed two of their citizens.

Jamal al-Dardsawi, public relations director of the electricity company, says that Israel has started to gradually cut supplies to Gaza from its Israeli companies, where the Gaza company is a client. Meanwhile, Israeli F-16 and drone missiles have also severely damaged electricity lines, which Gaza purchased from Egypt.

According to al-Dardsawi, 13 electricity lines have been badly damaged by either Israel's continuous air strikes or artillery shelling within the past 24 hours alone.

He indicated that Israel also refused to let his company workers repair the damaged lines, even to just relieve some of the darkness across the Gaza Strip.

"The electricity company is bordering on total shutdown with Israel constantly and deliberately bombing domestic power lines."

Gaza needs 360 megawatts in order to cover the needs of 1.8 million Palestinians living within the Israeli blockade, with 46 percent of Gaza being children under 14 years.

Gaza buys its electricity from three sources: Israeli lines providing 120 megawatts, Egypt's lines supplying 28 megawatts and Gaza's power plant that produces between 40 and 60 megawatts.

Eyewitnesses in East Gaza City say Israel is deliberately targeting electricity lines to cut off communication between the people of Gaza. In previous wars, this was also one of the first tactics used by the Israeli military—to isolate and disconnect everyone from each other and disrupt their utilities, whether telephones, TV or water. Telecommunication infrastructure is usually the first to be targeted.

On Thursday, Israel announced that the Kerem Shalom Crossing, which is the only access point for industrial fuel into Gaza, would be closed. The electricity company says that due to this closure, even the 40–60 megawatts it provides will no longer exist.

Gaza is running on dwindling reserves, enough only for a few days at best and at 10 percent of the basic capacity needed for Gaza.

The Interior Ministry says that it is in contact with the International Committee for the Red Cross in order to ensure the safety of workers who fix the broken lines.

During the war, several utility workers have been killed and injured. The last was killed in Rafah when a municipal car, which was clearly marked, was targeted by an Israeli missile, killing the worker and injuring his colleagues.

The fact that Israel is blocking technical teams from fixing damaged lines will bring Gaza to the edge of an unavoidable crisis, al-Dardsawi says.

"This is definitely collective punishment. It's like breaking an already broken arm."

Gaza's infrastructure on the verge of collapse

Experts warn of "catastrophic" consequences as power, water and medical facilities struggle to cope under the bombing

When Umm Ali Abu Sada visits her kitchen, she can see that her refrigerator is leaking. Its melting contents mix with blood from a kilo of frozen meat and flow onto the floor—the mother of six can do nothing to stop it.

Electricity outages over the last 24 hours have left Umm Ali, from Jabaliya refugee camp, with more damage and loss than she can cope with.

"It's unbearably hot, and I can't do anything without the electricity to run my refrigerator," she says.

Despite abject poverty and a disabled husband, she has stockpiled food for herself and her children. She knows the coming days will not be easy, with water supplies almost completely cut off for the past 48 hours.

In order to access water from the tank on the roof, she needs the water generator to work, and that is only possible with the electricity on. Even flushing her toilet is no longer an option.

Her home in northern Gaza is in an area under heavy bombardment, directly in the path of the Israeli offensive, intensifying the crisis Umm Ali has to deal with.

"Things have become much worse since the ground invasion," she told Al Jazeera.

According to Jamal al-Dardsawi from the local power supply company, 13 electricity feeder lines have been hit by Israeli air strikes and artillery shelling. That means 90 percent of electricity in the Gaza Strip is out.

The 10 percent that remains is not enough to cater to all the needs of Gaza's 1.8 million people, which results in prolonged blackouts.

Depending on the area they live in, residents of Gaza get between two and four hours of power every day, although some districts have had no power for two days.

For the past two weeks, workers at the power company have been targeted by Israeli gunfire—making Dardsawi reluctant to send his staff members out to investigate and make repairs.

Three workers have been killed trying to make critical repairs, and continuing hostilities have made such work too dangerous in many areas, said Philip Luther, Middle East and North Africa program director at Amnesty International.

A report by the UN's Office for the Coordination of Humanitarian Affairs (UNOCHA) also highlighted the dangers the workers face.

"The lack of protection during damage repair, operation and assessment remains the biggest constraint, impeding the immediate repair of water and waste water pipelines," the report said.

UNOCHA added that damage to technical equipment is affecting a majority of Gaza's population, despite repairs to two lines with the cooperation of the Israeli authorities.

"This has further undermined the operation of water and sewage facilities, many of which have been damaged," the report stated.

Gaza's infrastructure is expected to be damaged even further by the knock-on effects of having no power.

That is what Umm Ali is experiencing at her home—the sewage system is flooding and the garbage, sitting in the hot sun, has not been collected for days.

According to the Emergency Water and Sanitation-Hygiene Group (EWASH), 50 percent of sewage pumping and treatment systems no longer operate. This directly affects about 900,000 Palestinian inhabitants in Gaza.

"Gaza's infrastructure is on the verge of collapse and the consequences of a continuing lack of clean water could be catastrophic," said Luther.

EWASH says this situation is extremely dangerous, issuing a warning that the mixing of sewage and drinking water heightened the risk of a serious public health hazard from waterborne diseases.

With the ongoing Israeli attacks, the majority of hospitals are focusing mostly on urgent medical cases. The bombing has prevented thousands of patients from getting access to medical care.

Several human rights groups in Gaza have expressed concern about Israel's targeting of health facilities in Gaza over the past 13 days. So far, 16 medical facilities have been damaged since July 7, including two hospitals, 12 clinics and two nursing care centers, according to UNOCHA.

One case that caught international attention was the al-Wafa Rehabilitation Hospital, which was forced to evacuate many of its disabled patients before it was bombed for a second time by Israel.

Gaza's Health Ministry announced that 13 out of 54 primary care centers have been closed, particularly in areas targeted by the Israeli air force, artillery and navy warships.

On Saturday, Gaza hospitals announced that their medical supplies were rapidly declining, and some essential surgical operations had to be stopped due to a lack of provisions.

Dr. Yousef Abuelresh, the Deputy Minister of Health, sent an appeal to international organizations to immediately send desperately needed medical supplies.

His call for help has not had much of a response. Some states have sent money, but hospitals cannot do much with it when the Israeli blockade of the coast is in place.

At least 39 fishing boats have been destroyed or severely damaged since the beginning of the war, says Amjad Shrafi, secretary of the Palestinian Fishermen's Syndicate.

UNOCHA estimates that 3,600 fishermen are still in need of help to reestablish their livelihoods.

Shrafi calculates the cost of the latest damage to the fishing sector. Each day, the numbers mount.

"We have lived a painful experience, with the last few days of bombardment targeting fishing harbors and boats," he told Al Jazeera.

At midnight, Israeli warships fired missiles. Over 800 shells were fired from Israeli boats, mostly hitting equipment belonging to fishermen.

Some of their boats were burned, and since the fire department on the harbor was bombed, it was not possible to bring the fires under control in time.

Those fishermen whose boats have survived remain unable to access the sea due to constant bombing by the Israeli navy.

The killing of four children from the Bakr family in the harbor by the Israelis has turned it into a ghost town.

Gaza's Shejaiya carnage at Shifa morgue

Palestinians rush to search for their loved ones at Shifa Hospital following Israel's deadly strike on Gaza, but for many there is little good news

"No, it's not him," says the brother of Mohammed al-Mobayed, as he moves on to the next body searching for his brother. Half of the family is at the reception desk, and the other half at the morgue.

The ambulance arrives, asking crowds to clear the road so as to pass through and off-load the casualties and dead. As ambulance doors open, people run forward looking for their missing relatives.

"No, that's not him, Dad!" screams one of the brothers to his father as the ambulance arrives.

A shout comes over the air to all of the al-Mobayed family: "Here is Mohammed." The whole family runs to him, thinking he is alive.

But Mohammed's body arrives with scores of other bodies and bags of assorted fingers, heads, chests, legs and feet.

It's up to ambulance crews to sort through the body parts to match them for identification before preparing them for shrouding and burial.

The screams of grief begin among all members of the family. But everyone else is still looking for their own missing loved ones—hundreds of people are here. All are worried that the next ambulance will bring their relatives to the hospital doors.

The human carnage of Shejaiya began this morning when Israeli tanks started a massive shelling barrage on people's homes. The heavy tank shells hit houses directly; some of the people were able to run away under gunfire, but many others were hit.

Umm Ahed al-Qanou, 55 years old, had to walk five kilometers with her eight children until she could find transport to take all of them somewhere safe—here at Shifa Hospital, she does not know where her husband is.

She does not know the whereabouts of either her husband or her ninth child. One young man helps her look for them.

She still hopes they are alive—but no one knows for sure yet.

Ambulance crews say they were unable to evacuate bodies that were laid out on the street or thrown there by bombs. "It's a massacre. Dead and injured men, women, children are on the streets, and we are unable to evacuate them because we are being shot at too," screams the ambulance driver to *MEE*.

Apparently four Israeli soldiers died last night in a fierce battle with Palestinian resistance fighters. At least 100 Palestinians were killed on Sunday and over 300 injured, say doctors at Shifa Hospital. The numbers are increasing, as more bodies are dug out from under piles of rubble that used to be homes. The death toll since the start of Israel's attacks stands at 425 people, with 2,900 injured, the majority being civilians, says the United Nations.

The Red Cross attempted to organize a cease-fire to evacuate bodies, but medics say the cease-fire proposal provides too little time to dig for bodies that are not visible on the streets.

This has been the fiercest night of fighting since Israel's war began two weeks ago. Most families were bombed while sleeping, while others were killed while fleeing their homes in search of shelter, says 28-year-old Osama al-Orbaji.

"We were in our homes when we heard an exchange of fire at 2:30 this morning. I thought it would end soon."

Just before the sun set on Shejaiya, east of Gaza City, tank shells started to land everywhere. *MEE* counted 14 tank shells in 45 seconds.

"Each time my family and I attempt to get outside, we are faced with tank shells coming toward us. There is nowhere to escape to," says al-Orbaji as he searches for the bodies—or body parts—of his cousins.

"I saw the massacre of the Ayyad family, when tank shells hit them over and over again. Twelve people were trying to flee but were blown to pieces, splattered all over the walls and concrete," says Osama while he looks at the ambulances still arriving and the crowds of people screaming in fear.

"Ayyad's mother was holding her children by their hands. But I saw them disappear when the Israeli tank shell hit," he says.

Then he saw a small child's face—the top of a child's head. The rest was split into pieces. His mother's body was blown into small pieces, he says as he weeps.

"I started to run with my family. Under our feet were the bodies of our neighbors, and blood was everywhere," he says. He shows *MEE* the blood on his bare feet and trousers, and what appears to be a piece of someone else's flesh sticking to his forehead.

"They bombed mosques, schools, homes, cars and everything. The area has been turned into just the ruins and rubble of bombed homes and bodies," he adds.

"My relatives are still indoors. My in-laws are stuck there and we still don't know if they are alive," he adds.

His only option is to wait for the ambulances to come. If no ambulances come, Osama is afraid that no one will recover the bodies that are still underneath the buildings.

"The infant son of my in-laws is two months old. I know he was killed early this morning in his house next to Al Motasem mosque," he says.

He has not yet found the tiny body he is looking for among the burned, cold bodies in the morgue.

"Tank shells were falling like hot raindrops"

Survivors of the Shejaiya bombardment recount horrific tales amid their frantic search for lost family members

SHEJAIYA, GAZA—Mahmoud al-Sheikh Khail, 36, one of the few survivors from Shejaiya, stood nervously at the gates of Shifa Hospital waiting for the next ambulance to arrive. His frightened eyes spotted an ambulance making its way through the crowd with difficulty.

The ambulance doors opened and the dead were unloaded. He burst into tears as he recognized a familiar small face. He shouted: "Samia al-Sheikh Khail!" Three-year-old Samia's body has been torn to shreds by an Israeli tank shell. Yet she was still recognizable despite the burns.

Khail learned that the bodies that remained wrapped in white burial shrouds were his cousins. He collapsed: "We were trying to run but the tank shells were chasing us wherever we went," he told Al Jazeera.

"Around 6 am, I was inside my house. I heard the neighbors screaming for help after a blast. I managed to get outside to try to rescue them but it was a massacre: woman and children all torn to pieces."

Shejaiya, in eastern Gaza City, has been under the most horrendous attack since Israel began its assault on Gaza 14 days ago. Yesterday's carnage left 72 people dead, according to a Palestinian Health Ministry statement. Nearly all of the dead are women, children and elderly men.

According to Ashraf al-Qidra, spokesperson for the Health Ministry, Gaza's death toll has climbed to 506 people, with more than 3,150 injured since the start of Israel's assault on July 8.

Those like Khail who have survived say it's a miracle.

According to several eyewitness accounts, some Shejaiya residents were waving whatever white cloth they could find: white shirts, undershirts, tablecloths. They wanted to get out of the targeted area, which was under constant heavy Israeli bombardment. After the bombing, the white cloths were either ripped apart or covered in blood.

Iman Mansour, another survivor and mother of three, managed to escape with her children.

"Nowhere was safe to run to," she told Al Jazeera. Her three children, all injured, are receiving medical treatment at Shifa Hospital. "We were forced to leave our house because tank shells were falling like hot raindrops."

Her mother-in-law, Umm Wael Mansour, who is also being treated at Shifa Hospital, had her house destroyed by a tank shell. "I lived through the 1967 war and all the following Israeli wars but this war is indescribable. It's crueler than the massacres of Sabra and Shatila."

When her house was hit, she screamed out. As neighbors tried to help, they were killed right outside her doorstep. "The bodies of men, women and children were scattered all over and no one could come to help save them," she said as tears fell.

The smell at Shifa Hospital is of burned human flesh. The morgue is filled with all kinds of carnage: dismembered human body parts and burned bodies, including the burned faces of dead children.

The morgue has more bodies than it can hold. Many of the victims are unrecognizable. Those searching for their loved ones struggle to remember specific physical details—skin color, old scars, height, weight—in order to identify very badly damaged bodies.

During the two-hour cease-fire, ambulance crews struggled to collect dead bodies. When they came across people who were still alive, some were taking their last breath as they bled to death.

In one instance, a paramedic saw a stretcher on the floor. Underneath it was the body of his colleague Fouda Jaber, killed by an Israeli tank shell. "Oh my God, Fouad . . . Fouad is one of them. He has been killed!"

screamed the medical worker, before carrying away the body of his friend and colleague.

Jaber was on a rescue mission to save a family of 10, most of them women and children. He died inside the house. The ambulance was also destroyed by tank shells.

"Instead of targeting medical facilities, in violation of international law, Israeli forces must protect medics and patients and ensure that the injured can safely reach medical facilities in Gaza and, when necessary, outside the Strip," said Philip Luther of Amnesty International.

Back at the hospital, more survivors await the ambulances, searching desperately for their family members.

Khail stayed until the end of the day, looking in vain for more relatives. Paramedics confirmed that seven of his cousins were dead.

All he is hoping for now is another cease-fire so he can get back home to search for his missing family members.

Al-Aqsa Hospital hit as strikes on Gaza's medical facilities continue

Latest strike on hospital and ambulances wreaks havoc on an already stretched medical infrastructure

DEIR AL-BALAH, GAZA—At least five Palestinians were killed and 70 others injured by several Israeli tank shells fired at Al-Aqsa Hospital in Deir al-Balah, central Gaza.

The bombing carried on throughout much of the day and well into the evening, according to hospital sources.

One patient was killed while other patients, visitors and hospital staff were among those injured. Some 20 medical workers were caught up in the shelling, said Dr. Ashraf al-Qidra, head of public relations at the Health Ministry in Gaza.

The strike has left the hospital unable to receive or treat medical cases, with ambulances forced to ferry the wounded to other facilities.

Two ambulances that tried to move the wounded to Shifa Hospital, in Gaza City, were hit by tank shells.

According to Qudra, the missiles damaged several operating rooms as well as key equipment, including an oxygen production unit that is used in a wide range of operations and procedures.

The third and fourth floors, the reception area and the upper floor were all badly damaged, medical sources told the *Middle East Eye*.

Subsequent rounds of shelling then damaged the x-ray facilities and maternity wards.

Israel has repeatedly denied targeting medical facilities, although it does routinely insist that Hamas uses civilian infrastructure—including houses, schools and hospitals—to hide weapons.

"You are allowed to hit targets that their [Hamas] war machine is using to hide rockets," said Mark Regev, spokesman for Israeli Prime Minister Benjamin Netanyahu, to Al Jazeera.

"I have no doubt that Hamas uses, has used and continues to use hospitals. . . . We do not target civilians. But I am not aware of this specific situation."

Dr. Khalil Khattab was operating on a patient who had been injured in a separate strike when the shells first hit. He quickly ran downstairs and saw many of his colleagues injured. Many had been hit while trying to treat patients. Patients, doctors and nurses alike lay injured and bleeding.

"The elevator is destroyed and all hospital assets are badly damaged," Khattab told *MEE*, inspecting the destruction around him.

Al-Aqsa Hospital in central Gaza is the only hospital providing services to several refugee camps, including al-Maghazi and al-Nuseirat, as well as to some nearby towns and villages, including Deir al-Balah and Juhu al-Dik. Health officials estimate that Aqsa is the main hospital, serving over 350,000 residents of Gaza.

Since the start of Operation Protective Edge, more than 550 Palestinians, mostly civilians, have been killed, with at least 3,350 injured. One Israeli civilian and 25 Israeli soldiers have also been killed in the fighting.

Gaza's medical infrastructure was already hard-hit by the conflict, but the strike on Aqsa has further stretched resources.

Seriously injured patients have now been evacuated to the ground floor, leaving the hospital crammed, grossly under-equipped and with both staff and patients in sheer panic.

Dr. al-Qidra, another doctor caught up in the Aqsa shelling, was performing surgery in the Intensive Care Unit (ICU) when the first Israeli tank shell hit the hospital.

Qidra is calling on the World Health Organization and other groups to intervene immediately to stop Israeli attacks on hospitals, patients, medical crews and ambulances.

Human rights groups have also intensified their calls for greater protections.

"Today's attack on the Aqsa Hospital is the latest in a series of attacks on and near medical facilities in Gaza, which have been struggling to cope with thousands of injured people since the Israeli offensive began on 8 July," said Philip Luther, Director of the Middle East and North Africa Program at Amnesty International.

"There can be no justification for targeting medical facilities at any time. Attacks on medical facilities underline the need for a prompt, impartial international investigation as mandated by the UN."

It is unclear whether the hospital will be able to function in the days to come. There have been serious attempts to evacuate all patients and staff to other locations so they can receive appropriate care.

"It's not possible for doctors to do surgical procedures while Israeli tank shells are continuously dropping from overhead," says Khattab.

Last week, Israeli air strikes hit al-Wafa Rehabilitation Hospital, despite international peace activists announcing that they would be acting as human shields at the building.

Following the strike, doctors were forced to evacuate 18 people to another hospital, although only minor injuries were reported.

Gaza European Hospital has also been hit by Israeli air strikes, which damaged the operating room.

This kind of targeting has made patients and civilians feel unsafe in and close to hospitals, which were previously regarded as safe havens protected by international law.

"Are we going to wait for our wounded to be hit again? Israel knows this is a hospital, but still they bombed us," says Abuel Abed, a 44-year-old who lives close to Al-Aqsa Hospital.

"This war is between two parties: but why target a hospital that has nothing to do with politics?"

"Such hospitals provided vital public services to victims and families, and there is no valid reason to bomb them—no rockets are fired from nearby," he adds.

Nor is it just patients and civilians who are afraid—even doctors, who are trained to deal with high-intensity situations, are struggling to cope under the pressure of near-constant Israeli bombardment.

Now, Abuel Abed says, "Israel will let our patients die, even without bombing them."

Hundreds of families seek refuge in Gaza's Churches

With Israel bombing UN buildings, schools and hospitals, desperate Gazans seek refuge in Strip's churches

GAZA CITY—Umm Abdullah Hijazi holds her one-year-old son, Yousef, as she pours water on a bar of soap and tries to wash the boy and his clothes.

Although she scrubs hard, the soapy mixture proves inadequate. Hijazi cannot wash away the dirt and bloodstains that spattered the boy's body as his family fled their home under a hail of Israeli bombs.

"We ran outside as fires broke out all around us. Israeli tank shells fell on our heads and killed some of our neighbors," says Hijazi, who fled with her husband and six children.

The first idea that came to her mind after the shelling was to run to one of the UNRWA schools that act as makeshift shelters for the internally displaced. But with almost 120,000 people now taking refuge in 77 UN-run schools and medical centers, Hijazi found no room for her and her children.

With nowhere else to turn, she sought sanctuary in Gaza's Roman Orthodox Church in Gaza City's Zaytoun neighborhood. It's here where she now hides with her six children. She stubbornly scrubs her baby's bloodstained clothes, hanging what she can on the railings of the ancient church's altar.

In recent days, Gaza's three main churches have all taken in hundreds of terrified Palestinians who have flocked there in hopes that the religious structures—and their relatively sturdy roofs and walls—will provide them with some semblance of protection.

Crowds started flooding in as soon as it became clear that Israel was bombing hospitals, schools and mosques in addition to homes, leaving "literally no safe place for civilians," according to the UN.

While water, food and medicine are all in short supply, Gaza's small but active Palestinian Christian community is trying to do what it can. Bottles of milk are brought in during the day to feed the children.

"We don't have enough fluids or food. Just the basics are all we can offer, but neighbors are helping too," says Kamel Ayad, public relations officer for the Roman Orthodox Church.

Nowhere left to go

"We came to the church to feel safe," says nine-year-old Mustapha Hijazi, although he is still clearly terrified.

Tears roll down his dusty face as he watches his mother hang up his little brother's clothes in the burning sun.

"We used to rent an apartment in the building we just escaped from," says Hijazi.

"If you look now, it's gone, with everything we had. Only rubble exists now."

Hijazi and her children escaped from Shejaiya with only their lives over the weekend. The family has nothing else—no money, no extra clothes, no blankets, no food or water.

"We were terrified by Israel's tank shells. We couldn't sleep at night, or cook and eat because the power was out. The children have just been screaming and crying," says Hijazi.

The children are barefoot, and some are only wearing their undershirts, pants or diapers because they left in a hurry. They still consider themselves lucky in some ways. All they have are the bloodied clothes they managed to escape with.

Shejaiya was pummelled by Israeli air strikes over the weekend, with more than 130 people killed and 300 injured in the massacre. Umm Abdullah's family says they are lucky to have survived, even if their home is gone and no one can sleep at night or during the day. They are all tormented by nightmares.

"There was no time to grab anything—I just gathered up my children and we all ran," says the mother who's still dressed in her in-house prayer outfit.

"I only hope and pray that the walls of this church will shield my children from Israel's artillery shells."

No end in sight

But 19-year-old Anwar al-Jammal is not so sure. Having arrived the previous evening, Jammal bore testament to Monday's heavy shelling, which raged very close to the church. After just one night, all her hopes that a church might be safer have vanished.

"Bombing and shelling was heavy last night, and we were so scared," says Jammal, who is sheltering at the church with her four brothers and five sisters. "This blue window cloth and these heavy iron church-service pieces were knocked down and scattered all over."

"I don't think Israel would hesitate to bomb a church," Jammal adds.

The damage is clear to see. Some of the church windows are shattered and parts of the roof are cracking, with tiles and stones falling off. As the families know, this church is not far from Shejaiya, a neighborhood that has seen some of the worst bombing.

"One woman taking refuge inside here had a miscarriage and lost her baby because she was so terrified from the attacks," says Ayad. "Israeli tank shells also damaged 15 Christian graves and a funeral-service car."

In Operation Cast Lead in 2008–09, Israeli air strikes hit Gaza City's Anglican Church with two missiles, causing enormous damage. Not many people here in this Roman Orthodox church are aware of that.

But Hijazi still insists that this is her only option. "I don't want to see the children killed like my neighbors," she shouts out as she stops rinsing Yousef's trousers, just as another bomb flying overhead makes the entire church tremble.

One of her children, Khalil, complains, "Mom, I am hungry." She sits and says nothing because, as new arrivals, they haven't been registered by the church yet. A woman nearby has leftovers from last night and she offers the boy a piece of a tomato to eat, but with resources dwindling by the day, this daily scramble to get even basic food may well only get harder.

The church is overflowing with people, and there are not enough beds for everyone. Hijazi doesn't know what she will do tonight, except gather the children around her on the floor in a corner that she has claimed for them.

Her traumatized children want to go home when it's safe, despite the blood and the horrors of the massacres everywhere. However, their father knows that the house is now in ruins and their mother says she plans to cling to the church's protection even after a cease-fire is signed. Throughout the day, news filters in that more neighbors have been killed and more families and loved ones have been buried beneath the rubble.

"We don't have a home, everything is destroyed and we don't know where else we can go," says Hijazi.

Gaza's only cell phone network may go down

Cutting cellular phone service in Gaza means that journalists cannot report events and families cannot receive warnings of Israeli shelling

GAZA CITY—Behind the headlines dominated by bombings and killings, a more subtle yet extremely dangerous story is unfolding.

After weeks of heavy bombardment, the Palestine Cellular Communications Company (Jawwal) has begun warning its customers that services in Gaza will have to be cut in the coming days.

The company, a cell phone provider that operates throughout Palestine, knows that cutting communication is bad news for the civilian population. It's through this network that people sometimes receive warnings about possible Israeli strikes. The network is often a critical channel of communication for families, many of whom have been scattered and displaced across the Gaza Strip.

A network suspension would also be bad news for the hundreds of Palestinian journalists who rely on their cell phones to communicate with their editors abroad. They use their phones to get vital information out to the wider world.

Gaza TV reporter Abdelnasser Abueloun says that concern is growing that the lines of communication will soon go dark, which could have dire consequences for Gaza's 1.8 million people.

"This will contribute to the humanitarian crisis when people are [no longer] able to communicate with rescue teams," says Abueloun.

Despite the very real worry that cuts will further isolate an already trapped Gaza Strip—which has seen 17 straight days of shelling and almost a week of ground assaults by the Israeli military—there has so far been no notable international uproar regarding the possible blackout.

"For 17 days, 25 percent of our operations have been down. Much of our capacity has been damaged through homes with antennas on the rooftops being bombed and demolished," says Younies Abu Samra, General Director of Jawwal in Gaza.

With the widespread damage to its infrastructure and the likely continuation of attacks, Jawwal says that the company was left with no choice but to issue a warning to customers on Monday.

In total there are 328 operational stations across the Gaza Strip, according to Jawwal. One-hundred and twenty of them were forced to stop due to a shortage of fuel, while 12 others were damaged by Israeli bombs. The rest are powered by electricity or some sort of battery power, but with widespread power outages rocking Gaza, only about 10 percent—or some 30 stations—are fully operational.

"We have no power or fuel to function at full capacity," says Abu Samra.

Damage to Jawwal's network so far is estimated at around $4m, but that figure is set to rise. It only accounts for the damaged equipment, with total damages likely to be higher.

The equipment, at least in principle, can be repaired. But Jawwal has lost more than that. The company transmits its signal by paying people to place antennas on the roofs of their homes. The widespread destruction across Gaza and subsequent lack of structures on which to install the company's equipment make the task of rebuilding much more challenging.

Two of Jawwal's roof hosts were killed recently when a Jawwal technician tried to fix their antenna. The technician had to have his leg amputated but he survived the Israeli strike.

Jawwal strives to do what it can for its customers. It recently issued a free 10-shekel ($3) "top-up" to its Gaza customers as a gesture of good will, although this gesture should not be mistaken for optimism.

"The service will deteriorate but will not disappear completely, unless more networks are bombed and destroyed," says Abu Samra.

Breaking the silence

Jawwal staff are largely reluctant to comment on politically sensitive issues. They are very careful to stick to technicalities so as not to create misunderstandings with Israel and endanger their work. However, even these snippets of information paint a disturbing picture.

According to Abu Samra, technical staff simply can't keep up with repairing all the damage caused by Israeli strikes. With the remaining infrastructure continuing to come under attack, Jawwal says it had no option but to publish its Gaza-wide warnings.

Internet companies in Gaza have also been complaining that internet service has been very slow over recent weeks. Some experts link this to the damage caused to network providers that also offer internet, with frequent electricity outages further fuelling the problem.

Abu Raed, a 51-year-old resident of al-Zaytoun, says he has desperately been trying to check on his sister, who lives close to the border with Israel. But has been unable to get through.

"Without a mobile phone, I can't connect with my family," he says.

His part of Gaza City has been one of the worst hit. It's likely that al-Zaytoun will see yet more Israeli strikes if the crisis is not resolved.

"The longer we wait, the more catastrophic it becomes," says Jawwal's Abu Samra. "The solution is in the hands of other states [which must act] to stop the aggression and make sure the network is not affected."

In the 2008–09 war on Gaza, damages to Jawwal came to around 5m Jordanian dinars ($7m). This was roughly made up of $950,000 in network damage, $85,000 in infrastructure damage and just under $6m in other damage.

The toll is not just financial. Gaza TV's Abueloun says that network and internet interruptions have a huge impact on news-gathering.

Not only will this prevent journalists and other media professionals, who rely on cell phones, from making contact with their sources across the Strip. Local journalists may well find themselves increasingly squeezed out by international reporters who can gain access to Israeli satellite networks when times get truly tough.

With local news sources unable to compete for breaking news, a vital source of local income will be lost. But just as importantly, an increasingly incomplete picture of the situation on the ground will likely emerge, which could undermine the diplomatic response or inhibit things like aid delivery.

"This is what we don't want, particularly during war," says Abueloun. "Communications should be kept out of conflict and squabbling."

International moves to broker a cease-fire are heating up. There is hope that shells on both sides will stop firing in time for *eid*—the period at the end of Ramadan—when families and friends usually get together, or at least call and email one another, to mark the holiday.

However, with the death toll in Gaza at almost 700 and likely to rise, even an early cease-fire may not be able to get the lines of communication functioning again.

Hiding in the shadow of the pastor in Gaza

Gaza's churches provide families with shelter but they remain a possible target for Israel's war machine

GAZA CITY—Gaza's Greek Orthodox Archbishop Alexios has not had much sleep in the past few days. He has been busy ensuring that scores of Palestinian families that sought refuge in his church, the Church of Saint Porphyrius, are getting all the help they need.

"People did not know where to go. We had to help by opening the church's doors for women, babies, young and old people," Alexios told Al Jazeera.

On Sunday, a few hundred people, mostly families escaping the death and destruction of Shejaiya, came to the church, increasing the number of those sheltered in the church and the neighboring mosque to at least 1,000.

The gesture by the Greek Orthodox church sparked much solidarity in the community.

This is not the first time that churches have been turned into refugee centers during times of war. Alexios recalls that in previous wars, there were fewer families.

"Now there is much destruction," he said.

The Israeli assault on Gaza, which is entering its third week, has left at least 658 Palestinians dead, including 161 children and 60 women, and over

4,000 injured. Thousands of families were forced to flee their homes in search of safe haven. The UN estimates the number of internally displaced persons in the Strip to be at 118,300.

The churches of Gaza are among the very few places left where Palestinians can seek refuge—so far. But on Monday night, a cemetery located in the Roman Orthodox Church's yard was hit by an Israeli strike.

As a result, five Christian graves were destroyed and a funeral-service car was hit by two Israeli tank shells, according to Kamel Ayad, director of public relations at the church. The attack also caused panic among the refugees. Some even left in the middle of the night, only to come back in the morning.

"If we ask why they hit [the church], they [the Israelis] will come up with an excuse. But what I know is that Israel announced that churches and mosques were protected areas. They are safe places," said Alexios.

During its 17-day assault, Israel's army has hit at least five mosques.

The Church of Saint Porphyrius, the Latin Catholic Church and the Holy Family Church have also taken in a large number of displaced people.

Umm Amjad Shalah, a mother of nine, has run out of options for finding a sanctuary where her family feels protected. Hers is one of the many families that sought refuge in the Roman Orthodox Church.

"I thought Israel would not bomb us here, in a church—so we are taking refuge in the shadow of the pastor," she told Al Jazeera while comforting her one-year-old baby, born with a birth defect.

Her 10-year-old son Salman is so traumatized by the war that he will not let go of her.

"Mother, don't leave me! It [the bomb] is going to hit me!" he screams at her. Salman is visibly terrified, his young face and wide eyes showing tension and hysteria.

"Sometimes he screams so loud, it almost sounds like he's laughing loudly. Like he's out of control," says Umm Amjad as she puts a hand on his head.

"We were so scared last night, even inside the church. Tank shells were pounding the area all around, hitting very close to us," she says.

Umm Amjad said that the way the refugee residents of the Shejaiya neighborhood had to flee their homes over the last few days served as a grim reminder of the Nakba days, when thousands of Palestinians were driven out of their homes and off their land by Israel in 1947 and 1948.

"This is the same Nakba that Israel inflicted on our parents in the past, and now on us and our children. This is the very same terrifying experience our parents went through," she told Al Jazeera.

Nadia al-Jamal, 20, is another Palestinian who was forced to flee the Shaaf neighborhood when the bombing intensified.

"We were all huddled in the living room when Israeli tank shells were falling—unable to go anywhere," Jamal said. Half of the Jamal family ended up in UNRWA schools, while the other half had to search for other places.

"The school's classrooms were overflowing," she said, adding that some classrooms had over 50 women squeezed into them, with little room to move or breathe.

Jamal has now spent two days at the church. "It was only yesterday, when Israel began bombing right around the church, that we began to lose hope that the church would be a place of safety."

Church leaders, however, caution that there is a limit to how much the church can offer, particularly given Israel's blockade of Gaza and the ensuing dire conditions.

"Banks are closed, and as of now, the church has insufficient funds to buy food and water for the incoming people," Ayad told Al Jazeera.

According to Alexios, many people—Christians and Muslims—have reached out to the church to offer help. "The baker provides bread, some provide water and blankets, while others offer whatever they can. It is one society here in Gaza, like a big village."

Several organizations have been providing food for the *iftar* meal every night, securing enough supplies to go through another day, said Alexios. He tries to address the most immediate needs first.

Local NGOs like Caritas, according to Alexios, have been bringing in water, food and most importantly a generator to pump water for the refugees.

"God brings good people here with a will to help. There is a committee from the neighborhood which takes care of those who fled Shejaiya, catering to their needs."

Following the church cemetery bombing, 36-year-old Najla Juha, a mother of 10, sent her children to their grandmother's house. They were too scared to stay in the church, she said.

"The priests are here, they try to help. But it is not enough. We have nothing—no mattresses, no food, no clothes. We couldn't bring anything with us because the children were asleep [when the attack happened], so we had to carry them as we escaped our house," she said.

Ayad said that his church was offering whatever it could and, as in all previous wars, Muslim Palestinians had sought refuge inside the churches after mosques were targeted first.

He added that the church would continue to offer a safe haven, though he was not sure if the church was immune from Israeli attacks.

Two dozen killed as several UNRWA schools hit in Gaza

Eighteen civilians and three aid workers killed in strikes on UNRWA schools today

BEIT HANOUN, GAZA STRIP—At Kamal Adwan Hospital, the ambulances arrived unusually full with several injured at once. While this is becoming an increasingly regular sight in Gaza, there was something new about these ambulances that rushed in people from a UNRWA school at Beit Hanoun.

Every one of those injured or killed had hoped that they would be safe under the UN's protection. But they were not. In recent weeks, people have been flocking to UN-run shelters. The UN said it was sheltering 117,469 displaced Palestinians at 77 schools before today's bombing. This is more than double the number at the peak of the 2008–09 Israeli incursion. Many of these internal refugees now feel like they have been left with nowhere else to go, now that even the UN schools have succumbed to the Israeli bombardment.

The scenes at the school in northern Gaza are horrific. The peaceful light-blue walls of UNRWA schools are still spattered with blood. The children who once studied here have suddenly been forced to see another face of their school.

The black-and-white floor is covered with pools of blood. A blood-soaked blanket and a pair of lonely sandals are scattered nearby. The blood belongs to the people who were fasting here, waiting to break their fast three hours later.

Medics informed *MEE* that in this one school massacre 18 people, including a baby, were killed and over 200 were injured.

Since the attack, the panic level among the already frightened families has reached new proportions. Women and children have now fled the school and are taking refuge in hospitals, but these are also full and struggling to cope.

The influx of wounded is too much for one hospital to deal with, forcing casualties to be sent to four other hospitals: Beit Hanoun, Kamal Adwan, al-Awda and Shifa hospitals.

It is an exhausting feat for a mother to go by foot and search haphazardly for her children, who could be in any one of these four hospitals scattered throughout Gaza. Several people have still not been accounted for, with relatives continuing their frantic search.

The family of 17-year-old Doaa Abu Awda was forced to scour the various hospitals for their daughter. The family ran to Gaza City's Shifa Hospital, despite the heavy shelling in the area, after they were told that she sustained injuries and was being treated there. Once they got there, however, they were told by the receptionist that she was not there. The family ran through all the corridors trying to find her, but couldn't find her anywhere. After exhausting all other possibilities, the family went down to the morgue and immediately their search came to a tragic end.

Abu Awda was with her family seeking refuge in a place that she trusted to be safe. More than a thousand Palestinians were in the school in Beit Hanoun seeking refuge with her when the bombs struck.

"I was sitting in the soccer field when five tank shells hit," says an injured child to *Middle East Eye*, although he struggles to get the words out.

Another woman, running in terror, screams, "My daughter, my daughter. . . . They had her legs and arms amputated!"

This is one of the deadliest strikes today, and the bloodiest on a UN institution so far. In the last 24 hours, seven UNRWA schools have been hit or damaged by Israeli shelling. Earlier on Thursday, three UNRWA aid workers were killed when an Israeli shell hit their school. Five people were also injured in a separate attack on a girls' school, according to the UN.

The incident has further ignited debate about Israel's targeting of civilian sites, especially UNRWA schools and medical facilities that are supposed to be designated safe zones.

Israel insists that it does not purposefully target UN buildings.

"We can't confirm that this is a result of errant fire. In any case, we do not target UN facilities," said military spokesman Lt. Col. Peter Lerner to reporters. Lerner stressed that the military had urged the UN and the Red Cross to evacuate the school for three days leading up to the incident.

UNRWA, however, has challenged this. Spokespeople on the ground told Arabic-language media that, while UNRWA was warned, it was not given nearly enough time to evacuate the building.

UNRWA spokesman Chris Gunness also separately wrote on Twitter about the incident: "Precise coordinates of the UNRWA shelter in Beit Hanoun had been formally given to the Israeli army."

The scores of Palestinians who had been sheltering at the school have now begun lashing out at aid agencies. People from the school say they were misled when the International Committee of the Red Cross informed them that schools were the safest places to go to. Eyewitnesses additionally told the *Middle East Eye* that shortly before the blast, they were told by the ICRC to assemble in one place so that buses could take them to a safer location. Before the buses arrived, however, the shelling started. With so many people huddled together, the casualty count was almost certain to be huge. Whether the allegations are ultimately proven or not, the result is the same. Many Palestinians say they have grown weary, even distrustful, of the aid group.

Hamas has also now spoken out about the incident, saying that the Beit Hanoun massacre was extremely ominous.

Sami Abu Zuhri, a Hamas spokesman, criticized the Red Cross for its silence. Hamas has vowed revenge.

"Unfortunately, the Red Cross is not playing any role to scandalize the crimes of occupation and violating humanitarian cease-fire," he told reporters.

Israel launched its military offensive on July 8, with the declared objective of deterring Hamas from firing rockets from Gaza. Yet the rockets continue after almost three weeks of war. So far the majority of the targets in Gaza have been civilian, according to the UN.

The bombing of civilian structures is forbidden under international law, although Israel says that Hamas hides rockets beneath many of these structures, declaring the bombings legitimate.

However, in a densely populated area like Gaza, it has proved impossible to find anywhere that is a safe haven from Israel's wrath. The cost to civilian lives has been huge.

Thursday's death toll now stands at 112 Palestinians, with further strikes expected throughout the evening. Thus far, evenings have seen some of the worst shelling. In the past 17 days of war, more than 805 Palestinians have been killed and another 4,800 have been injured, while 33 Israeli soldiers and two civilians have been killed.

The death toll is likely to keep climbing. As evening set in, in Gaza several of the Beit Hanoun families were still looking for missing family members, as were scores of other Gazans who have struggled to make contact with friends and family across the Strip.

To the east of Gaza City, the Red Crescent says there are between 30 and 50 people who are missing. No information has thus far emerged regarding their whereabouts.

Umm Mohammed Shamali has lost her three brothers and her niece. The last time she was in touch with her brother, he said, "Send me an ambulance, please. I am injured and bleeding." Then his mobile phone died and Umm Mohammed has heard nothing since.

International aid groups are trying to intensify search-and-rescue efforts, but to little avail. According to UNRWA's Gunness, "Over the course of the day, UNRWA tried to coordinate with the Israeli Army a window for civilians to leave, but it was never granted."

This leaves Umm Mohammed and countless others like her with little hope that aid agencies will be able to act as a barrier to further Israeli attacks. Israel seems set to continue inflicting a terrible toll on Gaza.

Gaza about to run out of fuel, electricity: officials

Gaza officials issue their most frantic appeal yet as Strip uses up last energy reserves

GAZA CITY—Gaza's only power plant is perilously close to running out of fuel, Palestinian authorities have said, sparking a last-ditch appeal for emergency supplies.

The Palestinian Energy Authority on Thursday stepped up its previous appeals to Palestine's unity government, aid organizations and the EU, calling on them to take immediate action to provide the plant with desperately needed fuel.

Tons of fuel donated by Qatar lies just across the border, but with Egypt so far keeping the shipments in the Suez Canal and closing the Rafah crossing, none of this potentially lifesaving fuel has reached Gaza for almost a month.

"We have informed the Palestinian Authority in Ramallah that we are unable to collect monthly bills from people because of the war that Gaza is now living through," said Fathi El-Sheikh Khalil, the Deputy Head of Palestinian Energy Authority, on Thursday.

He called on authorities to release the Qatari fuel, saying that now was the right moment to take action. However, so far no action appears to have been taken, and Gaza's last reserves are quickly running out.

In the last several days, Gaza has received 250 liters of fuel, half of the 400 to 450 liters needed to run Gaza's power plant. With Egypt's Rafah crossing closed on Fridays and the Israeli Sabbath on Saturday, this could leave the Strip with no new fuel shipments throughout the weekend.

During the past three days, the power plant has not received any fuel at all, with its last reserves due to run out in the next 24 hours, according to Khalil.

For more than a week, Gaza has been operating on at most two hours of electricity a day, but this could dwindle even further.

To make matters worse, the power plant was hit by Israeli shells early on Wednesday morning.

Jamal al-Dardasawi, head of public relations of Gaza's Electricity Distribution Company, said that his technical staff was able to fix the damage, but the situation remains tense and many workers are worried that the plant will be hit again. Some power-plant workers now say they will only return to work after receiving guarantees that they will not be bombed, although any reassurances may well ring hollow.

Dardasawi claimed that targeting civilian infrastructure, like the power plant, is an act of collective punishment, intended to hit the 1.8 million Palestinians living in Gaza rather than Hamas or any other organization Israel claims to be fighting.

Repair teams from the electricity company work around the clock, even under the most difficult circumstances. The company says that it usually manages to coordinate with Israeli authorities in order to avoid having its workers caught in the fighting. But the coordination does not always work. This morning in Bani Suheila, in eastern Khan Younis, workers wearing orange vests were hit and three staff members sustained injuries Dardasawi said.

Israel, which usually provides Gaza with the vast majority of its electricity, has already damaged much of this infrastructure or shut off the supply completely.

This has left Gaza with an 80 percent energy deficit, according to Dardasawi. The power plant could never hope to compensate for this, even if it could get enough fuel to run at full capacity.

"After restarting the power plant, it will produce 113 megawatt, while Gazans need 480–500 megawatt at this time of year," Dardasawi said.

Wider impact

Fuel and electricity are not just needed to turn on the lights or power up mobile phones. Power is also desperately needed for a wide array of critical services, from health care to sanitation.

Water filtration and sewage pumps have all been affected by the cuts, as have hospitals and shops.

The United Nations Office for Coordination of Humanitarian Affairs (OCHA) estimated that 1.2 million people have no or very limited access to water or sanitation services due to the damaged electricity system and the lack of fuel to run generators.

International aid agencies have openly called on Egypt and Israel to allow in more supplies, with Amnesty International saying that both countries "must ensure that urgently needed medical and relief supplies, as well as sufficient amounts of fuel, are allowed into the Gaza Strip on a continual basis." So far these calls have fallen on deaf ears.

The crippling power shortages have already prompted many shopkeepers to frantically sell their goods at whatever price they can fetch.

In West Gaza City, shopkeepers are still defying the ongoing bombing by opening their shops to sell meat. But they too know that the lack of refrigeration means that their dairy and meat products may go rotten.

Abu Taha, 32, said that if he does not sell all his meat now, he will have to throw it away.

"Even if people take meat on debt, it's better than dumping it in the garbage," he said.

Some pharmacies are also complaining that they have been forced to dump medications that have to be kept cool, which is only compounding Gaza's already mounting health crisis.

Hospitals have likewise begun calling Gaza's electricity company and begging to have their power restored. Many hospitals have generators, but these are unreliable. They can often cause the voltage to spike, which damages equipment and causes medicine to go bad, Khalil said.

The only power Khalil feels he has is through the media, which he hopes will inform the world about what is going on, prompting a stronger international response. The Palestinian Authority and Israel don't seem to be listening.

"Only stones remain": Gaza lies in ruins

Palestinians in Gaza have been shocked by the scale of Israeli destruction, as long-term truce efforts continue

BEIT HANOUN, GAZA STRIP—Umm Ahmed Abu Sahwish holds stones in her hands. They are all that's left of her demolished home. "My home is gone and only stones remain," the 65-year-old says.

Hundreds of homes have been destroyed and unexploded Israeli missiles litter the ground in Beit Hanoun, a town at Gaza's northern tip near the border with Israel. The local hospital, emergency rescue equipment and critical infrastructure have also incurred heavy damage from Israeli shelling.

Another woman, from a family of 20 people, cries as she tries to dig through the rubble of her house. "Lifetimes of personal and household belongings are gone with one Israeli missile. Where can we go? We have no food, water, bedding or extra clothes," she says.

Driving the length of this tiny stretch of land—1.8 million Palestinians live on Gaza's 360 sq km—scenes of devastation are everywhere. The trip from the north to the south of Gaza was only possible during a 12-hour humanitarian cease-fire, agreed to by Israel and Hamas on July 26.

On Sunday, Israel resumed its military operation in Gaza as the Prime Minister's office declared: "If residents are inadvertently hit, it is Hamas which is responsible given that it has—again—violated the humanitarian truce that Israel acceded to."

Hamas and other Palestinian factions reportedly agreed to a 24-hour humanitarian truce in the Gaza Strip, starting at 2 pm local time on Sunday.

At least 1,052 Palestinians have been killed and more than 6,000 injured since Israel's military offensive began on July 8. Forty-three Israeli soldiers have also been killed, along with two Israeli civilians and one Thai worker.

In Gaza City, there is little to salvage from beneath the destruction.

The eastern neighborhood of Shejaiya is a ghost town. Electricity cables are severed and sticking out of the debris of homes. Cars lay burned out, and human remains are scattered along the streets; the air is thick with the smell of decay. "I am 45 years old, and I have never seen destruction like this," says a resident, who didn't give Al Jazeera his name.

At least 120 Palestinians were killed and hundreds more injured when Israel heavily bombarded Shejaiya overnight on July 21. The cease-fire provided the first opportunity for families to return to their homes to survey the destruction and salvage their belongings.

Ambulance sirens ring out, announcing the discovery of more dead bodies beneath the rubble. At least 90 bodies were pulled out from the destruction in Shejaiya during the cease-fire on Saturday.

"This is more ominous than Sabra and Shatila," says Umm Hesham, referring to the killing of about 2,000 Palestinian refugees in the Beirut-area refugee camps in 1982, as her son helps her avoid stepping on bodies.

Outside Shejaiya, on al-Wehda Street, traffic was closed off. Residents busied themselves with trying to get food, water and medicine during the cease-fire. Abu Haytam, a father of eight, stood at a market looking for pasta and lentils. He said he didn't know what would happen in the coming days: "With electricity out, we can't buy meat or chicken. It will rot too quickly in the heat."

Nearby, a man selling vegetables was surrounded by customers, while at least 300 men waited for bread at Tal al-Hawa Bakery. Banks were crowded, while money-wiring centers were overflowing with people clamouring to get cash.

There are two roads linking north and south Gaza: Saladin Road and Beach Road. Both are damaged, the former from Israeli tank shells and the latter from the Israeli warships lining the coast.

Along Saladin Road, dairies and a local beverage factory had been destroyed, while technical teams worked to restore power to electricity and water installations. Al-Aqsa Hospital in Deir al-Balah was damaged after Israeli strikes hit the operating theater and the radiology department on July 21, killing five people and injuring more than 70 others.

In Khan Younis, a burned-out crater left a gaping hole in the main road—the aftermath of an Israeli F-16 missile strike. The residents of nearby Khuza'a, which was under heavy Israeli bombardment, are sleeping on the streets. Access to water is extremely difficult; a man who usually sells water tanks for 15 NIS ($4) is now asking for 100 NIS ($29).

The road to Rafah, at Gaza's southernmost end, is equally precarious.

Two days ahead of Eid al-Fitr, the celebration marking the end of the holy month of Ramadan, Dahra Market in Khan Younis is buzzing with activity, but no one is in the mood to celebrate. Most are only there to stock up on supplies.

But in Rafah, a barbershop is full of young people getting haircuts. Spirits are high, but talk quickly turns to stories of death and destruction. The youth criticize neighboring Egypt for not opening the Rafah border crossing, only a few hundred meters away.

"The [Israeli–Egyptian] siege has hit every aspect of life; spare parts for my shaving machine are unavailable," says 29-year-old barber Abuel Bara. "Before, we would buy it from tunnel merchants, but tunnels are now closed."

The machine provides the only income to feed his two daughters, his wife, his parents and his siblings, he says. "But Israel sees no humanitarian need [to lift the siege]."

Rescue teams: on Gaza's front lines

Gaza's first responders are on the front lines as Israel bombards the coastal strip, often targeting emergency services personnel

It has become the norm for Ayman Sahwan to round up injured civilians. It's a job he has done for 15 years and continues to do.

"Every day I see new faces, and meet new people in similar high-stress, painful situations" he says.

Sahwan just received a signal from the emergency operator informing him of another Israeli air strike on Gaza City—an Israeli drone missile has slammed into another family home. So he runs with his colleague to the ambulance.

The door of the ambulance is hardly closed before the ambulance rushes off to the next mission.

"These Israeli 'knock on the roof' drone-missile warnings are injuring and killing so many people, demolishing homes and bringing the roof down on top of their heads," he says, driving toward the Nasser Street area in central Gaza City.

The ambulance arrives amid a mass of anxious people. Sahwan sees a man, his wife and children all wearing short-sleeve tops as if they had just been asleep in bed. Sahwan then sees the deep wound, about 10 cm wide, in the man's head.

"I've seen so much blood and injury lately, it doesn't affect me anymore" he says. "But I am still affected by witnessing the horror and terror in the people's eyes and hearing the screams, cries and shouts of the children, women and men as they run from their beds and homes, some almost naked, to escape Israel's missile attacks and death."

Everyone is running everywhere and nowhere, because there is nowhere to hide. Everywhere is under threat of attack. The ambulances are a destination for many, but even the ambulances are not safe. For Sahwan, there is not much more he can do, other than bring the injured and dead to the already overcrowded hospitals in Gaza.

Sahwan acknowledged that his greatest fear is heading into the unknown. He knows that an Israeli missile has hit, but his real fear is that another missile will strike the location where he's going, or even target the ambulance directly, in the same way that so many other ambulances have been targeted.

The red flashing lights of the ambulance won't protect him—so he tries to work in partnership with another ambulance, as backup, for the task that lies ahead.

"Sometimes I feel the impact of the missile when it hits—but it's too late to react or reverse," he says.

He has gained a lot of experience doing this work. He's familiar with the various types of missiles that Israel fires at Gaza—the different sounds they make, the various pitches and the interval of time between when the F-16 or drone launches its bombs and when they strike their targets.

Like his colleagues, he makes the rounds to all the hospitals in an attempt to match up ripped and shredded body parts left in the rubble or scattered on the streets by Israel's military. It's important to put back the human body parts that Israel blew up so inhumanely.

"This is very common. More than in previous military strikes on Gaza, Israel is using lethal weapons which split bodies into even smaller pieces of burned flesh."

On Thursday, Gaza's Interior Ministry again accused Israel of using white phosphorous, as well as flechette weapons containing miniature metal darts that pierce the flesh and embed metal shrapnel fragments into the body and organs.

Human Rights groups familiar with Israel's use of such weapons—including DIME (Dense Inert Metal Explosive) weapons—don't need to inform or remind Sahwan about this. During his 24-hour shift, if he gets a chance for a break to eat or pray with his colleagues, they already know and discuss the symptoms they have witnessed first hand from such weapons, their impacts evident on the bodies of the people around them.

As they sit around the ambulances next to the emergency operator, they talk about many topics, including food recipes and their families, to distract them from thoughts of the next call that inevitably comes in.

Home is calling

Sahwan is a father of three children who call him immediately every time they hear of an attack involving an ambulance crew, just to make sure he is still alive.

When it was announced that Sahwan's colleague, Fouad Jaber, had been killed by shrapnel and rubble in an Israeli air strike on Shejaiya, in eastern of Gaza, Sahwan's relatives called many times to check on him.

He tends to avoid too many phone calls when he needs to focus on his work and tend to so many victims, injured or dead.

The calls he will always answer are those of his children, like the call he is taking now from his youngest daughter, 12-year-old Shahd, who constantly worries about her father's safety and wants to know when he's coming home.

Sahwan's family knows his 24-hour shift is almost done. It's early in the morning. Now comes his return journey back to Khan Younis in the south of the Gaza Strip. This journey is another risk that scares his children. He does not go home by ambulance, which further maximizes the dangers of the journey.

"Take care of yourself daddy. I need you!" says Shahd.

When Shahd calls her father, he tries not to contemplate the possibility that something might happen to her and the rest of his family. His family is familiar with stories of ambulance crews being held hostage and injured by Israeli troops, while others are arrested and detained.

"Sometimes I fear not getting home to my children" he says.

But when morning comes, he's relieved that at least his shift is over and his worries, for now, will diminish when he gets back to his family in Khan Younis and they are all together again.

"I always worry about what might happen to my wife and children, if I'm killed in an Israeli air strike."

The fire department is in no less danger. The firemen all have their share of concerns and suffering. If Sahwan needs to evacuate victims from homes bombed and burned by Israeli missiles, he must first wait for his fire department friends to come and contain the fire.

Firefighting under gunfire: another difficult task

Ahmed Joudeh, a 24-year-old firefighter, recalls when Israeli warships bombed their fire department building at Gaza Beach. They had to evacuate and then run to help fishermen and their boats, which were burning. "We were trying to put out the fishing-boat fires and then another Israeli navy missile struck nearby. We tried to keep away, moving into another fishing boat, but we were hit again, and again" he says.

Meanwhile, Omar Abu Owdah, 44 years old and in charge of tonight's shift, says it is understood why Israel targets fire departments and emergency service departments, even though they are so clearly marked and visible.

As father of nine children between two and 16 years, his family constantly tries to reach him. He says it's only in Palestine where emergency first responders are targeted in wartime.

A difficult aspect of his job is teaching new recruits who are replacing those who have been injured or killed by Israeli attacks. It's not easy to explain to them why they are now so often the target.

In total, seven Palestinian ambulance medics have been killed and 16 others injured since the offensive began three weeks ago, according to the Health Ministry. One of the last ones to be killed was 32-year-old Mohammad Alabadla, who was killed in Khuza'a, in the southern Gaza Strip.

Another, Hamed al-Borai, was killed when his ambulance was bombed by Israeli tank shells in Beit Hanoun. He was burned inside the ambulance while others inside sustained critical wounds.

Meanwhile, Hussam Radi, a medical analysis specialist, died of his injuries today.

The Health Ministry says such attacks go against the fourth Geneva Convention and are in violation humanitarian international law.

Gaza pulverized beyond recognition

During a brief cease-fire, Gazans return to the places they knew as home, only to be met with the stench of death and sight of destruction

"You either give me the bodies of my two brothers so I can bury them, or tell me they're alive so I can hug them," screams a mother in her mid-forties as she searches for her two brothers in Shejaiya, eastern Gaza City, during a 12-hour humanitarian cease-fire.

She's not alone in her desperate search for loved ones. The search takes hours amidst the smell of death and burned flesh that fills the ruins and rubble of what were recently family homes. During the cease-fire on Saturday, 155 bodies were found across Gaza Strip, deaths which resulted from the last Israeli bombings.

Ahmed Al-Hassan, 32, is one among many in the Shejaiya neighborhood searching for lost relatives. He is searching for uncles he lost contact with over two weeks ago.

Al-Hassan was here a month ago, but nothing he sees looks anything like what he remembers before Israel's missiles started falling.

"I can't tell which part used to be the street and which the house," he says while carefully stepping through the huge pile of rubble to see if he can find anyone, dead or alive.

Rescue teams are using masks because the smell is very strong. Ambulance crews have been shot at, as Israel has barred them from entering this area. Seven medics have been killed, while many others have been injured.

Al-Hassan continues treading slowly through what's left of homes destroyed by Israel's F-16s, drones and tank shells. "This is a tragedy of the century, and the world is letting Israel get away with it" he says while removing a destroyed copy of the Quran from the ruins of the houses.

"See, even holy sites and mosques are bombed. . . . Look, this is where I used to pray when visiting my grandmother. I recognize this," he adds, his eyes tired and his face covered in dust as he keeps searching through the destruction for anything else he recognizes.

He is able to identify a mosaic piece from the mosque.

He can't find the stone pillar in the middle of his uncle's home, nor the tiny garden at its entrance or the silver-colored door he remembers from childhood. Only ruins remain. He continues the search for the corpses, in line with the Islamic tradition that requires the dead to be buried quickly as a way of honoring them. It's a practice shared by the Jewish faith.

"But they won't allow Gaza that human and spiritual dignity," says Al-Hassan. "God created human beings to be treated with dignity. But in Gaza, even our dead lose their dignity and respect, humiliated by the Israeli occupiers."

Still confused and trying to visualize the plan of the house and link it with the rubble around him, he says, "I think that was where my children used to be. It was full of love and beautiful memories."

Al-Hassan will have to adapt to the new reality—but he is saddened every time the rescue teams shout out that they have found more bodies, some of whom he recognizes as his grandmother's neighbors. The smell around Al-Hassan gets stronger.

Key to ruins

When the humanitarian cease-fire was announced, Haider Abu Hussein, 34, took the key to his house with him as he left the park where he had taken shelter to go to his house and find clothes for his children. But he could not find the house.

"We had to make holes in the walls of our home so as to escape through them and get to the side street," he says, explaining the miracle of how he is still alive when so many of his neighbors are dead and buried under the rubble. His face becomes tense as he smells the dead bodies.

Abu Hussein's family had to split up: some went to the park and others to the UNRWA school or to relatives' houses. He is one of 170,000 people forced to flee their homes by Israel's strikes. A baby in the park cries for food, but Abu Hussein can't offer anything—as all his house's contents have been destroyed and burned.

Walking along Nazaz Street in Gaza City, people know the 12-hour cease-fire is crucial in finding relatives and grabbing as many supplies as they can before Israel attacks again.

The cease-fire has exposed the extent of the destruction wrought by Israel's 19-day offensive. The heaviest bombardment was here in Shejaiya, when Israeli strikes killed and wounded hundreds.

As ambulance and rescue teams continue their recovery work, friends, neighbors and colleagues of the victims use this 12-hour window to look for who they can find. Over 150 bodies have been found, bringing the Gaza death toll to 1,015.

When Abu Hussein gets to what he thinks was his home, he stands in shock.

He says this this is a man-made Israeli hurricane. He received no warning call or "roof knock" from Israel before the bombing. It just came.

Now, dead bodies are under the building and health officials are calling for an urgent clean up so as to avoid making a humanitarian crisis and human catastrophe become worse.

However, for Abu Hussein there is not much left, not even an ID he can use to prove he once lived here.

This is the immediate reality he cannot change—his legacy is nothing but a home reduced to rubble and a homeless family. Many others around him have to face the same horror and deal with it in the best way they can.

"There are the mattresses my children used to sleep on," says Abu Hussein's neighbor.

"But every time we Palestinians are killed under Israel's occupation, we pick ourselves up and carry on as best we can. This time, our resistance is stronger and we have to rely on it, instead of relying on lame world leaders."

Many people are crying around him, while others collapse after seeing bodies pulled gently out of the rubble, pulverized beyond recognition.

A neighbor of Abu Hussein says: “Homes can be rebuilt, if Israel allows construction materials through to Gaza.” He doesn’t expect this to happen.

“If we could turn the bones of our bodies into bridges to our freedom, we would do that to escape this ominous Israeli siege.”

As Gazans mark Eid, killing is still Israel's "favorite sport"

This year's Eid al-Fitr celebration will not take place for 170,000 displaced Gazans, but their strong spirit resists as they have nothing else to lose

GAZA CITY—Amjad Habeeb should be celebrating Eid al-Fitr on Monday with his children and his wife. Marking the end of the holy month of Ramadan, Muslims celebrate Eid al-Fitr by exchanging visits and gifts with relatives and friends.

This year, however, the devastating impact of Israel's Operation Protective Edge means that the 33-year-old has nothing to offer his family except goodwill. He has nowhere to receive relatives, as his house is located in the Shejaiya area, which was razed by Israeli strikes.

The reality of this year's Ramadan for Amjad is that he is dependent on what the United Nations Relief and Works Agency for Palestine Refugees in the Near East (UNRWA) can offer him—he and his family are sheltering at a UNRWA school.

There is no need to ask him how or what he feels. He had earned his living as an electrician, but can no longer house or feed his family.

"A week ago we ran away from our home," he says, pausing to watch his four children: 12-year-old Mohammed, 10-year-old Laila, 7-year-old Shams and 4-year-old Abdel Rahman.

"We ran away under Israeli artillery shells at 6 am," he says as he touches the hands of his daughter Shams, who is sleeping in a dusty, bare classroom. Amjad's family and others sharing the room have hung spare clothes up across the windows to create some shade and keep temperatures down, while also creating a semblance of privacy.

His voice seems tired and cracked—but he can still speak about his experience of Israel's offensive. "The target was never the resistance. The aim was to kill us, destroy our homes and uproot us all again," he says.

Despite the 24-hour cease-fire agreed upon by Israel and Hamas, he still finds it difficult to return home. This year the Eid celebration will not take place for Amjad and his family and 170,000 displaced inhabitants of Gaza.

In previous years, he was one of the lucky few Gazans who could afford to buy new Eid dresses for his daughters and suits for his two boys.

"[Israeli Prime Minister Benjamin] Netanyahu did not intend for us to celebrate. But he underestimates our strong spirit to survive."

Amjad echoes the voices of hundreds of displaced families who have no connection to Gaza's resistance, or to the resistance in their neighborhood of Shejaiya either. The only link is that they all happen to live in Gaza.

"We hear rockets still being fired from Gaza—but Netanyahu can't pretend that he has achieved anything apart from hurting more trapped civilians."

Failed military target

Gaza-based political analyst Hani Habeeb sees Israel's offensive in Gaza as a failure on two points: targets and ending the resistance's crude rocket attacks.

"As long as Netanyahu continues this war, it means he did not achieve his goals."

Habeeb says that Netanyahu knows that in the eyes of the Israeli public and voters, not achieving his objectives means that both he and his party are out of Israeli politics as a whole.

In Gaza, there is a belief among the population that the continuation of the offensive reflects the fact that Netanyahu is in trouble. But Amjad and people sleeping in UNRWA schools question why they must pay the price for Israel's internal politics.

"The last time I saw fighters in my neighborhood was seven years ago."

Habeeb says that certain ambitious Israeli leaders see themselves as Netanyahu's future successors.

"They pushed him more, to perform a bigger show of war so they can take his position when Israel sees his failure to crack down on the Palestinian resistance."

Meanwhile, Palestinian resistance groups in Gaza say they will continue their retaliation until their conditions are met: ending the long blockade of Gaza, releasing prisoners arrested in the past two months and opening all borders.

"Naftali Bennet is waiting for Netanyahu to fail, to present himself as a harder candidate in the next election," adds Habeeb.

Habeeb also says that Palestinian blood is the "price" for Israeli votes. The more Palestinian blood is promised, the more Israeli votes are won.

The UN-initiated 24-hour humanitarian cease-fire appears not to have held as Hamas and Israel exchanged accusations of violating the cease-fire. Hamas accused Israel of bombing Khuza'a and other places within the cease-fire time. Sixteen Palestinians were killed and 30 were injured on Sunday, while one Israeli was injured.

Habeeb says the offensive will continue for some time, but a cease-fire for humanitarian reasons will be the norm.

"I think both parties want a cease-fire. The Palestinian resistance and Israel are pressuring each other to accept cease-fire conditions."

Regional and international parties are unable to end the offensive on Gaza. Hamas is at odds with Egypt for supporting the Muslim Brotherhood in Egypt.

Habeeb believes that with or without Gaza's resistance, the killing will continue. He says killing is "Israel's favorite sport," especially prior to its national elections.

For him, the Israeli public must be aware that Israel's military offensive has failed in achieving its objectives. He invited the world to start bringing those responsible for killing Gazans to international criminal courts.

Habeeb says people who had lost their homes and children have nothing more to lose. Support for the resistance is increasing among people. He himself did not support the resistance a few months ago, but now he says there is nothing left to do, since all else has failed.

"I shall remain patient because this is my home. I belong here and will never leave Palestine."

When Habeeb is asked by *Middle East Eye*—as he wanders around the UNRWA school room with its blue-painted walls, looking for a piece of carton for his daughter Sham to sleep on—what he would say to the Israeli public if given the chance, he responds:

"Allah is watching and only he will judge Netanyahu and his military." He then pauses to comfort his impatient child, who is crying from hunger and the heat.

"Your prime minister has failed his objectives. The resistance fighters are still alive. It is we civilians who are killed with our children."

Gaza mourns the dead during a joyless Eid

Palestinians in Gaza mark a somber Eid holiday as the death toll from Israel's bombardment mounts

GAZA CITY—Izzddin Akila knew what he wanted to do on the first day of Eid al-Fitr, when Muslims around the world celebrate the end of the holy month of Ramadan. But the 35-year-old's wishes—to exchange gifts, visit relatives and watch the children in his family play games—didn't go as planned.

Holding brown prayer beads and white flowers, he instead spent the first day of the three-day holiday digging a small hole in which to put flowers at the head of his 20-year-old cousin Mohammed's grave.

"You have always been the moonlight and inspiration to your brothers," said Izzddin, sitting beside the grave.

"Come back Mohammed. Return to your weeping mother. She has your Eid gift," another cousin cried as people tried to comfort him. There wasn't a dry eye at the grave site.

Mohammed was killed last week when an Israeli tank shell hit his home. He was sitting in his family's living room. The blast also injured his aunt's husband, and eight children. "In one second, an Israel missile ended his short 20 years of life," said Izzddin, unable to hold back tears.

Before he died, Mohammed and his father had opened their home to displaced Palestinians fleeing Israeli bombings in Shejaiya. They shared food and drink with women and children who had been driven out of their homes.

"He hadn't planned his future yet, but he was intelligent and keen and had already managed to memorize the whole Quran, verse by verse," Izzddin cried, as his fingers moved across the sand on top of Mohammed's grave.

At least 1,110 Palestinians in Gaza have been killed and more than 6,200 others have been injured in the ongoing Israeli offensive. Fifty-three Israeli soldiers have also died, along with two Israeli civilians and one Thai worker.

Monday night saw some of the heaviest Israeli shelling of Gaza, as more than 30 Palestinians were killed. The Israeli military called and sent text messages to people in Shejaiya, Zaytoun and eastern Jabaliya, instructing them to evacuate their homes.

For most in Gaza, the widespread death and destruction of the last three weeks of violence has made this a somber Eid, devoid of celebration.

"We should be celebrating Eid with happiness and family love. Usually, our children would enjoy themselves and play together. But the Israeli occupation has denied us that right and has forced us to take our children to the graveyard to say goodbye to murdered relatives instead of letting us all celebrate the joy of life," said Izzddin.

Thousands of Palestinian families across Gaza have been displaced. According to United Nations figures, more than 10 percent of the local population—about 215,000 people—are now taking shelter in UN-run facilities or are staying with host families. At least 3,695 families, or 22,200 people, have had their homes completely destroyed or severely damaged.

At least 22 hospitals or medical centers have been affected by Israeli shelling, while the UN estimates that 133 schools across Gaza have been damaged.

The main cemetery in eastern Gaza has also endured heavy Israeli air strikes, making even burials dangerous. As a result, the Akila family had no other option but to bury Mohammed somewhere else.

"We had to dig into the grave of Mohammed's grandfather in order to use his space," said Izzddin, as his brothers wept beside him. "It's like opening up the old wounds of [my] grandfather's body to lay the newly wounded body of Mohammed next to him."

While Izzddin and his brother, Khaled, visited the grave, Israeli drones hovered overhead. This cemetery was bombed on Monday by an Israeli F-16 missile; bones are now scattered across the sand. "Then we had to rush to bury him immediately, under Israel's constant bombing," said Izzddin. "At least Mohammed is warm, with his grandpa."

At 6:30 pm on Monday, the first day of Eid, the graveyard was full of people coming to visit their loved ones, some of them killed during Israel's latest offensive. As the crowds of people tried to comfort each other, Khaled and Izzddin poured water and sand into the grave to remould it and make sure it stayed intact.

"We cry for those we have loved and lost," Khaled said. "But we say that God is also watching these atrocities [committed] against innocent people."

Death toll soars in Gaza as Israel unleashes "fiercest" bombardment

At least 60 Gazans were killed in a night of intensified air, naval and artillery strikes by Israel while the home of Hamas leader Ismail Haniyeh was hit

GAZA CITY—Palestinians in Gaza say that Israeli attacks last night and this morning were the most aggressive since Israel's offensive began three weeks ago.

According to local health officials, an estimated 60 Palestinians were killed as a result of some 60 air strikes. This raises the death toll in the conflict to 1,137 Palestinians, mostly civilians, since July 8. Israel has lost 53 soldiers and three civilians, while a Thai worker was also killed.

Israeli F-16 fighter jets bombed Gaza's fishing harbor, with the targets including a statue that was erected for the victims of the Mavi Marmara aid flotilla attack in May 2010, as well as a fish market, a mosque and rooms used by the fishermen of Gaza.

"This is the most fierce night we ever had," said Aya Humaid to *Middle East Eye*, adding that the bombing lasted for 10 hours. "This is the night when Israel has used a scorched-earth policy."

The bombardment came on the second of what should be three of the most joyous days of the Muslim calendar. Monday's holiday of Eid al-Fitr was also marked by mourning and bloodshed in the Gaza Strip, following three weeks of merciless fighting.

On Monday afternoon, Israeli troops told civilians in Jabaliya and Gaza City to evacuate their homes to central and western Gaza. However, last night's bombings in Gaza City focused on those western and central areas.

Tuesday morning saw several attacks in western Gaza city. An Israeli missile hit the home of Hamas' deputy political chief in Gaza, Ismail Haniyeh. The son of Ismail Haniyeh commented on the incident some hours later: "One drop of blood from a Palestinian child is more precious than all our homes."

The escalation comes after Israeli Prime Minister Benjamin Netanyahu vowed not to end the Gaza operation "without neutralizing the tunnels," warning of "many more days" before a truce.

However, the attacks carried out on Tuesday morning focused on residential areas and civilian infrastructure, including the fuel tanks of Gaza's only power plant and carton and soft drink factories on Salahddin Road.

Firefighters have been unable to cope with the massive fire damage caused by the attacks early Tuesday. Other governmental buildings were also targeted by F-16 missiles, including the Finance Ministry, witnesses said.

The only power plant supplying electricity to the Gaza Strip was knocked out of commission by Israeli shelling, said the deputy director of the energy authority in the Palestinian territory on Tuesday.

Several mosques were hit, including the al-Amin mosque, which faces the house of Palestinian President Mahmoud Abbas. The mosque was hit three times Tuesday morning.

Netanyahu said on Monday that Israelis should ready for a long military campaign in Gaza, after Hamas mortar fire from the enclave killed four Israeli soldiers.

Mazen Hawleh from Jabaliya says there is a clear escalation in the targeting of civilians.

"Israeli warplanes have targeted all aspects of life. Even a shop that sells paint has been targeted." Hawleh wonders what threat there could be in this. "Artillery shelling continues only hitting us civilians in Jabaliya," he adds.

"We must be prepared for a lengthy campaign," said Netanyahu in a speech that was broadcast live. The speech came soon after the news of the shelling of the Eshkol region of Israel, which reportedly wounded at least 12 soldiers.

In Khan Younis, citizens say that the humanitarian crisis is intensifying as electricity outages have affected telecommunications services for the 250,000 inhabitants.

A local resident of Khan Younis, Abu Fouad, says that he was unable to connect with ambulance crews to inform them about injured people in his neighborhood.

An Israeli F-16 missile hit the homes of the al-Najjar family. Twenty family members were killed. The air strike hit the family without prior warning. Families were unable to make phone calls to ambulances and rescue teams because the telecommunications network is down. Instead, dozens of private cars transferred victims of the attacks to Nasser Hospital.

On Tuesday morning, neighbors of the al-Najjar family said that there are still more family members under the ruins and that they were waiting for bulldozers to dig out their bodies.

Entire families were wiped out in overnight strikes from southern and central Gaza to Rafah. One of the homes targeted without prior warning was in Rafah. It belongs to the Abu Zaid family.

Abu Yousef al-Najjar, a doctor, said seven people were killed in the attack on the Abu Zaid home, with dozens injured. Rescue teams are still digging out more bodies from the three-story house. Residents in Rafah say there was no reason the family should have been targeted.

The home of the mayor of Buriej, in the central Gaza Strip, was hit by several Israeli missiles. So far health officials have said that four people were killed in that strike.

During early morning hours, Israeli warplanes targeted al-Shrouq Tower, a building which hosts several international and local TV channels. The target seems to have been Hamas' Al-Aqsa Voice Radio.

A live announcement released by the Qassam Brigades, referring to a press statement about rockets being fired on Tel Aviv, was cut short.

Among the five other buildings attacked was the headquarters of the Al-Aqsa Satellite Channel in Gaza City.

The Palestinian Journalists Syndicate has condemned the attack and called for the International Federation of Journalists to send a fact-finding mission to investigate crimes against press freedom and journalists.

In a press statement, the Al-Aqsa network said that the attack will not stop it from broadcasting the suffering and steadfastness of the Palestinian people. "Targeting media shows bankruptcy and blunder, and what happened is a clear violation of press freedom"

In Gaza, even the dead get no peace

The targeting of cemeteries by Israeli jets has stirred much anger in Gaza City, particularly as families are now tasked with the ordeal of reburying their loved ones

GAZA CITY—The deeper 58-year-old Inshirah al-Najjar digs, the more she comes across the bones of dead bodies—she only hopes that these bones do not belong to the child she gave birth to.

"My heart was burning when my son came early this morning to tell me Israeli F-16s had bombed the cemetery and Hani's grave is missing," she says, crying.

Al Najjar is the mother of a fisherman, Hani al-Najjar, who was 27 in 2006 when an Israeli gunboat killed him while he was trying to catch fish to feed his family.

She continues to dig down, deeper into his grave, still crying—a mother coming here alone with Israeli warplanes dropping bombs overhead. Just a few hours ago, the Sheikh Radwan Cemetery was hit by missiles from Israeli jets.

Al Najjar digs deeper still, while another man from the al-Kateeb family comes to rebury the body of his relative after approximately 20 grave sites were hit by Israeli missiles. Broken bones lie scattered around and it is difficult for relatives to determine which parts come from which grave.

The man standing nearby starts screaming while holding a piece of skull by an eye socket. His loud cries of anguish can be heard across the cemetery, shouting back at Israel's fighter jets for disturbing and abusing the graves of the dead.

"These are our dead, why attack them again, why?" he says. "The bones were not firing rockets."

Al Najjar has found a man to share her pain of looking for a family grave in the churned-up ground. "Israel has no civility and no respect for the dignity of the human body—alive or dead," says the man.

"This is the work of cowards who fear even the bones of human beings," he shouts at the sky.

Al Najjar weeps as she eventually gets near the bottom of her son's grave that has sustained so much damage. But she's still not sure his bones are intact, among many others disturbed and scattered.

"I am a mother who loves her son and, although he may be dead, I will still protect his grave as any mother around the world would," she says, breaking down in tears again.

Her son Ikrami came earlier to visit the grave of his brother to tell him how much he misses him. Ikrami has done this on the first day of every Eid since Hani was killed. But this Eid, Ikrami did not find the grave—he ran away in horror upon seeing the bones scattered on the ground. He ran to his mother, screaming about what he'd seen.

"The burning sadness I had in my heart is stronger than when I heard about his killing some years ago," she says, trying to steady her voice.

Al Najjar says that Hani's two children wanted to come to visit their father's grave, as they had done on every Eid since he was killed in 2006. But she did not want them to see the shattered grave of their father or the other graves nearby.

"They would have been terrified and upset at what I have seen. I just couldn't bring them," she says

Sixteen-year-old Mohammed Khader, who lives nearby, witnessed the bombing. He works at the normally peaceful graveyard, where he tends the graves.

He arrives today with some water to rinse the gravestones off and to take care of the flowers, so visiting families can enjoy fresh and clean graves on the first day of Eid.

"I don't know how to tell people that the bones of their loved ones have been displaced by Israeli bombs," he says.

Targeting the dead

Residents of the area say that they have seen no fighters and know of no reason why Israel would target cemeteries and graves. Last week, the Roman Orthodox Church in the city center reported that 15 Palestinian Christian graves were also damaged by Israeli artillery shells.

For the past four years, Khader has worked as a volunteer at the cemetery, tending the graves, sometimes getting paid by families to look after the grave sites.

"We need more stones to cover the bodies, but because of the war, people don't know where to find them," he says, holding on tightly to a yellow water container that he uses for washing the gravestones.

When the grave sites are bombed by Israeli jets, families in Gaza have no other option but to bury all the bones together, instead of going through the pain and trauma of sorting through them to identify individuals—male or female. In this case, the local resident who discovered that the cemetery had been bombed decided to lay every scattered and shattered bone together in the same area.

Israel's attacks on the grave sites have stirred much anger. Abu Suhaib, 46, is extremely upset: "To Israel, everything is a target: the gravestones, trees, living humans and now our dead."

The first day of Eid is special to Palestinians who spend the day with their deceased loved ones—thousands made it here to Sheikh Radwan Cemetery. And everyone is wondering why Israeli F-16s would strike just before people flooded into the cemeteries to pay their respects to the dead.

Abu Suhaib thinks the real aim is to intimidate Palestinians and make them fear that whatever they do, wherever they go, they could be a target for Israeli weapons.

"This is a pure form of terrorism—Christian and Muslim cemeteries are targets. Even the dead are Israel's targets."

Gaza families bake Eid "cake of resistance"

Under Israeli bombardment, displaced Palestinians are baking traditional holiday cakes to bring joy to their children

GAZA CITY—When Elham Elzanin fled her home in Beit Hanoun, she only had time to grab her terrified children and evacuate. Now sheltering at a school in Gaza City, Elzanin's nine-year-old daughter Nima cries over missing one of the sweetest parts of the Eid holiday: cake.

"I said to myself, 'We ought to make the children feel the atmosphere of Eid, even if warplanes are bombing,'" Elzanin, 39, told Al Jazeera. She said that the idea quickly spread among the children seeking refuge with their families at al-Hud school, and soon, a group of mothers began baking.

"The Israelis should know they will not stop us [from] finding some joy in making Eid cake," she said. The cake, she added, represents "resilience and resistance."

The cramped al-Huda school provides shelter to many internally displaced Palestinian families from across the Gaza Strip.

According to United Nations figures, more than 240,000 Palestinians have now sought refuge at UN or government-run schools, at informal shelters or with friends and relatives. At least 747 residential buildings in Gaza have also been destroyed or damaged.

On July 20, Israeli shells hit a UN school that was sheltering displaced families, killing at least 19 people and wounding dozens more. In response, the Israeli military said Palestinian fighters had been firing from near the facility.

It was the second time in a week that a UN school being used as a shelter was hit by Israeli attacks. The UN has reported that at least 133 schools in Gaza have been damaged by Israeli strikes, while 23 health facilities have also been hit.

More than 1,303 Palestinians have been killed since Israel's military operation in Gaza began over three weeks ago, while more than 7,203 others have been injured. Fifty-three Israeli soldiers have also died, along with two Israeli civilians and a Thai worker.

Meanwhile, at al-Huda school, Khitam al-Fayomi, a 46-year-old mother of nine, said that her son Abdullah, seven, and daughter Fatima, nine, begged her to make Eid cake. "We can't deprive them just because of what Israel is doing to us," Fayomi, who fled her home in Tuffa, near Shejaiya, told Al Jazeera.

Sitting in a long corridor, she was among a group of 40 women rolling the cake mixture and pressing crushed dates inside. These Eid sweets are well-known throughout the Gaza Strip as marking the Eid al-Fitr holiday. Usually, families compete over whose version of the cake is tastier.

Next to Fayomi, Nawal Abu Asi smiled as she helped make the treats. Eighteen members of Abu Asi's family fled their home in Shejaiya after heavy Israeli bombardment two weeks ago. She told Al Jazeera that she witnessed the bombing of their house with her own eyes.

"The more you displace us, we will remain. The more you kill us, we will plant happiness in the hearts of our children," said the 24-year-old. She lost everything in the bombardment, including her wedding dress, which she planned to wear for her nuptials, planned for August 15. "My wedding dress, my clothes and my new bedroom have all turned into ruins."

Khader Abelkas, 48, was the only man among the women making the cakes. An Israeli F-16 missile hit his home, forcing him, his wife and their six sons and three daughters into the shelter. "We also want to tell Israel [that] despite the siege, destruction and killing, we will continue to make [the] cake of resistance," he said.

Israeli buffer zone tightens Gaza chokehold

A buffer zone surrounding Gaza has been continuously bombed, with a high rate of civilian casualties

GAZA CITY—Israel declared a three kilometer buffer zone inside Gaza's borders last week, an area that represents 44 percent of Gaza's territory. Anyone within the zone has been warned by the Israeli military to leave or risk being bombed.

This buffer zone has only exacerbated Gaza's siege. To the east, Palestinians in Gaza are fenced in by Israeli artillery tanks, mortars, cannon shells and snipers. On Gaza's western side, Israeli warships form a blockade and allow only a three-mile fishing zone. To the north are more military checkpoints and soldiers. To the south, the Egyptian military has closed off the Rafah border.

The buffer zone has tightened the Israeli chokehold around Gaza's small strip of land.

Essam Dogmush, 25, ran a family business renting out apartments in the residential tower where he and his family also lived. He said the building was reduced to rubble immediately after he received a phone call from the Israeli army at midday. The caller on the other end of the line simply ordered him to evacuate the building. Dogmush rushed to each apartment screaming, "Israel is going to bomb the building."

The bombing of the seven-story residential building left 21 families homeless.

"Why our building? I don't know. These are poor people who haven't been able to pay their debts due to lack of access to [their] salaries," he said, while holding a bill he found on top of the rubble showing the debt of someone in his building.

Dogmush believes this present Israeli policy deliberately tries to drive people away from the Hamas resistance. But he insists that his business is politically neutral. "I usually check that people are not affiliated with political factions before renting to them," he told Al Jazeera.

Dogmush sat on top of the rubble counting how many people lived in the building. On average, 10 family members lived in each apartment.

"Nowhere is safe," he said.

Jalal Jundia, 41, has been displaced for the second time in 10 days.

"Last week, our home was demolished in Shejaiya. I sought shelter with relatives in this building, but it was bombed," he said while trying to comfort his terrified children.

Jundia was a Palestinian Authority (PA) civil servant who got laid off seven years ago due to internal Palestinian political strife.

He is the father of six children—aged three to 15—who are now left with nowhere else to go.

"We had no time to evacuate the building—the drone missile struck while we were still inside. We only just managed to get outside before the F-16 missile hit," Jundia told Al Jazeera.

Suliman Jarboe, 51, lives nearby. He described how "women and children had run from their homes, some still wearing [just] underwear."

"I had to protect them in my home, and now they have nothing to wear and nowhere to hide," he said. Jarboe was also laid off eight years ago after working most of his life in construction in Israel.

After performing Umrah in Saudi Arabia recently, Abdullah Nassar was hosting some friends when he received a phone call that told him, "Mussa speaking from the Israeli Defense Army. Evacuate because we will bomb the house." The first missile came from a drone and hit a house nearby.

"Israel says that we are targeting civilians. But they know that we are also innocent civilians here," he said as he gathered decorations from a guest room.

Nassar expressed concerned about the future of his family—his entire neighborhood had to evacuate and he feels that his new location is not safe enough to stay.

"With schools and hospitals also being bombed, we have no alternative other than making tents and waiting to die in them."

Gaza: no place to bury the dead

Under continuous Israeli shelling, Palestinians in south Gaza face a shortage of space and supplies to bury loved ones

RAFAH, GAZA STRIP—Umm Mohammed Abu Sada uses her headscarf to block the stench of bodies, some of which have been lying outside for days. Excluded from Israel's humanitarian cease-fire in the Gaza Strip, this city in southern Gaza has suffered under continued Israeli shelling and air strikes.

"The smell of bodies knocks people down—it is horrible to see human bodies thrown onto the streets like that," Abu Sada told Al Jazeera. "The missiles are hitting everyone. . . . There is nowhere for us to seek shelter."

Corpses of dead Palestinians have overwhelmed morgues at Rafah's hospitals, and relatives have been left with no option but to keep their loved ones in commercial refrigerators. At the city's Kuwaiti Hospital, a stream of ambulances negotiated its way through crowds of medical staff and families, delivering bodies to be laid out on the gravel outside the building.

Many of the dead have no one to bury them except distant relatives, an Israeli air strikes on Rafah have killed several members of the same families.

On Saturday, four members of Mohammed Ayyad Abu Taha's family were killed when Israel struck their home, including two children and one woman. An Israeli air strike on the al-Ghoul family home in Rafah killed eight family members on Sunday, including two women and three children—aged one month, three years and 13 years—according to UN figures.

Relatives crowded around the bodies at Kuwaiti Hospital, stroking the blood-stained faces of six-year-old Malak and 13-year-old Ismail. Doctors had no space in the hospital's morgue for the family, so those small enough to fit were placed in ice cream freezers.

Ibrahim Abu Moammar, of the National Society for Democracy and Law in Rafah, told Al Jazeera that not allowing Palestinians to bury their dead was a form of humiliation. "Keeping the bodies in ice cream and vegetable refrigerators is a violation of the most basic human rights," said Abu Moammar.

Since Israel's military operation in Gaza began nearly one month ago, at least 1,830 Palestinians have been killed and more than 9,406 have been injured. Sixty-three Israeli soldiers have also died, along with two Israeli civilians and a Thai worker.

Israel announced a seven-hour humanitarian cease-fire in Gaza on Monday, to take place across the whole territory except for the area east of Rafah, "where clashes were still ongoing and there was an Israeli military presence."

The city has been excluded from cease-fire deals over the past few days, as Israel's shelling has continued unabated. Abu Moammar said that at least 300 people in Rafah had been killed in recent Israeli bombings.

On Sunday, Israel struck a United Nations school being used as a shelter, killing 10 Palestinians. UN Secretary-General Ban Ki-moon condemned the attack, calling it "a moral outrage and a criminal act."

Meanwhile, Palestinian officials in Gaza are struggling with the dozens of bodies that cannot be identified, either because of the nature of the wounds, or because there are no family members left to do so. The persisting Egyptian–Israeli siege of Gaza has also made proper burials almost impossible.

"Usually in such situations, we build 500 graves, but since cement is not allowed into Gaza, we are unable to build graves," Hassan al-Saifi, Deputy Minister of Gaza's Waqf Ministry, in charge of religious affairs, told Al Jazeera.

For now the ministry said it is putting bodies into a temporary mass grave until the Israeli assault on Gaza ends. But the task of holding funerals has also become precarious due to Israel's shelling of the Rafah cemetery. "Where else can we bury our relatives when Israel is bombing the cemeteries?" said Abu Mohammed Abusuliman, a resident of Rafah, as he wept over the death of seven family members.

"This fierce aggression on Rafah has no justification, especially now that the tunnels [in Rafah leading to Egypt] have been shut completely and no one is able to access the tunnel area for many months," said Maher Tabaa, a Gaza City–based economist who specializes in Gaza's commercial crossings and the tunnel economy.

In addition to those killed, Rafah's residents are deprived of access to vital infrastructure. Engineers have not been allowed to get in and fix damage caused to water and electricity lines, while phone networks and the internet have also been cut off, leaving the city's 180,000 residents isolated from the outside world.

Back at Rafah's Kuwaiti hospital, Umm Mohammed walked towards the garage where dead bodies were being laid out, complaining about the UN's inability to end the Israeli occupation. "Our faith and trust is in God's hands," she said.

When a shelter is a target

After an Israeli strike hit an UN-run school in the night, Gazan children are fearful of going to sleep. Meanwhile, their parents know that the schools and hospitals traditionally seen as shelters have clearly become targets

GAZA CITY—"In the night, I am frightened by the bombings, missiles and the thought of the blood of injured people in the street," says eight-year-old Karam Abu Shanab.

"I can't sleep in the night. My mind is filled with bad images from the Israeli bombs," he tells his mother, who says her other three children, Saleh, Malak and Sjoud, are all unable to sleep after hearing how children were bombed in their sleep at the UNRWA schools in Jabaliya.

Karam is now taking shelter at al-Rafdeen School in Gaza City. Among the children, there is constant talk about it being bombed and how parents cannot put a stop to it all.

At least 19 died in the attack on Jabaliya refugee camp and another 200 were injured. Israel has been accused of breaking international law over the strike, which was also condemned by the UN as "a source of universal shame."

Families such as Karam, his mother and his three brothers went to the shelter believing that it would be safe place to take refuge—but no one is safe.

"Everyone is a target here, but where else should we go?" asks Umm Karam while holding children, who fear the next Israeli air strike. "Every day I look at my children and hug them to make them feel safe and sound."

About 10 days ago, Karam Abu Shanab lost his home and all of his clothes and belongings in the bombardment of eastern Gaza City. Now, al-Rafdeen School is the only shelter he has. His home was one of the 747 homes that have been damaged or totally destroyed since Israel's current offensive began more than 3 weeks ago.

According to the United Nations, more than 240,000 Palestinians have now sought refuge at UN or government-run schools, at informal shelters or with relatives and friends.

Inside the UNRWA schools, Gaza's refugees don't feel safe. Some fled the schools to find other shelter after Israel attacked its second UN school in a week on Wednesday—a UN school that Israel knew was being used as a civilian shelter.

According to the United Nations, this brings the toll of schools attacked and damaged to at least 133 facilities. Another 23 health facilities have also been targeted.

Umm Ahmed Suhawil, 54, knows that schools are targeted, so she has considered trying a hospital, but this is not a safe option either because hospitals have also been directly targeted by Israeli gunfire.

On Thursday morning, an Israeli artillery shell hit Al-Aqsa Hospital in Deir al-Balah, central Gaza, leaving one nurse injured. The week before, the same hospital was hit by 10 Israeli tank shells, leaving five dead and 70 injured, says Dr. Khalil Khattab.

Some families decided to split up and go to different shelters hoping that when Israel attacks again, at least some members might survive.

As a mother and grandmother, Suhawil takes care of 17 children in their family home in Beit Hanoun, in the northern Gaza Strip.

"I had to leave the house when Israeli troops called telling me I must evacuate the house—which I did, by coming here," she says as she hangs children's underwear out to dry on a window of a classroom.

She adds that she did not leave immediately, as she waited until she saw her neighbors leaving. "Luckily, we left, because moments later Israeli tank shells came down like hot raindrops."

She and her family had no time to gather anything for emergency supplies. They left with just the clothes on their backs, not knowing if they would ever return home. Some of the children were barefoot.

"It was early morning. I dragged everyone out of bed with the help of my son and his wife," she says, trying to comfort her 10-year-old daughter Fatima Suhwail, who is crying again at the sound of an Israeli missile hitting nearby.

"Now the children fear everything, every sound. Even a door banging makes them tense. They scream and tremble and hold on tight to me," she says as she holds Fatima's hands.

Suhwail described the moments of horror when they were leaving the house. She feared that she might leave behind one of the children, so she ran back and forth and kept looking behind her to ensure that all the children were still with her as she led them away.

When Israel and Hamas agreed on a 12-hour humanitarian cease-fire last week, she ran to the house to get some spare clothes—but she didn't recognize the area after Israel's bombing.

"It wasn't possible to tell which part was the street, and which had been our home, until I saw our burned clothes and belongings in the rubble—none of which were usable anymore," says Suhwail with tears in her eyes.

Her daughter Fatima insists to her mother that she does not want her fate to be the same as the children that were killed and injured in Wednesday's bombing of the UNRWA school. In tears she asks: "Mom, let's leave here, please?"

Her mother tries to comfort her, with little success—she doesn't know where else they can go. She explains that Fatima has been very sick for over a week from the constant bombings and living in a crowded classroom.

"At night, I fear the bombing. I can't sleep, my stomach hurts and my ears hurt," says the child softly, as she is hardly able to speak without pain.

"The rockets and bombs make me scared and feel pain—the humming sound of the tanks scares me," Fatima adds.

Ten days ago, she could hear the noises of tanks and bulldozers, but now in the shelter she hears F-16s, drones and shelling by tanks and warships.

Fatima had asked her mother to bring back her favorite toy—a bride doll—when she went back to her destroyed home to find some more clothes.

"I want to go back home, mom, and sleep in my usual room with my sisters and get ready for school," she says.

But whether Fatima likes it or not, this is their reality and the al-Rafdeen School is now home for the Suhawil family. However, when school begins again in September, students and teachers will need their classrooms back.

"Where we go from here? I have no idea," says the mother of Fatima Suhwail.

Palestinians struggle to "dig out bodies"

Dozens of dead bodies remain under the rubble in Rafah, as Israel's assault on southern Gaza kills scores of civilians

RAFAH, GAZA STRIP—Under continued Israeli air strikes and artillery fire, Issa Akel has no other choice: the 50-year-old bulldozer driver must stop unearthing the dead bodies buried beneath the rubble in this southern Gaza town and seek safety for himself.

In Hay al-Junina, east of Rafah, Akel went on a mission to rescue the dead, but he soon realized that his life was in danger. On Saturday, the town's roads were littered with dead bodies, left bleeding for hours without any ambulance crews arriving to rescue them.

"We are now unable to dig out bodies of people from under the ground," Subhi Radwan, the mayor of Rafah, told Al Jazeera. He explained that his office receives hundreds of calls for help, but the municipality's trucks can't access most areas.

Local medics said that at least 110 people have been killed in Rafah in the past 24 hours, while hundreds more have been injured. At least 1,680 Palestinians have been killed and 8,500 others hurt in Gaza since Israel's military offensive began on July 8.

On Friday, an Israeli tank shell struck an ambulance in Rafah, killing three medical crew members: Yousef Elshiekh Eid, Yousef Darabeh and Atef Alzamli. Meanwhile, the city's only hospital, Abu Yousef Al-Najjar, has been under constant Israeli artillery shelling, forcing doctors to evacuate their patients and the dead bodies.

The killings in Rafah occurred just two hours after an internationally brokered, 72-hour humanitarian cease-fire between Hamas and Israel came into effect. Israel blamed Hamas for shattering the truce, while the Palestinian group said Israeli troops used the short-lived deal to storm into Rafah and kill residents.

Meanwhile, Ashraf al-Qidra of Gaza's Health Ministry has appealed to international groups to ensure that ambulances have a secure route to evacuate victims to the nearby town of Khan Younis.

With nowhere safe left to take the dead, people in Rafah have begun storing the bodies of their loved ones in refrigerators usually used to store food items. Al Jazeera saw dozens of bodies stuffed into one such refrigerator.

Nearly half the city was under Israeli bombardment on Saturday, making it difficult to arrange proper burials. "Injured people [are] calling us . . . but we can't get to them," said a local ambulance driver. "No one is safe. Ambulance crews, municipality workers and civilians in their homes are hit," Mayor Radwan told Al Jazeera.

The crisis in Rafah has resulted in a lack of electricity, water and sanitation services. "We are receiving hundreds of phone calls from people who have no water and they can't move under constant artillery shelling," said Radwan, explaining that between 30,000–40,000 people have been left without drinking water in the eastern part of the city.

The violence has also created thousands of new internally displaced persons, according to the United Nations, including many who have sought shelter in overcrowded UN schools. At least 280,000 Palestinians across Gaza have now been displaced.

The UN estimates that 76 families have lost three or more members in the same in incident, totalling over 400 deaths.

Radwan said he had never seen a war like this in his 62 years, more than half of which has been spent working in public services in Rafah. "In the past I have dealt with [the] Egyptian and Israeli military," he said. "But it has never reached [this] level of no consideration for [the] humanitarian crisis."

Butchery in Rafah: the dead are kept in vegetable refrigerators

As Gaza stranglehold tightens, full morgues have forced people to store dead bodies in refrigerators

Abu Taha, a farmer in Rafah, opened the refrigerator in which he normally keeps his potatoes and carrots. In it were the corpses of children, young men and women lying on top of one another, soaked in blood. Many were impossible to identify and only a few have been placed in white burial shrouds.

Such was the savagery of Israel's bombardment in Rafah, such was the quantity of dead bodies, that there was simply no other option but to use vegetable refrigerators as makeshift morgues. The closure of hospitals that came under bombardment led to a cascade of corpses. It started when medical staff were forced to abandon Rafah's main hospital, Abu Yousef al-Najjar, which came under constant bombardment by artillery shelling from the east of the city.

They evacuated the injured to Kuwaiti Hospital, a facility totally ill-equipped to deal with major trauma injuries from the battlefield that the Gaza Strip has become. Several bodies were left lying on the road, bleeding for hours without any ambulance crew arriving to rescue them.

Meanwhile, three ambulance crew members have been killed. Their bodies were unidentifiable after they were hit by an Israeli tank shell directed at their ambulance. Several of the victims close to the hospital gate were not reachable by rescue teams, says Abu Ahmed, an ambulance driver. "Each time I drive through, tank shells are fired nearby," he says. He is a couple of hundred meters from dozens of victims bleeding on the road.

Most of those killed in Rafah are civilians slain by canon shells that wiped out several homes in the Hay al-Junina area. Israeli warplanes fired missiles on several homes in Rafah, targeting the houses of Abu Suliman, Zorb and Alshaer. The death toll in Rafah in the past 24 hours is now 110, with hundreds injured. Medics say there were more bodies they could not reach.

The corpses were put into vegetable refrigerators in Rafah, which have their own electricity generators. Even burying the dead was full of hazards, as the cemetries in the east of the city have also endured Israeli artillery shelling over the past 24 days.

"We had no option but to put the bodies in the refrigerators," Subhi Radwan, Mayor of Rafah, told *MEE*.

Al-Najjar hospital has only enough beds for a few dozen patients, but the evacuation of the hospital has meant that there is nowhere to go for victims of the attacks.

Radwan says that his staff is unable to offer any utilities to people on the ground. Water and electricity lines were destroyed by the strikes.

"We appeal to international organizations to step in and help us evacuate injured people lying in the east of Rafah," he says.

International groups have tried to help evacuate victims, but to no avail.

Survivors of the 24-hour bombardment said they had seen nothing like it in their lives. They were bombed from the air, sea and ground simultaneously.

"It is terrifying. The Israeli military has gone out of control. They bombed a building of families fleeing and killed 23 innocents," says Abdelraouf Ayyad, 33. He fled his home in Hay al-Junina when the bombing started 24 hours ago.

"No one is safe—no home, no hospital, no shelter," he says as he runs to Tal al-Sultan to seek shelter at his cousin's house.

Ashraf al-Qidra of the Health Ministry has appealed to the international community to allow ambulances to evacuate injured people from roads in eastern Rafah and near Kuwaiti Hospital.

"We need safe routes for ambulances to evacuate victims to other hospitals in Khan Younis."

Israeli tanks could be seen to the east overlooking Rafah, home of 180,000 inhabitants. The town is in far southern Gaza, on the border with Egypt.

The massacre in Rafah occurred two hours into the 72-hour humanitarian cease-fire announced yesterday. Hamas and Israel exchanged accusations of breaking the cease-fire. Despite the truce, Israel insisted on carrying out a military ground operation near the eastern border.

Israel announced that one soldier was missing after the ground invasion, while Hamas' Qassam Brigades say they lost communication with some of their members who were in combat with Israeli troops before the cease-fire started. The Qassam Brigades said in a statement that the Israeli soldier was probably killed during an ambush, along with Qassam Brigades members.

Since the war began 27 days ago, the death toll across the Gaza Strip is 1,680, with 8,500 injured—a majority of them civilians, according to the UN. Meanwhile, three Israeli civilians and 50 Israeli soldiers have been killed.

Israel and Palestinian factions were expected to travel to Cairo for talks with Egypt on a long-lasting truce, but the presence of Israeli tanks around the Rafah crossing means that this is unlikely to happen anytime soon.

Nowhere to hide in Gaza

The UN reports that 215,000 Palestinians are now seeking shelter in UN facilities, while 133 schools have been bombed since Operation Protective Edge began

GAZA CITY—"Netanyahu has turned our homes into ruins and our neighborhoods into ghost towns," says Anaam Bannar, a 56-year-old homeless Palestinian.

Bannar has nowhere to go except al-Rafdeen School to seek shelter—but even schools are targeted by Israel. Ten days ago, her home was razed to the ground by Israeli tank shells. When she cautiously returned during a 12-hour cease-fire, she didn't recognize the location or house, and no familiar landmarks were left to identify exactly where she was.

More than three weeks of horror and trauma fill the hearts and minds of people in Gaza. Those who are lucky enough to be alive have still lost everything and have no safe haven from Israel's heavy military bombardment. The whole of Gaza is in the crosshairs.

"You can run in any direction," she says, "and you are still a target, because you are Palestinian." In Operation Cast Lead, the 2008–09 Israeli war on Gaza, Bannar lost her husband and four sons in a massacre. This brought immense sorrow to her family. Now, her home is demolished and she still questions why she is being targeted.

For 56-year-old Inshirah Abuelkas, it is difficult to contemplate what Israel considers to be a target, as she has no affiliation or connection to the resistance or militants—she just lives in Gaza.

"Israelis are failing to reach the resistance fighters, so they punish all civilians instead. They bomb our homes, families and children."

She tells of how she ran away from Israeli mortars in Shejaiya, fleeing to a new shelter at al-Rafdeen School in Gaza City. But even here in the school with her family, she can't escape the attacks and her children are still chased by gunfire.

"And where do we go in September when schools are due to open?" A neighbor speaks up and suggests, "We only have the beach to run to . . ." before another person interrupts her: "No, remember what Israel did? Killed four children on the beach, firing missiles at them from navy warships."

"In the dark night, as the drones hover, we are hit by Israeli warships. Then in daylight, we are hit by F-16s," she says.

The debate goes in circles, with no one knowing of any safe place to shelter, be it homes, schools, hospitals, parks, cemeteries, beaches, mosques or churches. All areas are being bombed by Israel.

"The option that we surrender and leave completely is not on the Palestinian 'table.' This is our land, our home; we belong here and will stay."

A few days ago, Israel bombed another UNRWA school—a UN-designated "safe haven"—killing at least 16 people and injuring hundreds of civilians who were sheltering there after being ordered by Israel to leave their homes.

The UN reports that 215,000 Palestinians—more than 10 percent of Gaza's population—are now seeking shelter in UN facilities, as well as in schools and with their relatives. Chris Gunness, an UNRWA spokesman in Gaza, broke down in tears when he was interviewed by international media yesterday.

As a wife and mother to 12 children, Abuelkas says she cannot think of any safe place to go. The constant threat from Israel means that she counts her children every few minutes to make sure none have wandered away from the fragile refuge of the school.

The UN reports that 133 schools have been targeted by Israeli tank shells. Gaza is a small piece of land, tightly packed with 1.8 million civilians—considered to be the most overcrowded residential area on the planet. Because of Israel's occupation and the restrictions it imposes, Gazans don't even have the option of fleeing to neighboring countries. It's like shooting fish in a barrel!

The death toll now stands 1,730 Gazans, with 9,200 injured. This surpasses the Palestinian death toll of 1,417 in Operation Cast Lead.

What do Gazans think of Hamas, Abbas and Israel's strikes?

Ordinary Gazans are asked about their views on armed resistance, Hamas, Mahmoud Abbas, Egypt's role and what the future may hold

GAZA—During an unusual moment of quiet, residents of the Gaza Strip were asked by *MEE* their opinions of Israel's latest war on the Gaza Strip and the Palestinian response. Here are some of their very thought-provoking responses.

Nashaat al-Wehidi, 47 years old, author:
"Today there is a national consensus on the resistance as Israel continuously attacks. I refer to a group of Palestinian military factions who have brought hope and spirit to occupied Palestinians, as well as all Arabs. The Palestinian resistance has the ability to crack down on the Israeli army, known as 'the army never defeated,' one of the most strategic and powerful military forces in the world.

"Palestinians have hope that Palestinian political leadership headed by Abu Mazen [Mahmoud Abbas] will return to the same stage of combining Islamists and nationalists together, in order to lead the national project to end the Israeli occupation of Palestine, release prisoners and return Palestinian refugees.

"I have a seven-year-old daughter; she has already lived through three wars with Israel, which killed around 5,000 Palestinians. When we talk about wars, we include the physical, psychological and emotional impact on Palestinian children from the first moment they are born. Many children in our world can't imagine this.

"As far as Egypt is concerned, we, as Palestinians, are looking for an Egyptian leader to take on a role that has long been absent from the Arab scene, since the time of Mustafa Hafed—the Egyptian who was killed in Palestine by an Israeli explosive device, whose name is still honoured, with a school named after him in Gaza. Abdelaziz was killed in Palestine at the hands of Israeli occupation forces. We remember Ahmed Abdelaziz who was killed when Egyptian officers and soldiers were killed in Sinai at the hands of Israeli forces who took them as POWs, disarmed them, tied their hands behind their backs and executed all but one or two—making them dig the mass graves before executing them too. Israel's orders were to take no prisoners. Egyptians need to remember these things, and we, as Palestinians, need Egypt to work with us toward Arab reunification. The relationship between Egypt and Palestine is not simple. Our two nations have both human and historical relations. Egypt is considered to be, for all Arabs, the beating heart and pulse that combines the hopes and pains of all Arab nations.

"When I talk about my daughter Areej, I have to mention the defeat in June 1967. I was born in that era, which was tough for Islamic and national movements. Since then, I have lived through several wars up to the present: 2014.

"Despite our pain and Israel's heavy weapons splitting Palestinian bodies into small pieces, I emphasize the principle that elders die and the young never forget."

Hekmat Abu Zakary, 32 years old, public administrator:
"Hamas is a Palestinian resistance group which defends the Palestinian lands that Israel occupies. I disagree with it ideologically and some of its policies. The difference in ideology appeared at the period of contest for governance over Gaza, in military confrontations with Fatah and PA security forces led by Abu Mazen. This made Hamas lose popularity, because it wanted to impose its principles and beliefs on the Palestinian people. However, as a legitimate resistance movement, I respect them, especially for resisting Israel as it has continued its massacres against Palestinians for so many years.

"As for Islamic Jihad—it's a movement that has always avoided political squabbling, earning many people's respect. It sidelined itself from political work and focused only on resisting Israel's occupation. This makes them very respected among the Palestinian public, even though some Palestinians may view them as an extension of the Iranian regime in Palestine. But that is not a problem for me.

"The foundation of Palestinian resistance is to defend Palestinian rights, and I respect that, as long as the gun is directed toward the Israeli occupation and its aim is to resist the occupation for Palestinian freedom.

"I believe Egypt, as a neighboring country, will remain the defender of the Gaza Strip. The geographical and human relationship between us means that Egypt is always present, even if they are absent from the scene because of a struggling political system. But there is no alternative to Egypt, it has to come back.

"As far as Mahmoud Abbas, he is still president of Palestine, regardless of how much we agree or disagree with him. He implements a policy that he sees as a service to Palestinian people and their aspirations, while Islamic movements may have different opinions. But I think a large sector of Palestinian people support him, despite his mistakes."

Abdelmajeed Abu Nasser, 22 years old, student:

"I believe Hamas is a movement which defends Palestinian rights—I see it as a potential defense army and I respect that highly. Islamic Jihad is also an extension of Hamas, working for one objective—to liberate Palestine from occupation. I respect Islamic Jihad for not getting involved in Palestinian politics, but instead fighting the Zionist project in Palestine.

"I see Mahmoud Abbas as a legitimate Palestinian president and I respect him for carrying the cause of Palestine to the international arena. Now Abbas is standing for his people in Gaza, after he realized that Israel had little to offer him in real negotiations.

"As for Egypt, with [Egyptian President Abdul-Fattah] al-Sisi in charge, the government in Cairo stands by Israel from A to Z in endorsing Israel's blockade of Gaza and closing the Rafah crossing to sick and injured people stuck inside Gaza. In [former Egyptian President Mohamed] Morsi's era, life was easier for us. During the 2012 Israeli war on Gaza, Morsi sent his prime minister to monitor the situation closely. I miss the time of Morsi, when we felt some freedom and care from our neighbors."

Hassan Nakhala, 23 years old, academic:

"Hamas is a resistance movement working for the liberation of Palestine from the Jordan River to the Mediterranean Sea. It tries to resist occupation with all available means. We have seen Hamas develop over the years—any person who resists occupation, I respect very much. Hamas brings pride to us by capturing Israeli soldiers to exchange for our Palestinian prisoners. Israel is unwilling to release them.

"Islamic Jihad is also a resistance movement with aims to liberate Palestine by adopting the Islamic project. I don't know why they have reservations when it comes to joining a government, but I know in the previous war of 2012, Islamic Jihad played a role in the cease-fire, and now it has a vital part in mediating between Egypt and Hamas.

"Regarding Abbas, he is the president of Palestine, but he is supposed to stand by all his people. He should stop security-coordination (PASF) with Israel. The power of Hamas resistance in Gaza is stronger because of their intention to fight collaborators. In the West Bank, the security forces of President Abbas are not allowing people to resist illegal occupation.

"During Morsi's time, Egypt played a different role in the 2012 war on Gaza, but now we are under siege still and even medical supplies are not coming through. In the first war, during Mubarak's era, the war was announced from Cairo, but Mubarak pledged that he would not allow Palestinians to starve. But now, during this Israeli war, our lifeline tunnels are shut, and water and electricity supplies are seriously low. Egypt no longer plays the role of mediator. I do see Egypt as a party involved in imposing Israel's siege. We hope that Egypt, as we knew it, returns to its old role, by bringing about an honorable cease-fire deal for Palestinian factions."

Ibtisam Al-Khalili, 48 years old, housewife:

"Hamas: I think they are good. May Allah bless them for the work they do. They are the ones who will rescue us from Israel's long-imposed siege. We have only Allah, then Hamas. I have always respected them for the work they do. They have helped through charity; helping many women and orphan children when the rest of the world turned their backs on them.

"Islamic Jihad: may Allah protect them for defending us with their rockets, when we are attacked by Israel daily. They will rescue us and give us life. We live in the shadow of their resistance now. Before we were killed for no reason, and today we are killed, but at least we have resistance. The more Israel hits us, we have no one to turn to except them. Borders are closed and our Arab brothers have forgotten us.

"I am unhappy with Egypt. Sisi is supposed to be Muslim, but he is watching our children's bodies torn to pieces by Israel's weapons and our homes demolished over our heads. The Egyptian government is supporting Israel and not Palestinians. Didn't Sisi see the small Gaza child whose brain poured out of her head? He should have acted more humanely. Sisi can't moderate a cease-fire and help the Israeli oppressor at the same time.

"Abbas is still watching, like the rest of the community—Abbas and Sisi are not standing fairly. They have sold themselves to Israel and the US. I always remember both of them in my prayers and ask Allah to punish them. Abbas deals with us as a country needing charity, sending us medication as if we are a poor country in Africa, and not his own Palestinian nation."

Othman Swaliem, 38 years old, taxi driver:
"I never liked Hamas, because I disagree with their approach to ending conflict, but I am afraid we could not achieve our rights through other methods. Israel failed Abbas in negotiations and empowered Hamas by making people like me see them as the only option for changing a grim reality. The siege is killing people like me who need to feed eight children. Now, Hamas sacrifices their lives and are owed our respect for trying the new approach—which is armed struggle—to end Israel's siege and open the borders to freedom.

"Islamic Jihad has always been a good fighter in the field. I've never had problems with them. They are softer than Hamas, but their relationship with Egypt will open doors for Hamas in Egypt, after being shut by Sisi after Morsi was pushed out.

"As for Abbas, I wish he'd pay more attention to people like us who are lost in seven years of siege and Palestinian factional divides. I understand he did his best with Israel, offering so many compromises. But my advice to him is that he dismantles the PA and tells the world, 'We are finished and occupying Israel must assume responsibility for providing services. If you keep an animal in a zoo, you are obliged to take care of it. You can't just leave it to starve and die.'

"When Egypt is mentioned I can't help but see the image of Sisi. He's done so much damage to us, bringing us to a strangulation point, because some of us stood and cheered for Morsi. I am personally being punished, because before Sisi ordered the closure of the Rafah crossing, I did two or three trips from Gaza City to Rafah to meet international visitors arriving with money to spend here and new faces that brought a few smiles here among the depression. None of that exists today. Egypt carries the responsibility. I can't say I am outwardly angry with them, but I remain silently unhappy, because although revolution ended an era of tyranny in Egypt, that tyranny has expanded to us through Israel and Egyptian regimes working together. I wish we could have back the old Egypt that we loved."

Gaza's voice from under the staircase

A group of brave and dedicated radio journalists continue to report the news from Gaza—despite their building being targeted by Israeli air strikes

GAZA CITY—It is no wonder that listeners tuning in to Ahmed Said's live broadcast are amazed that his radio show is still on air, especially when you consider that the building housing his office and studio has been targeted three times already by Israeli strikes within the past four weeks.

The voice of 30-year-old Said reaches his audience with the help of a group of exhausted, but dedicated, youngsters on Al Shaab Radio (People's Radio), which offers live coverage of each day's traumatic events and news from around the Gaza Strip.

Now Said sits under the staircase, with a microphone, mixer, transmitter and the will to resist with words. Said's real-time interaction with the community can be deeply moving.

A mother calls in from Shejaiya, eastern Gaza City. She has only a few minutes of battery life left on her cell phone—Israeli missiles targeted the sole power plant in Gaza and there are numerous power outages.

"I appeal to you! My children are scared! Israeli tank shells are hitting my neighbors!" screams the mother on the live broadcast. In the background listeners can hear the sounds of tank shells pounding and children screaming.

"I feel powerless myself and realize how much our role as journalists is limited to reflecting people's true pain, but we can't rescue the people from their suffering," said Said during break.

But Said's job goes beyond journalism now, as he opens the airwaves and directs the messages to officials of the International Committee of the Red Cross, urging them to intervene and rescue families hit by Israeli air strikes.

As a concerned father of two children, he says he can visualize his own children screaming when he hears other people's children suffering.

Under the stairs lie cell phone chargers, a computer and some spare clothes. The youth who work with Said are familiar with his commitment to serious journalism. He could just stay home and say it's unsafe to show up. But he still comes. His rationale? "Nothing compels me to do this except the urgency of making sure that the people's calls for help is heard."

In general, all Palestinians speculate about the Israeli mindset and strategy. Over the years, Said has developed his own deeper analytical sense of how the Israeli government thinks. This insight has compelled other media channels, including Al Jazeera and other Arab stations, to approach him for his viewpoints and analysis.

"I believe this is a national message which I have to transmit as a journalist. It is a price I feel I must pay," said Said.

This price could be the loss of his own life, like the dozens of reporters killed and injured by Israeli troops. When asked if he is scared while broadcasting under the staircase, Said said he was more frightened when phone calls came from his family after they heard him announce Israel's bombardment of the tower where he and his radio colleagues are located. Said said that women taking shelter under the stairs, in Shejaiya, have been hit by Israeli missiles.

"I fear a random tank shell could harm us more than a deliberate targeting of our building as journalists," he said.

Mahmoud Elyan, the 29-year-old Executive Director of Al Shaab Radio, works all night long—at 2 am he is organizing shift changes and checking on his 25 reporters around the Gaza Strip. The decision to go under the staircase was for the safety of his staff members. Israel has special bunkers to protect its citizens, but this is just a makeshift shelter.

"We felt that the Israeli cannon shells were reaching far behind and around us, so our building was a possible target," he said.

Elyan's decision to broadcast from under the stairs proved to be wise, as an Israeli missile hit their building once more in the past week, damaging the two floors below them and some floors above.

A uniting force

Al Shaab Radio began broadcasting in 2006, with the aim of bringing people's voices together and inviting leaders from Fatah and Hamas to speak on the same show—an initiative that would not be possible on other factional media outlets.

"We try to work on whatever can unite all Palestinians and end internal Palestinian division," said Elyan.

For the past four weeks the work of Al Shaab Radio has focused primarily on the Israeli strikes, and helping to connect urgent-case victims to rescue teams and medics.

International groups have always criticized Israel and Palestinian security forces for imposing censorship on the media. However, Elyan views this as a form of "healthy monitoring," which he seems not to mind.

"We have been approached with positive communication, rather than authoritarian obligation," he said of such censorship.

To him, Israel's falling missiles are more dangerous than censorship. He said that the latter helps guide the work of his station when instructions are received from the Gaza-based Interior Ministry.

"If Palestinian resistance fighters launched rockets from specific locations and we broke that news, it could endanger the lives of the resistance fighters," he said.

The Interior Ministry in Gaza has been proactive on local and social media by not providing information harmful to the internal front. This tactic only began in this war—it was not used in the 2008–09 or 2012 wars.

"We also try to advise listeners not to heed dubious Israeli messages meant as a form of psychological warfare," said Elyan as he reported the breaking news that a car had just been hit in east Gaza City.

According to Rami El-Shrafi, secretary of Al Shaab Radio, his 25 reporters in the field and in the studio are on a mission to fight with words against Israel's psychological warfare on the Palestinian civilian population.

"We have volunteer correspondents determined to provide honest and professional messages, making the public feel more secure," he said.

Palestinians left facing the odds alone after cease-fire

Families return to Beit Lahia in northern Gaza to pick up the pieces but find their homes almost completely destroyed

BEIT LAHIA, GAZA STRIP—When Israel and Palestinian factions announced a 72-hour cease-fire, Umm Feras Abuelneen, 35, had few choices left except to return to her apartment at al-Nada residential towers in Beit Lahia.

She expected little, but what met her eyes when she reached her home in the northern Gaza Strip was worse. The whole apartment was bombed and smashed. Dust and debris lay scattered everywhere, as if a hurricane had smashed straight into the center of it.

"They [Israel] bombed the hell out of our homes, with their Hellfire missiles, drones, tank shells and gas which irritates the skin and eyes of my children," says Abuelneen.

When Israel launched its offensive four weeks ago, Abuelneen managed to stay home for three days, but as Israel began to shower the north with leaflets warning of its planned escalation, she knew she had to go. Situated in the first line of residential homes facing the northern border with Israel, her home was one of the first to be targeted by Israeli tanks that lined up close to, and set their sights on, the apartments.

"We tried to run away. I called the ambulance and the International Red Cross, but they told me there was nothing they could do and I would have to manage as best I could, on my own," says Abuelneen as she inspects the massive holes in what remains of her house as well as the craters around her neighbors' now levelled homes.

While the horror has impacted everyone in Gaza, Abuelneen has been left particularly vulnerable. She is originally from Iraq, and has no real family in Gaza.

Her in-laws are based in Egypt while her husband, Mohammed Abuelneen, was killed in 2002 by Israeli gun fire, shortly after he went to work as a bodyguard for former Palestinian President Yasser Arafat in Ramallah.

"There are so many people, families, fleeing—many barefoot—trying to reach some place safe which hasn't been hit. But everywhere has been hit," says Abuelneen.

Frightened, tired, hungry and with sore feet, Abuelneen at last decided to leave her home and dragged her five children to a UN school, already filled with local refugees seeking shelter.

"The school we ran to, Abu Hussein School, was filled with civilians. Later on, Israel bombed that school too," she says.

With her home, and then the UN shelter, destroyed, Abuelneen's only option was to run to anyone who could offer even the semblance of protection.

As the sun set, Abuelneen and her five children were lucky and managed to find a sympathetic family that offered them refuge, but this shelter did not endure for long either.

"When we ran into their home, the cemetery facing them was under constant bombardment," says Abuelneen. Eventually even the host family's home was damaged after an Israeli drone struck the house next door.

An uphill battle

Tears now flow freely down Abuelneen's face as she holds her son Feras. The 13-year-old sustained injuries to his back and arms last Sunday, and his ears still buzz from the noise of the missiles that hit him. He is just one of thousands of children who have been injured during the grueling Israeli onslaught.

"Thank God he is still alive. I only have my children in this life," says Abuelneen.

But the current truce brings only mild relief. Abuelneen is paperless and is unable to travel to her in-laws in Egypt, or to her parents in Iraq.

She can only stay in Gaza with her five children. But she insists that she remains firmly committed to raising and educating them, despite the extremely difficult security and economic situation.

How a widow will do this now that her apartment is severely damaged and has been burned by tank shells is not immediately clear.

The whole area has been turned into a disaster area. Under the family's tower stand hundreds of others who have also lost their homes. In the damage, one can see the remains of a supermarket. Diapers, toothpaste, spices and the remains of various other products are all seen strewn across the ground.

Men, women, and children have all come back to collect whatever they can retrieve from their homes: documents, bedding, clothing, food, pots, pans, cutlery and anything else they can carry away. But those desperately fumbling around for their possessions are the fortunate ones. Other families have come back to the dreadful task of digging out their loved ones who were asleep when Israeli missiles hit.

In the 2012 war, Abuelneen's home was also damaged, but not remotely as seriously as in this Israeli attack. Back then, mostly window frames cracked and glass panes were shattered.

"I never received any compensation then because the apartment we live in is not in my name," says Abuelneen. "It's annually leased from the government. The same situation applies now, and most people living in government-leased homes may not get any reparations."

Abuelneen knows that no officials will come and help her with the damage, but her resilience is reflected in her eyes that show a determination to carry on and try to salvage and rebuild a home from the ash, the dust, the rubble and the chaos that was left behind by Israel's artillery shelling.

As sundown approaches, Abuelneen stands in the rubble sorting through dusty items, looking for a small corner where she and her children might be able to sleep and take shelter, at least for the duration of the 72-hour cease-fire. Her children meanwhile gather together, trying to collect some photographs from the cupboard that is riddled with holes.

The Iraqi widow says she misses her husband, as she holds her children close and runs her fingers through her son's hair. She explains that Feras, at 13 years old, is the man of the house now that he husband is gone.

"I shall remain here with my children. We are not going anywhere."

Ahmed's story and heartache for Gaza's lost

Tragic human tales from Israel's brutal four-week offensive on Gaza are only now emerging amid a fragile cease-fire

GAZA CITY—A cease-fire that ended a four-week-long Israeli offensive on Gaza held for a third day on Thursday, while talks in Cairo on a longer-lasting truce took place.

It has remained relatively peaceful at Shifa Hospital, although hundreds of displaced families are still camping on the floor there. But among the crowds, Narjes al-Qayed, 21, grew more anxious as the days passed. She was waiting for her 12-year-old brother, Ahmed.

Ahmed had returned home with his 14-year-old older sister, Walaa, on July 25 amid reports of a cease-fire. The plan was to bring mattresses and new clothes for the Eid festival back to the UNRWA school where they were sheltering.

Narjes said she remembered his smile as he told her, "Make sure you get me an Eid gift."

But the brother and sister never made it back to the shelter—and never saw Eid: an Israeli drone missile hit them both on their way back to the UN shelter, killing Walaa instantly. Her young body was collected in small pieces by an ambulance crew and brought to the Al-Aqsa Hospital in Deir al-Balah.

But Ahmed's body was not there when the ambulance crew arrived—raising both fear and hopes among the family who desperately phoned hospitals and aid workers for news. To their relief, officials from the International Committee of the Red Cross (ICRC) said they had found out that Ahmed was still alive and had been taken by Israeli troops for treatment at Sorko Hospital in Beersheba.

"We were so relieved to hear he was alive," said Ahmed's brother-in-law.

Waiting for 13 days with no news about his condition or injuries proved terrifying for the family. The only person, Walaa, who would know about Ahmed's injuries was now buried in Deir al-Balah's cemetery.

When a more durable cease-fire was announced last week, the family ran to their home and found leftover supplies of IV fluid bags and bandages there. They took this as a sign that the Israeli military, controlling the area, had offered medical aid to the boy.

Palestinian ambulances generally evacuate patients and bodies to hospitals for triage treatment or storage—they have meager ambulance supplies to treat patients en route to the hospital. The Israeli army has more than adequate medical supplies in the field.

The family was in limbo, with Narjes frantically wanting to see her brother. On August 5, the family heard that some injured people had been discharged from hospitals and brought back by the ICRC.

Narjes took the Eid gift she had kept for Ahmed and, with her husband Adham al-Qayed and sister-in-law Amal al-Sayad, jumped into a taxi on Saladin Road in Deir al-Balah and rushed back to Shifa Hospital.

Upon arrival at the hospital, she ran to every corridor and corner to check the patients on stretchers and beds—but Ahmed was not there. Nor was his name on medication charts or the patient registry.

Her husband tried to reassure her that perhaps if Israel was treating Ahmed, he wouldn't be released until he was considered stable enough for discharge home.

Shifa Hospital staff was not able to provide much information, other than the message they received from the ICRC: "Ahmed al-Qayed is injured and alive."

Narjes was more reassured, but still wanted to hold him and give him his Eid gift, after almost two weeks of grieving the loss of her younger sister. After a time, a medic dressed in a white coat came and asked, "Are you al-Qayed's relatives?" When they said yes, they followed him to the southern part of the hospital.

Narjes, her husband and his sister knew little about the layout of Shifa Hospital or where they were headed. They just followed nervously behind hospital staff, hoping to see Ahmed.

"May Allah bless his soul," said the man while opening a white metal door. When the morgue door opened, Narjes broke down sobbing and stepped forward to try and wake Ahmed, his little face cold and stiff and part of his head shaven, showing some sutures.

"Ahmed! Brother Ahmed, my Ahmed!" she screamed, banging against the wall and then collapsing on the ground in tears.

Her husband—also in shock—tried to help her stand up, but she couldn't.

Ahmed and Walaa had both been killed. In 2002, their brother Mahmoud was also killed by Israeli gunfire when he was just 12 years old.

Narjes called out again, "Ahmed, I love you. Wake up, I brought your Eid gift darling."

But Ahmed was dead, from injuries sustained to his head, chest and leg.

He may have survived a few days, before his body was brought back to Gaza.

"It breaks my heart that both my children were killed for no reason. They just wanted to celebrate Eid," says their mother, with no home left to receive her family and friends offering condolences.

Saying a final goodbye to Ahmed wouldn't happen at their home, destroyed by Israel, but at the UNRWA school, their new home for an indefinite period of time.

"If my two children had been Jewish, would the world have been so silent?" Ahmed and Walaa's mother asked, through tears.

Voices from Gaza: Survivors speak out

The cease-fire holds for now, but many in Gaza fear it will be broken unless the demands of the Palestinian factions are met

GAZA STRIP—A month has passed since the Israeli offensive on Gaza began. Palestinians in the besieged territory are still tending their wounds after four weeks of war and destruction.

Israel said on Wednesday night that they are willing to extend the 72-hour cease-fire that took effect on Tuesday. However, this comes amid a general feeling among Gazans that the offensive could begin again tomorrow, since Hamas has announced that it has no intention of extending the current cease-fire so long as the Palestinian factions' conditions are not met.

Palestinians have demanded an end to the eight-year Israeli blockade of Gaza and the release of Palestinian prisoners, but Israel has resisted those demands.

Al Jazeera toured the north, central and southern areas of the Gaza Strip to hear what people are saying about the offensive.

Jamal Salman, 56, farmer:

"We were forced to leave our homes and seek shelter in an UNRWA school, as protection. But sadly, bullets of hatred chased us even into the schools where we thought we would be safe. It is only today that we have been able to receive condolences. Our hearts are burned. We lost our loved ones, which can't be estimated at any price.

"A month later, we have survived to tell the story of how our family members were slaughtered by Israeli tank shells. Civilians are looking for a life that is free of this harm."

Abu Osama Nofal, 51, teacher:

"Three minutes before the start of the 72-hour cease-fire, and rockets are still being fired on Israel. If it was about making us lose our children, I can assure Israel that all Gaza women are birth-giving by nature.

"A month later, I stand on the ruins of these demolished homes and say, we won this war. What has Israel achieved? They killed children, women and elders, but the resistance fighters remained untouched.

"You kill one, we will bring 10. I stand now and say, Israel won the war over stones which it has destroyed, but the Palestinian resistance has beat all of Israel."

Abdullah El Hageen, 54, unemployed:

"I never blame Hamas or our Palestinian resistance factions. The destruction we live in is caused by Israel on this ground and Arab silence on the other end. I am homeless today because my home was bombed. A war that struck civilians for a whole month can happen only because of the silence of Arab leaders.

"It's a choice we have to make—either we die, or we live a dignified life."

Eid Sabaat, 60, engineer:

"As long as the resistance exists, this is, itself, a victory, and, *Inshallah* [God willing], in the coming period, the resistance will make victory tangible. A month later, I would like to tell Israel, which made the decision to start this war: as for this destruction, we will fix it.

"As for this destruction, it's not necessarily us who will rebuild, but our sons will.

"Israel has an agenda, but there is no justification for targeting a civilian population."

Umm Yousef Shabaat, 50, housewife:

"They want to end the last Middle East issue. But I can assure them that we will remain resilient, and one martyr will bring forward 1,000 more, as the Palestinian people will not quit. I blame the Arab states for not standing by us. This war should not have happened. I feel all Arabs are conspiring against us, because they want to get rid of us, the Palestinian people.

"I have lived here for 14 years, and I know God will compensate us for such damage."

Yousef Rashwan, 28, baker:

"He [Palestinian Authority President Mahmoud Abbas] is in agreement with Israel to maim people, so that he can politically cleanse the Islamist party in Gaza. Israel failed in this war. After all, killing civilians is not the way to go. Abu Mazen is a traitor who left us alone. [Egyptian President] El-Sisi has also been part of this war in order to bring Abu Mazen back to Gaza.

"Thanks to God, Hamas achieved so much by its steadfastness. People were rushing here to buy bread during the war and we fear no war, like this one from the air, by cowards."

Ismail Radwan, 45, Palestinian Authority civil servant:

"This is a war that will not end—this is just a pause for a time but, whether we like it or not, we should forget about the scenes of fleeing like during the al-Nakba [the forced expulsion of about 750,000 Palestinians after Israel's creation in 1948]. One month later, tens of thousands of homes have been damaged. We lost so much in this war after, no doubt, tens of tons of Israeli explosives were dropped on Gaza.

"Resistance won the war, but so did the resilience of the people of Gaza. Nowhere to go now, we have Israel ahead of us, and the beach behind us. We must face the challenges, because this is our land."

Mohammed Kullab, 56, construction worker:

"I shall hope that Egypt will make the conditions of resistance succeed. Arabs were watching us. I am appalled by the Arab silence. Why are they just watching Gaza being slaughtered? Where is the Arabism? Where is the Arabism? No Arabism.

"I am confident in the resistance."

Osama Ejelah, 9, student:

"Even our apartment has been bombed. The aim is to make us displaced in UN schools and then be a target for tank shells. As you see we had our three shops completely destroyed, but I know fully in my heart that God will compensate us.

"Till the last day of the war, we remained in our apartment, but when the apartment next door sustained damage, we ran to seek shelter at my grandpa's place in Shejaiya, and there it was bombed again.

"We ended up going to relatives in the west. There is nowhere safe. Even Shifa Hospital has been targeted.

"Nobody won the war, not any of the sides. I only blame one side: the Arab states for their silence which gave the green light to Israel to kill indiscriminately.

"All Arabs don't like us Palestinians, because we are, after all, fighting the filthiest occupation, sticking to our land and maintaining Arab courage."

Umm Salam Abuelbayed, 35, homemaker:

"And I say to the resistance: go ahead, we are behind you. I say this despite losing my home and some family members being injured. I say this despite my pain and deep wounds. If I were to describe this last month: It was a war of terror.

"This war made me believe only in the resistance, and the resistance will bring an end to this occupation. It is the resistance which defends us and our souls—the world is watching us, but they are doing nothing for us."

Missing in Khuza'a: Dead or arrested?

While many families have learned of the fate of killed relatives, many still don't know if loved ones are alive, arrested or buried under rubble

Fareed al-Najjar, 50, does not know which way to turn—his home has been bombed by Israeli tank shells in Khuza'a and he stands lost in the middle of the rubble of his family home.

"It is not about money or assets; all that can be rebuilt. But not knowing about our loved ones is the biggest catastrophe today."

That feeling of catastrophe is shared by all families in Khuza'a—who sit among the ruins of their bombed-out homes, not knowing if their family members are alive or dead.

"Here are the bodies of four elderly men who were killed in front of me. Their bodies were dragged to the side of this gas station." He described the moment when tank shells began falling on them and snipers were shooting people.

"A donkey cart arrived carrying more dead bodies—the man on the donkey cart could not go further, so he had to put the bodies down here and left them," he said, while on the other side of him the body of a donkey lay lifeless on the road, covered with what looked like shrapnel wounds.

Fareed is a taxi driver—his orange taxi is smashed underneath the building—but he said nothing about the business that feeds his nine children. "There is worse that burns my heart," he said.

His 54 year-old brother Hamdan al-Najjar also doesn't know what to do next.

He described a moment of death that he and his family had to face—the details of that moment filled with pain and sorrow, as everyone from the area listened to his testimony.

"This is not Khuza'a, the peaceful place where I was born," says al-Najjar. "Escaping from our homes, we will be hit by Israeli tank shells and snipers, but staying inside means we are still in danger from the bombs overhead," he explained.

His neighbor, 106-year-old Abu Mustafa al-Najjar, popped his head out of his window, telling Hamdan al-Najjar, "We have never seen a war like this—not even the 1947–48 Nakba."

The old man's body was buried after he was killed by an Israeli tank shell. Many in al-Najjar's family know he is dead, because his body was retrieved and taken away. But many others in the family don't know yet.

The al-Najjar family knows that 82 of its family members have been killed, either by tank shells or F-16 missile strikes: "The explosives the soldiers put under our homes are terrifying. . . . You don't know which home will be blown up next when soldiers are everywhere," said a man whose eyes were bloodshot from crying.

Even those who were injured but were rescued from inside their houses had to lay on the side of the road near the gas station, only to be killed later by more Israeli attacks.

"The Israeli soldiers even shoot at anyone who has sustained injuries and is bleeding—some injured people were killed in front of me, while bleeding," he said, showing bloodstains. Seventeen people had been allowed to leave by Israeli troops to find safe shelter. "But four of them did not make it—they were shot in the head by Israeli snipers," he explained.

"The soldiers told them that they were safe, but then shot them," he said.

The 35 years that al-Najjar spent constructing his home are all gone—and he's never been a resistance fighter or lived near any.

"All my cousins have been taken by Israeli soldiers. We know nothing about them—if they are alive but arrested, or dead under the ruins."

Al-Najjar and his people have been to the International Committee of the Red Cross (ICRC) to check on their relatives, but little information is provided on the whereabouts of dozens of people from his neighborhood. Now they are appealing for more information on those missing. He explains that they also need bulldozers to dig down to see if missing relatives are under the ruins of homes.

Some of those arrested were released after a few days. The terrifying account that 23-year-old Baker tells is about a man who was forced to strip naked and was beaten up by soldiers.

"The soldiers made two lines, one tank ahead and one behind us, and burning sand beneath our feet," he told *MEE*.

Baker said that they interrogated them about tunnels and rockets, of which he knew nothing. For a few days, the soldiers kept him handcuffed, blindfolded and wouldn't allow him to sleep. He said to them that he was only a farmer and only saw rockets flying in the sky.

Baker said there were more arrested young people left behind when he was released with his brother and a few others.

"It all depends on the moods of the soldiers interrogating us," he added as he gazed at the ruins of his demolished home.

Baker is not familiar with what Hamdan saw, when 15 young men were rounded up from their homes, held inside a bathroom and handcuffed.

"They were executed, shot in the head point-blank. We found their bodies with arms handcuffed beyond them in a kneeling position on the floor."

Hamdan said that the Nazis led the way in human atrocities, but Israel is committing the same atrocities now.

The 15 execution victims are known by people in Khuza'a, and their families now know of their fate. But many more still do not know about their loved ones.

Hamdan noted that scores of people are missing. In a war zone, usually an army announces the names of captured prisoners, but not Israel. They have not made any such announcement during the four-week war. Many families remain unsure of the whereabouts of their children and relatives.

"I have lived through 1967, 1982, the Iraq War, 2008, 2012 and now 2014. But this is the most aggressive one—Israel acts as if it's fighting a powerful, equally sized entity, but we only have the resistance, so they arrest, injure and kill our children."

Gaza fishermen demand end to blockade

Gaza's fishermen are particularly hard-hit by Israel's offensive, with many decrying the bombings as "economic war"

GAZA CITY—Ayman Alamodi was 18 when he began working as a fisherman in the Gaza Strip. But that was 30 years ago, long before the Egyptian–Israeli siege on the Palestinian territory made it nearly impossible for the father of four to provide food for his family.

"My experience from this ongoing war has been the worst; the intensity of air strikes and destruction has forced me to stay home," Alamodi told Al Jazeera, explaining that fishing has been nearly impossible under a near-constant barrage of Israeli air strikes and naval shelling off Gaza's coast.

At least 1,922 Palestinians have been killed, and 9,806 others have been injured since Israel's military operation in the Gaza Strip began on July 8. Sixty-four Israeli soldiers have also been killed, along with two Israeli civilians and a Thai worker.

A 72-hour cease-fire that began on Tuesday in Gaza provided a brief opportunity for local fishermen, but Alamodi said he was unable to catch anything of substance when he went out on the water. Alamodi currently shares a boat with nine other fishermen, all members of his extended family, and their catch provides for about 70 people.

"Today there is no fishing. We went out during the 72-hour cease-fire to try and get food for our families, but we got nothing," he said, while removing crabs from his fishing nets. Holding one in his hands, he added: "This is all you get when allowed to fish not more than two or three [nautical] miles out."

Since the war began, Palestinian fishermen have suffered severe financial losses after Israeli F-16s struck sheds storing fishing equipment. Amjad Shrafi, deputy head of the Gaza Fishermen's Syndicate, told Al Jazeera that Israeli shelling has cost the fishing industry about $3m in the past month along the Gaza coastline.

"Bombing the workrooms of fishermen [where fishing equipment, including motors and nets, is kept] is meant to drive us away from the sea," Shrafi said. "It's a [form of] collective punishment."

Over the past several years, hundreds of Palestinian fishermen have been arrested, injured and even killed off the Gaza coast. Meanwhile, the Israeli navy has confiscated 54 fishing boats, Shrafi said. In the first half of 2014 alone, Israeli navy ships fired at Gaza fishermen at least 177 separate times.

Over a month ago, on July 6, the Israeli authorities reduced the fishing area off Gaza's coast from six to three nautical miles. This was the fourth time restrictions were placed on access to Gaza's coastal waters since a cease-fire agreement came into effect following Israel's 2012 military offensive in Gaza.

Israeli officials gave no explanation as to why the recent limits were imposed, "nor whether [they are] permanent or temporary," according to Gisha, a legal center advocating for Palestinian freedom of movement.

Under the Oslo Accords agreement, Palestinians should be granted access to 20 nautical miles off the Gaza coast.

"It's a waste of time: there are no fish within three [nautical] miles now, but further out, beyond six [nautical] miles, there are natural stones where we can find a variety of fish," said Alamodi, adding that he remembered when he was able to go beyond 12 nautical miles and catch all types of fish in the Mediterranean.

Even in 2012, when Egyptian President Mohamed Morsi was in power, fuel came cheaply from tunnels linking Gaza to Egypt, and fishermen could enter Egyptian waters, Alamodi said.

Dr. Moeen Rajab, an economist at Al-Azhar University, said that Israel has purposefully targeted Gaza's fishing industry to stem its profits and sever Palestinians from the historic profession. “This economic war [is] to force fishermen to rely on charity and eventually leave Palestine,” Rajab said.

According to the United Nations, at least 95 percent of Gaza’s fishermen rely on international aid to survive, while the number of fishermen dropped from approximately 10,000 in 2000, to 3,500 in July 2013. Palestinian fishermen lost approximately 1,300 metric tons of fish annually between 2000 and 2012 as a result of Israeli restrictions, the UN found.

But these challenges haven’t kept a younger generation of Palestinian fishermen out of the water.

Alamodi’s nephew, Mouneer, 34, makes a living from the family’s boat, but told Al Jazeera that whatever he earns has never been enough to meet his family’s needs. It costs 200 NIS ($58) to run a generator to power the boat each day, while what he catches only brings in 50 NIS ($14). Those earnings are then divided between his relatives: each of the 10 fishermen receives only 5 NIS ($1.44).

“We are living on debt owed to the gas stations; we pay [them] half of what we earn and we live on the other half,” Mouneer said, adding that for the past month he hasn’t been able to work at all. The family boat’s motor was also destroyed, and replacing it will cost 25,000 NIS (about $7,210), he said.

Another fisherman, Saleh Abu Ryala, had his workroom destroyed in an Israeli bombing. With all his belongings and work tools now unusable, the 45-year-old fisherman said that it might take years to get back on his feet.

“Even motors for fishing boats are not available to us because Israel won’t allow us to use them on our boats,” he said. “So what is destroyed, is gone forever. . . . This is Israel’s aim for Gaza.”

Alamodi added that lifting the siege on Gaza—a main Palestinian demand in ongoing negotiations between Israel and Palestinian faction Hamas to end the violence in Gaza—is crucial to ensuring that their profession can continue.

“We just want freedom to fish,” Alamodi said, “and sustain our families exactly like our grandparents did.”

Gazans return to looted homes, dead livestock

"Even my child's savings were looted by Israel troops," a resident of the Gazan town of Khuza'a tells *Middle East Eye*

KHUZA'A—The beautiful, dark yellow–colored villa of Al-Najjar appears to be in pieces. In Khuza'a, it's the closest Palestinian home to the Israeli tanks on the border with Gaza—and the first one Israeli troops broke into two weeks ago.

"They were here. They destroyed all my belongings—windows, front door, lamps, furniture and my bedroom. They stole the money I'd saved," said Mohammed Hussein al-Najjar, 35.

Najjar's claims were checked by *MEE* when we went to verify his details and inspect the damages.

Al-Najjar walks us through his villa, lying just behind another large villa where his cousin lives with his wife and children. There are no bullet holes in the damaged door, but it seems the door was broken open by metal instruments, and the lock was destroyed.

"They opened the kitchen vacuum bag and turned the sofas upside-down to cut through them," Najjar said as he inspected the massive damage caused to the villa.

His kitchen is in a mess—onion boxes are thrown around, his dishes are destroyed, the refrigerator door left open. In the bathroom, the toilet seat is totally destroyed as water pours out into the living room. A soldier seems to have forgotten his sunglasses, and scattered around are bits of bread and strawberry jam among bags with Hebrew writing on them.

Najjar inspects his bedroom. He doubts that they slept here, but he says a hole that he carved out of the left-hand side of the bed was opened by force.

"Come, I will show you my bedroom where I had my savings," he said. "I designed a hole in the side of the bed—no one would think to look for money there, not even my wife."

When the Israeli troops broke into his house, one soldier asked him to hand over the key to his chicken farm nearby. Najjar always kept the key in the leg of the bed. Najjar gave it to the soldier, inadvertently revealing the location of his safe.

The next day, the same soldier returned the keys, before ordering Najjar, his wife and children to leave.

"After 12 years working in the chicken-farm business, I saved $40,000 to expand the business to another area and hire my relatives," Najjar said.

When he and his family heard about the 72-hour cease-fire, they went home, but on arrival found the $40,000 gone. He doubts if any Palestinian would have known the money was there, and his family was the first to return.

As night falls, no sign of life is left in Khuza'a, east of Khan Younis. A resident tells *MEE* he is hungry. A neighbor tells him the local falafel man has gone and has taken his business with him.

The loss to Mohammed al-Najjar is not just his savings: forced to stay away for seven day, his chickens went without food and died.

The Najjar family, like most in Khuza'a, have a different life from the rest of the community. Many of the families here were the first to arrive in Gaza in 1948 after the Arab–Israeli War and the creation of the state of Israel, when an estimated 700,000 Palestinians fled or were expelled in what is called the Nakba ("catastrophe" in Arabic).

Families like the Najjars bought their land very cheaply at the time because of its close proximity to Israel. Today, the land is now worth millions of dollars, but the families hold down similar jobs to other Gazans. Still, they have been able to build more expensive villas hardly found anywhere else in Gaza.

"We went through almost certain death here, with Israeli gunfire," Najjar said, while putting his hand into the empty hole in the bed leg. The makeshift safe was protected with a lock, the remains of which lay on the floor of the dusty room.

Najjar had no option but run to the International Red Cross, who said they were assessing damages and that he should return on Sunday.

"They told me to find an Israeli lawyer to litigate this in Israeli court," he told *MEE*.

Israeli officials say they will open investigations about such claims. Mohammed al-Najjar doesn't expect much from these investigations, but he said he is not going to let this go. He is now starting to litigate the case.

The case of alleged theft by Israeli soldiers is not the only one in Khaza'a. It's similar to other stories being told by Gazans living in towns near the border where troops were concentrated during the ground invasion.

Mohammed al-Najjar's cousin, Baker al-Najjar, 29, also returned to his home this week—after he was forced to undress down to his underpants and was taken by Israeli troops for five days. He found that the home had been vandalized.

He believes Israeli soldiers raided a cupboard where he had stashed $2,000 and a certificate to allow him to marry his fiancée.

As a farmer, Baker is better off than his cousin—he worked hard to save the $2,000 he had in his cupboard.

"The money the soldiers stole was money I'd been saving for our wedding next September," said Baker Najjar.

In the same neighborhood on the outskirts of town stands Ghaleb al-Najjar, 34, who runs a falafel restaurant that competed with the other falafel man who has fled. Najjar developed the habit of saving 10 Israeli shekels every night in coins. His money has also disappeared.

"I kept this money as emergency funds, in case my three children had any health issues," Najjar said. "Even my child's savings were looted by Israeli troops."

The blue plastic teddy bear bank belonging to his child, Mohammed, was broken open and the coins looted by Israeli troops, he said.

Najjar said he does not mind going to court, even if he has to save more coins from his falafel business to get an Israeli lawyer.

"No rights are lost, as long I am alive and demanding them," he said.

“Please don’t shoot me”: evidence of a summary execution in Gaza

Members of a family in Khuza’a say an Israeli soldier shot their relative point-blank as he waved a white flag, trying to negotiate the exit of women and children from his home

KHUZA’A—Raghad Qudeh had nowhere to run except the home of her uncle, Mohammed Tawfiq Qudeh, 64, who had a basement.

For two consecutive nights, Israeli forces had used all manner of weapons and missiles to hit her family home. “They use pesticides, as if they are just killing insects,” said Raghad.

Then on Friday, July 25, next door to Raghad’s house, the home of her neighbor, Helmi Abu Rejela, was hit and the bodies of his family lay under the rubble.

After the bombing, Israeli soldiers were shooting all around Raghad’s house. In a moment of calm, Raghad and her family found shelter at her uncle’s house next door.

In his basement, Raghad gathered with 21 members of her family, including her sisters and her mother. No one wanted to leave. Others in their neighborhood had tried to escape their homes and been injured or killed. Some who were told to evacuate by masked Israeli special forces were killed by snipers at the entrance of the town in southern Gaza.

"We stayed hiding until Friday at noon," Raghad said as tears fell from her eyes. "Israeli bulldozers came closer to my uncle's home, destroying the side. Israeli troops broke into the house."

As a bulldozer then crashed into the home and the family feared that the house would collapse into the basement, soldiers entered the house by breaking down a door.

"We closed the curtains and were terrified when a bullet hit the door and voices shouted to us to get out," she said.

"Please don't shoot me"

Raghad's uncle, Mohammed, told his family he would open the door and talk peacefully with the soldiers, explaining to them that there were only civilians in the house.

"He courageously went outside, with a white flag, just to talk with them, saying, 'I am a peaceful man and have only women, children and elderly here,'" Raghad said.

Her uncle, Mohammed, usually based in Spain, showed the soldiers his Spanish Permanent Residency card (he also held a resident permit) and spoke to them in English, Hebrew, Arabic and Spanish. He told his family that using multiple languages would help to avoid any misunderstandings.

He moved closer, speaking softly and politely in all four languages.

"Please don't shoot me," he said.

Suddenly, a muffled shot came from a short, blond-haired, blue-eyed soldier holding an M-16 in his shaking hands. He was only about 20 years old, Raghad said.

"I looked the soldier in the eye and his eyes seemed wet," she said.

"My father only said, 'Please don't shoot us, we are peaceful people,'" his 35-year-old daughter, Buthina Qudeh, said in despair. "But the soldier shot him anyway."

Raghad is still in shock. She never imagined Israeli troops would kill an unarmed civilian.

"I understand them killing a resistance fighter from close range, but to kill an innocent old man who was kind?" she said.

Buthina continued: "Usually my dad was a bit tougher with troops, yelling at them to stop using offensive ethnic slurs, but this time he seemed to realize that caution would protect the lives of those in the family with him."

"It was a cold-blooded killing, just a human killed in front of our eyes, without reason," said Raghad, a first-year English-language college student.

Helen Hintjens, a Hague-based human rights lecturer, said incidents like the one described by Raghad, when people shelter for safety and are attacked, remind her of the Rwandan genocide.

"There, too, women, children, old people and civilian men, not taking part in any fighting at all, were slaughtered in places of safety—churches, hospitals, schools," Hintjens said. "It is very reminiscent of the genocide. It looks like another genocide, for all intents and purposes."

"Your bullets forced us to stay inside"

After the soldier shot her father, Buthina said, all three soldiers backed away and threw tear gas at the family.

Raghad and her family ran indoors, as tear gas made it difficult to breathe or even see Mohammed's body.

Minutes later, the same three soldiers came into the house again.

"Why didn't you leave the house?" they asked the family.

"We tried," Raghad said she told the troops, "but you were shooting at us, your bullets forcing us to stay inside."

Raghad retells the events of that day outside the same home that used to be a small farm with goats, doves, chicken and dogs. All of the farm animals have been killed, their bodies scattered around what used to be a lovely garden amid the stench of dead meat. One can't tell if this comes from the animals or the human dead bodies next door.

Raghad said she communicated with a soldier in English, explaining why they hadn't left the house, but the soldier who executed her uncle did not say a word. He still had his hands on the gun, ready to shoot anyone.

"I told them, we are children and women—my cousin spoke in Hebrew, I spoke in English, and downstairs the children were screaming in Arabic," she recounted.

"After they executed my uncle, they told us to go," she said. Ordered by the soldiers, Raghad and her family had to go back to her parents' home, leaving the body of her uncle bleeding with his mouth open.

While Raghad and her family walked home to their house, many of the male members of the family, including Mohammed Qudeh's son, Ramadan Mohammed Qudeh, were kept behind.

For several hours, Ramadan said, the soldiers moved him and other relatives from room to room around the home, using them as human shields as they shot from windows.

At the time, there weren't any fighters returning fire at the soldiers, but the tactic scared Ramadan all the same.

"We could have been killed at any moment," he said.

Under the staircase

As Raghad and her family walked back to their home, soldiers standing about two meters away fired bullets around the feet of all the children and women, a common practice used to scare civilians.

"We are used to them bombing us from above, demolishing our homes with bulldozers, or firing tank shells—but to break into your home, and execute you in front of your family is something we have never seen. We are simple people who don't deserve this," she said.

"There is no humanity in them, they are cruel and heartless," she said while holding back tears, her voice staying strong.

When they returned to her parents' home, the family hid under the staircase, the only place they felt was still safe. Raghad told her dad and everyone to pray and prepare to die from the Israeli bullets.

Suddenly, a bulldozer made a hole in the fence of the home and bullets were fired at the staircase, she said.

A gun came through the hole that Raghad had made to try to see what was happening. A soldier screamed, "Raghad, come here. . . . Who is inside?"

"Just my family," she said. The soldier demanded they all come out, one by one.

Her father, in his sixties, was pushed around by the soldiers using the butts of their guns. "I felt so sad for my dad, an old wise man being hit by them," she said.

The family was taken again to the house they were hiding in before. When Raghad asked where her uncle was, the soldiers said they had given him first aid and he was okay. "I felt relieved when they told me he was alive," she said.

The children were screaming, asking for water, but two blond-haired soldiers couldn't care less about them and refused to let them use the toilet or drink water, she said.

"We were held at gunpoint, unable to do anything," Raghad said.

Only one Druze soldier came to them with a bottle of water. Speaking Arabic, he told them to cover their ears because of the explosions.

Raghad's brothers were handcuffed, blindfolded and taken to an unknown area. They screamed to the soldiers, "We did nothing, for God's sake," as smoke came out of nearby buildings.

Every time Raghad said she asked a soldier when they could leave and use the toilet, they responded, "Ask Hamas."

One of the soldiers wearing a dark-blue yarmulke told Raghad to say where the tunnels were in exchange for her safety. She told him she didn't know anything about Hamas.

"When women were finally allowed to use the toilet, the soldiers came inside the toilets to observe us," she said.

Military dogs passed by the children to scare them, while soldiers refilled guns, making noise similar to the sounds the family heard when their uncle, Mohammed, was shot.

"Someone will come to give you instructions on what to do," a soldier told Raghad and her family.

Moments later, Raghad's dad, Ramadan, came in and told her, "They have ordered us to leave one way, not look to the side or argue with the soldiers."

"Please be quiet," Ramadan told his daughter, confirming to her that her uncle had been killed. "Go quietly and say goodbye to him."

A final look and a question

All of the children and women ran up to the body that lay in a pool of blood. Some held onto their uncle and grandfather by his phenomenal moustache. They had a few seconds for a final look, some kissing his hands, others kissing his forehead and legs, but trying not to make a sound so that the soldiers wouldn't shoot them.

"I kissed him and told him how very proud I am of him," Raghad said.

The family was allowed to flee, but Mohammed's body was left behind. As they left, she lingered to ask one of the soldiers—who spoke in British-accented English—a question.

"Why did you kill my uncle, a peaceful man?" she asked.

"Tears fell from the soldier's face as he turned away," Raghad said.

Another soldier distributed chewing gum to the children, which they could not refuse because they were hungry and thirsty, "and our lives were still in the hands of the soldiers," she explained.

Raghad, her father and their family—four children, 10 women and six men—walked around 7 km from their uncle's home, passing several dead bodies as they walked through their town. During their walk along roads torn up by Israeli bulldozers, soldiers shot at them again.

"Sometimes the soldiers threatened us by saying, 'You will die on the way,'" said Buthina.

Soldiers, she said, lied to her family, saying they had offered her father medical care. His body had not been moved and remained in exactly the same spot, in the same position as when he was executed.

"It was a cold-blooded execution of my father, in front of us. He had a huge influence on me and the person I am today," Buthina said.

Outside the house, in the once lovely garden, the body remained for several days and was later unrecognizable when it was brought to Nasser Hospital. It was bloated and bruised, but in better condition than other corpses in Gaza, eaten by insects.

Israel's attacks in Gaza town "a war crime"

Witnesses say Israeli soldiers used Palestinians as human shields and fired on civilians in Khuza'a in southern Gaza

KHUZA'A, GAZA STRIP—An Israeli bulldozer crushed the outside of Mohammed Khalil al-Najjar's home, pushing rubble through his kitchen. Dozens of Israeli soldiers then entered his home, many of them masked, moving from room to room, weapons in hand.

"We are 14 family members inside this home, all civilian women and children, in addition to my two boys," al-Najjar screamed to the army commanders in Hebrew, a language he mastered over 30 years as a construction worker in Israel.

"I have built in Israel more than you," he added, as the soldiers ignored his pleas.

"I want safe haven for my 14 family members," the 57-year-old eventually told the soldiers, four hours after they first entered his home. Moments later, al-Najjar told Al Jazeera, the Israeli soldiers used the family as human shields—walking behind them through the streets of Khuza'a, a small town in southern Gaza.

The soldiers, al-Najjar said, told him to "take the women and go to Khan Younis, Rafah or anywhere."

Al-Najjar returned to his home during a short-lived cease-fire in Gaza between Israel and Hamas that expired on Friday. Israeli troops had ransacked his home, and destroyed all the family's furniture and possessions.

According to the United Nations, at least 1,922 Palestinians have been killed, and 9,806 others injured since Israel's military operation in the Gaza Strip began on July 8. Sixty-four Israeli soldiers have also been killed, along with two Israeli civilians and a Thai worker.

The Israeli military launched a ground invasion into Khuza'a, a town of about 10,000 residents near the city of Khan Younis, not far from the border with Israel, on July 23.

The Israeli army fired on and killed dozens of civilians in Khuza'a during the ground offensive, human rights groups have reported, with some calling the attacks that were launched between July 23 and 25 "apparent violations of the laws of war."

The Israeli army reportedly warned Khuza'a residents to leave the area, but many residents were trapped in the town as it was under heavy Israeli shelling. Israeli air strikes hit many civilian homes, and destroyed the local mosque.

A paramedic attempting to evacuate wounded Palestinians and remove dead bodies from Khuza'a was also killed, according to the Red Cross.

"Warning families to flee fighting doesn't make them fair targets . . . because they're unable to do so, and deliberately attacking them is a war crime," said Sarah Leah Whitson, Middle East and North Africa director at Human Rights Watch.

The Israeli army spokesperson's office told Al Jazeera via email that it could not comment on specific events that occurred during its current operation in Gaza.

The army said, however, that it "undertakes all possible measures in order to prevent civilian casualties" in Gaza, and would "look into all cases following the close of the operation."

"Without addressing specific events, it is important to note that the [Israeli army's] policy regarding fighting in urban areas goes to great lengths in order to avoid hurting civilians, while Hamas cynically uses its own population as human shields," the army said.

Jaber Wishah, Deputy Director of the Palestinian Center for Human Rights (PCHR) in Gaza, visited Khuza'a after the Israeli ground invasion, and spoke with three families from the neighborhood.

He said that according to PCHR's findings, Israeli soldiers ordered residents of Khuza'a to leave their homes, and forced them to pass through an army-operated checkpoint before allowing them to leave the area.

Between 70–100 residents were arrested at this checkpoint, Wishah said, and transferred to a makeshift interrogation center on the Israeli side of the Gaza–Israel border. For many, the detention lasted at least three days.

"I think the aim of this huge destruction was to make some sort of deterrence to the whole Khan Younis area," Wishah told Al Jazeera, explaining that control of the Khuza'a area would divide the Gaza Strip into two parts, one north and one south.

"[Future] inquiry committees and investigation committees will easily find verification that not [only] war crimes, but crimes against humanity and ethnic cleansing [were] committed. It was committed indiscriminately," said Wishah.

Israeli soldiers arrested two of al-Najjar's children, Baker and Saad, along with two of their cousins. HRW estimated that about 100 Palestinians from Khuza'a were arrested on July 23, most of them boys and men over the age of 15.

Israeli troops reportedly forced the imam of the town's main mosque at gunpoint to announce via loudspeakers, "Surrender yourself to the Israeli army and you will be safe," to draw the men out of their homes.

"They forced us to sit on the ground under the hot sun for about an hour," recalled Baker, 29. "All of us, together, from the same neighborhood, have nothing to do with the resistance."

The soldiers took the men to an unknown destination, and made them strip down to their underwear, Baker said. They were then handcuffed and blindfolded for five days, he added.

Baker told Al Jazeera that one of the soldiers shouted, "Sit on your ass or I'll shoot you," and he was forced to sit on hot sand against his bare backside.

His brother, Saad, was forced to sit on hot pavement. "The night was freezing cold, and we were naked except for our underwear," said Saad, 23.

"Every night, after sitting for the past five nights, we slept in a sitting position. They woke us up two to three times each night. We were handcuffed for 24 hours," Saad added.

The brothers were released from Israeli detention and dropped off at the Erez crossing, in the northern Gaza Strip. From there, they said they were picked up by the International Committee of the Red Cross, and driven back to Khan Younis. Their two cousins remain missing, and the family hasn't received any information on their whereabouts.

Baker, who is soon to be married, said he lost everything from his now-destroyed home in Khuza'a. "Even the $2,000 I kept in the safe for our wedding expenses was stolen by the Israeli troops," he said, adding that Israeli soldiers left only a stack of plastic handcuffs behind.

"We had no phone, water, electricity—no way of connecting [to] anyone," Baker, who is traumatized by his experience and speaks very little, told Al Jazeera. "My [skin] is still burning from that hot sun."

Gaza's new plague: scabies

The cramped and unhygienic living conditions in Gaza's refugee shelters are proving to be the perfect breeding ground for contagious illnesses

KHAN YOUNIS—It is a moment when a mother becomes frantic, not knowing what is causing the symptoms affecting her baby. She runs everywhere but, in war time, there is nowhere to go except the UN school where she now lives.

Arafa Abu Jamie, 29, arrives with her eight-month-old baby, Remas Abu Jamie, not knowing what is wrong with her. She has a visible skin rash and what seems to be serious stomach cramps, vomiting and other gastric symptoms.

"She is vomiting, and her temperature is elevated. She's never needed clinics before, except for routine vaccinations," said her frightened mother while waiting to see the emergency doctor at the Khan Younis UNRWA school.

Abu Jamie and her children are sheltering here after their home was bombed by Israeli missiles—28 family members were killed inside the home in addition to scores of others also killed by Israeli missiles in eastern Khan Younis.

With nowhere else to go, this UNRWA school is their home for the foreseeable future. This is not, however, her main concern right now. Her baby's health has worsened in the last 10 days, so Abu Jamie urgently seeks diagnosis and treatment for her baby's symptoms.

Challenging conditions

Dr. Yamen Alshaer, on the emergency team of UNRWA, finds it challenging to cope with so many different medical cases, especially as he has so few medications available to treat people, and he knows that scabies (the condition Abu Jamie's baby is suffering from) is difficult to treat in an overcrowded school, where around 100 people sleep together in each classroom.

More than a hundred people are queuing outside a classroom to see Dr. Alshaer, some with acute scabies and head lice, others with acute fever and gastroenteritis, diarrhea and vomiting. Others come with severe upper respiratory-tract infections.

According to Alshaer, not one day passes without seeing scores of children with acute gastric problems—some are treatable, others are not. And he is seeing more children arriving with severe dehydration who must wait patiently to be seen in the makeshift facilities at the school.

"Such symptoms come through a combination of a lack of hygiene, overcrowding, poor nutrition and inadequate hydration among people in refugee shelters," he said.

Abu Jamie is given enough medication for a day, but has to attend another clinic for follow-up—she knows hospitals in Khan Younis are overwhelmed with urgent cases from Israel's attacks, and patients with secondary symptoms are lower priority.

Abu Jamie is from east Khan Younis but can't get there due to Israel's military presence, so she must go to another UN clinic where the doctor says he's seeing around 200 patients in a six-hour shift. The long waiting period to see (for less than two minutes) the doctor is time enough for illnesses to spread further.

The emergency is now beyond the UN's capacity in Gaza—with more than 450,000 civilians displaced and needing shelter in UN and government schools, hospitals, public places, churches or with relatives. Everywhere is overcrowded and unhygienic, with people malnourished and dehydrated, and with a severe shortage of medical supplies.

However, the main problems affecting the people in shelters are scabies and head/body lice. UNRWA has handed out leaflets on how to avoid such conditions in normal circumstances.

But these are abnormal circumstances for Gaza's people. And avoiding the spread of these maladies is not possible in these circumstances.

A woman arrives at the clinic concerned that there is nowhere to shower in the schools. She and her children haven't showered for five weeks since Israel's attacks began.

Hosni Abu Rida is waiting in line with serious scabies on his leg, which is spreading to the rest of his body. He fears that his wife and eight children will contract the scabies. He arrived from a nearby school—Sheikh Jaber—where he couldn't get a doctor to check his family. This is extra humiliation for him, as his family lived comfortably in their villa for a long time. Now there is little left, his business is closed and his money is gone.

His 11-year-old child, Abdullah Abu Rida, has acute vomiting and is waiting in line to be seen. The stench coming from the sewage in the school where they are sheltering is intolerable, but this is the only "safe" shelter for his family. These schools are not built to cater to such a huge number of sick and desperate people under attack, so the school-shelter system is collapsing fast.

"For a second week we are sleeping on the floor, and right next to us is a flooding sewage well," he said.

Trucks have tried pumping the sewage four times per day, he explained, but within an hour, the floor floods again. The family huddles in the only small space they can find.

He feels that the UN should urgently open new shelters for Gaza's refugees, as space is running out and more people are forced to seek sanctuary on sewage-filled floors.

"In each classroom, there are 100 people sleeping—if each one carries a virus, it will soon spread to everyone," said Dr. Alshaer.

"I treat a child one day and the next day his sister, brother or neighbor comes to the room and pick up similar symptoms," he said, while trying to reduce the temperature of Remas Abu Jamie, which has reached 104 degrees.

There is a fear that if these conditions persist, it would expose the population to more deadly diseases, such as meningitis, dysentery and cholera.

Abu Rida has experienced a big trauma recently: both his son and brother were killed in eastern Khan Younis by Israeli air strikes last week. He fears these conditions will wipe out the survivors in his family too.

"We escaped almost certain death from Israeli gunfire, but now it seems instead of sending missiles to kill us, Israel wants us to kill us with disease," he said.

Gaza: "It's like the aftermath of a hurricane"

One Gaza family returns to a home reduced to rubble after leaving the cramped conditions of a UN school shelter

AL-FAKHARI, KHAN YOUNIS—"I am 70 years old, yet feel as though I was born today," said Mahmoud Abu Hadaeid, while surveying what is left of his family home. Abu Hadaeid is a well-respected man, known for his wisdom. He lives in the village of Al-Fakhari, in Khan Younis.

He made the decision to flee his home, under gunfire, to a UN school shelter. But then decided to leave and return home to build a tent, made from whatever bed linens and blankets he could salvage, to protect him and his family from the scorching heat of the day.

"I have lived through all wars, but this war is different from previous wars in that Israel focuses more on breaking bones and stones," said the old man, surrounded by his children as a fresh breeze blew around the remains of his home, which was recently destroyed by Israeli military attacks.

This is one of the most marginalized areas in the Gaza Strip. Most families here rely on farming and agriculture, the produce of which they use to supply Gaza's vegetable markets. The people in this village live about 3 km away from the Israeli border fence. Even now, under the cease-fire, Israeli tanks and bulldozers can be heard moving around nearby. The location of the area did not afford it constant media attention—emergency help in getting injured and dead people to the nearest hospital took longer than in other areas.

No stone untouched

"It's like the aftermath of a hurricane—silent like a graveyard with no signs of real life. No one would recognize our family home, lived in for 45 years and renovated by my children. But it's all history now," said Abu Hadaeid. The smell of bodies decaying under the rubble and dust is very strong—bodies of friends and neighbors not yet able to be recovered, as there is such a high demand for heavy machines to dig people out.

"Israeli troops left no humans, trees or stones untouched," he said. All that's left are the ruins he sits on, with memories lying buried underneath. They decided to leave after Israeli F-16s dropped leaflets, demanding that all residents leave their homes immediately.

"The Israeli troops broke into the house and occupied it for several days," said Abu Hadaeid. "We had no option but to go to the Gaza European Hospital for shelter." When they fled, he, his wife and 21 children and grandchildren had to run fast, dodging the Israeli bombs falling around them. He stumbled across his neighbor's donkey, lying on the ground bleeding from shrapnel in its neck.

"The night before the 72-hour cease-fire was announced, my house was still standing," said Abu Hadaeid. "Now it looks like it's been blown up by dynamite." He keeps watch on his home from a distance, waiting for Israeli tanks and bulldozers to stop moving, for the sand and dust to settle, and maybe some calm to return.

Abu Hadaeid and his wife have dug under the destroyed house—but not much can be identified, including their personal belongings.

"This is where the soldiers ate—see the food cans with Hebrew writing on it, and also the blue plastic bags holding their shit, left behind, over there," he said, grimacing.

One of his children was able to retrieve a gas cylinder, found a couple of hundred meters away from the site.

His wife, Umm Hani, 70, spent hours searching for some personal gold items inherited from her mother and grandparents. Many families pass personal heirlooms from one generation to the next.

She struggled to find something to keep for her granddaughter to pass on to the next generation.

"I can't retrieve anything from these ruins," she said as she continued to search for some gold and money left by a mother she knew who had asked her to keep it safe for the education of her orphaned child.

Grandfather Hadaeid has a new problem too: the injustice of aid distribution, which he views as based on favoritism and family affiliation. With some loaves of bread, milk and bits of tomatoes from a nearby farm, he is able to make a small meal, but the portions are nowhere near what he needs for the family.

He misses the tea kettle—a symbol of hospitality and friendship over the years. He used to enjoy sitting around the fire, making tea, swapping stories and resolving social disputes between families.

"All is well," he said, as he knocked on a piece of broken wooden shelf. "After all, my children and grandchildren are all unhurt, which is the priority."

Hadaeid fled the unbearably overcrowded conditions at Al Khalidi UNRWA School, and made the decision to return home. He said that Israel may have won a game over stones, but it failed at breaking his will to remain.

He said: "We have nowhere else to go—but I'd rather die here instead of going back to the UNRWA schools, where you can't get a clean toilet or bathroom to even prepare for prayers."

When night falls on displaced Gazans

Gaza families who left their homes and overcrowded UN refugee accommodations are now being forced to live in tents and beg for food

GAZA CITY—Eight-year-old Mariam Alejla was sitting outside the entrance to Gaza's biggest hospital, Shifa. Her leg was bandaged and she had a drip tube in her arm—but that's not why she was there.

The moment she saw this correspondent, she insisted on pulling me to an area behind the surgical department. "Come and see my mom and siblings. . . . Our home has been bombed," she said.

Her mom, Umm Nidal Alejla, 47, was lying on a mattress she recovered from a damaged home just behind the surgical building. She was tending to a kettle heated by a small fire.

The family home, for all 20 of them, was a makeshift tent with random pieces of cloth—a Shifa Hospital bedsheet and pieces of nylon.

"We ran to UN school shelters, but were told, 'You should have come earlier,'" she said.

But it wasn't a question of leaving earlier—the day the Alejla family decided to leave their home was dictated by the timing of Israeli bombs. She says she did her best to stay indoors until it simply became too dangerous to stay.

After two of her children were injured two weeks ago, she fled her home under Israeli bombardment. Since then she hasn't been able to find anywhere to stay but Shifa Hospital, with thousands of other Gazans.

Shifa Hospital's external clinic has also been attacked, but Alejla and hundreds more would rather be here than in an overcrowded school classroom—they are well aware of what happened in Jabaliya.

"We only ask mercy from Allah," she says as she prepares four mattresses for another night's sleep. Mariam disconnects her IV to sleep closer to her mom—she says it's the only place where she feels safe.

"It is cold at night, and we have two blankets to share between us all," Mariam says as her older brother tucks himself into "bed."

Ambulance sirens call out—Mariam says that initially the children were keen to see who or what was inside the ambulances, but now they are all familiar with the sound and the terrible sight of what they bring to the hospital.

"We lost everything in the house, all the cupboard contents were completely destroyed," sayd Umm Nidal, as her daughter Nida'a rinses mud out of the other children's clothes.

The mother wants at least a real tent that she can erect near the ruins of her home.

"We are like beggars here. I can't cope with all the children as some get sick, like the children inside the hospital," she says, pointing to four children showing symptoms of acute stomach pain and skin irritation.

Her daughter Nida'a Alejla, 24, summarizes the story of many. "Every day I have pains in my stomach. The doctors told me it's from the overcrowding, lack of hygiene and clean drinking water."

Unlike those sheltered in UNRWA schools, which are aid-distribution points, the refugees at Shifa Hospital have received no aid so far.

The children and their mom survive on donations from people passing by on their way to buy a little bread, cheese and thyme, which they use to make tea. "That's our breakfast, lunch and dinner" she said.

"I just ask Allah for some peace, so we can eat bread and salt on the ruins of what remains of our home," said Umm Nidal.

In another tent nearby sits Mervat Shanan, 22. She gave birth to a daughter yesterday, who is yet to be named by the family.

The baby is one of 4,500 new babies in Gaza born during the same period that around 2,000 Palestinians were killed, according to the Interior Ministry in Gaza.

Before coming to this cloth hut, Shanan lived with her husband, three other children, his 10 siblings and his parents in a simple home in the northern Gaza Strip, close to the American School, before an Israeli tank shell and drone missile hit their home, causing massive damage.

"During the last war, in 2012, an Israeli missile killed my daughter inside her bedroom. She was one week old."

This time, together with her husband Atta Shanan, 22, Mervat made the decision to keep the children safe by leaving the front line where Israeli missiles struck most areas. He had thought that the American School would be an ideal shelter, but he saw that it was also hit.

"When the cease-fire began, we ran back to check our home, but found everything burned," says Atta Shanan.

Afterwards he returned to the school classroom but found it occupied by another family. He did not want to make trouble so he dragged his family to other schools but found no free space. Now his only place to go is Shifa Hospital.

Shanan is one of 450,000 Gazans who fled their homes with nowhere else to go. Unlike other war zones, where some borders are open, Gaza is locked in, under Israeli siege by land, sea and air. Egypt only opens the Rafah border sporadically, and only to those with foreign passports.

Now his sisters have nowhere to sleep—everyone is squashed into a room no bigger than the garbage container outside the gates of Shifa Hospital.

Night begins, the temperature drops and the Shanan family sleeps close together to keep warm, before the hot day comes again. In this place, the baby breast-feeds, the children sleep, the mother slices bread and cheese and the father pokes his head through a torn bedsheet to smoke.

Sometimes he sits outside the tent just to get some cool air. For everyone, sleep is difficult while the hospital stays noisy and busy.

"It's tough because we can't just walk into the surgical unit to fill a bottle of water," he says while carrying his two-day-old baby.

His three daughters haven't showered for over 20 days. "We tried to use facilities inside the hospital but we know that the patients with severe injuries are the priority," he says as he hands over his baby to his wife and starts to tuck his daughters in under a thin blanket, the only thing that separates them from the hard floor.

"We sleep side by side to protect each other. This is another dark period which will pass," he adds.

New life is born amid Gaza destruction

Palestinian officials say that at least 4,500 babies have been born since Israel's military operation began in Gaza

KHAN YOUNIS, GAZA STRIP—Only a few hundred meters from Nasser Hospital's morgue, Palestinians are breathing new life into the war-ravaged Gaza Strip.

"I am telling the Israeli occupier, if you think killing Palestinians will make us cower . . . no way," Abeer Saqqa told Al Jazeera, only a few hours after delivering her newborn son, Anwar.

The hospital's neonatal unit is buzzing with activity. A 72-hour truce between Israel and Hamas has provided a reprieve after more than a month of Israeli shelling on the Palestinian territory.

At least 1,965 Palestinians have been killed, and almost 10,000 others have been injured, since Israel's military operation in Gaza began on July 8, according to the United Nations. Sixty-four Israeli soldiers and three Israeli civilians have also been killed.

"I am now more determined than ever to bring in more children, to compensate for those Israel has taken away," said Saqqa, 20.

Haneen Alfarra, 30, gave birth just one hour after her 34-year-old husband was killed by an Israeli air strike on August 1. "The air strike hit our home while we [were] fleeing," she said, crying.

Married for eight years, Alfarra has three other children, aged between two and five years. Her 10-day-old daughter is not yet named. "Her dad, grandfather and cousins were all killed by the missile," said Alfarra.

Since Israel's military operation began in Gaza, local officials reported that at least 4,500 babies have been born. In 2013, 66,600 babies were born in the Gaza Strip, according to the Palestinian Central Bureau of Statistics, or 5,550 babies each month. The population of Gaza is expected to reach 2.1 million by 2020.

Dr. Yasmine Wahba, of Nasser Hospital's nursery unit, told Al Jazeera that the number of births would've been higher, but several women have had miscarriages.

"Fear is a main cause for the high increase in premature births. . . . Most babies here are between 30 and 32 weeks, with full-term births being over 37 weeks," said Wahba, adding that the unit is running at full capacity, which is rare.

Fifteen hospitals and 16 public health clinics have been damaged in the current Israeli operation, according to the UN. The local Health Ministry also reported that 13 of 54 primary health-care centers in Gaza have been closed due to Israeli bombing, while seven out of 21 UN-operated primary health-care centers have also been closed.

This has forced several women to give birth at home, or at shelters, without proper medical care.

Despite these challenges, Palestinians in Gaza have not been deterred. "Israel cuts our electricity, so let them handle the increasing [birth rate]," said Abu Sami, a father of 13 from Khan Younis.

Meanwhile, from her bed in the Nasser Hospital maternity ward, new mother Abeer Saqqa said she would build a tent on the ruins of her family's demolished house.

Giving birth, she added, was part of her will to resist. "If they kill one [child] we will give birth to 10 more."

Not even animals are safe in Gaza

Thousands of farm animals fall victim to the Israeli onslaught in Gaza. Palestinian farmers call on animal rights groups to advocate for them

KHAN YOUNIS—"We are not one of those luxury states. We are simple farming people who use a few donkeys a lot in our lives, and always have."

Ali Alommor, 34 years old, is a Palestinian who relied on his donkeys for farming. Now they are dead—killed by Israeli air strikes. His house still stands, but his donkeys are all dead.

One donkey is riddled with bullets. Another looks like a bulldozer ran over it while it tried to escape. Alommor had to flee his home, at Israeli gunpoint, seeking any safe shelter that he could find for his wife and children.

His farm looks like it's been hit by an earthquake and he still can't fathom why Israel should be so desperate to target animals and destroy agriculture, Gaza's farming products.

"We escaped almost-certain death, leaving camels, donkeys, cows and birds. The tank shells hit the trees, the stones and even the animals," he said as he inspected the massive damage caused to his crops, surrounded by the stench of the decaying flesh of the dead animals around him.

Alommor lives in an agricultural area, and he, as well as many of his neighbors, sustained massive damage to property. Now, no bulldozers can reach the area to clear the rubble. The bodies of four missing people are believed to be decaying under the rubble. No one knows which building they could be under.

"We are used to being invaded by Israeli troops, as we live close to Israel's fence around us. This is an area which does not receive much media attention, despite Israeli special forces invading once or twice weekly," he said.

He acknowledged that animals that were lucky enough to avoid Israeli missiles or bulldozers on the farm eventually died from starvation. Food and water were unavailable when the family had to escape their home.

"Israeli troops shoot at anything that moves, even when they can see it's only a camel, donkey or chicken, kept outdoors in the summer."

He shared how he saw his neighbor's dog directly hit by an Israeli drone missile, blowing it into tiny pieces. Medical specialists in Gaza said that leaving these dead animals to decay among agricultural crops would cause human contamination and a long-term environmental crisis.

Thirty-six-year-old Sami Abu Hadaeid had no other option but to run away when tank shells began falling on his land, but he grieved to leave his 30 sheep behind. When the five-day cease-fire was announced, he returned to his home.

He arrived home to find that all 30 sheep had been savagely killed.

"I wish I knew that they hadn't suffered," he said. But his brother and neighbors doubt this. Some of the sheep were riddled with bullet holes. One had its head sliced off, and all were covered with flies and worms. Among more dead animals lying around, some were killed by tiny shrapnel wounds. Other dead animals had no visible physical wounds; they probably died from fear, hunger and thirst, with the land destroyed around them, the water polluted and Israeli bulldozers demolishing everything in sight.

"Come see inside. Some are even buried under a pile of bulldozed farm sand. I left them alive, now they're all dead."

Abu Hadaeid walked to the other side of his farm to find more sheep flattened by bulldozers. "You feel very sad to see an animal you raised and cared for, for years, slaughtered like this. Imagine how it feels to lose a brother," he said while following the tracks of the bulldozer as it flattened his land and whatever animals stood in the way.

He dug out more animals over the next few hours—ones that were unable to escape. "I doubt whether I'll find any more alive." he said. The financial loss is estimated at around $12,000.

He walked over to massive rows of cactus plants, all broken and crushed. The Israeli bulldozers seem to have avoided using streets, expecting explosive devices, so the only route for the bulldozers was straight through farms and homes to get to roads.

He continued walking through his farm. Bulldozers had come right through rooms, on top of mattresses and furniture, even flattening a teapot and fireplace.

One of his neighbors arrived to see the farm, or what was left of it—only sheep carcasses and destruction.

"This sheep belonged to another farm nearby. Now it's lying dead here," he said.

Israel's bombardment also hit the Gaza municipal zoo, Isaad al-Tifola, where several animals were killed. Mohammed Abu Ajwwa, 37, looked at his dead cows. "Even they paid the price for Israel's attacks," he said while inspecting damage during the cease-fire.

"Israeli tank shells killed over 500 of our cows, all of which supplied the Gaza market with milk," he said. Sixty of his family members make their living breeding dairy cows.

He tried to get the cows to a safe place when he saw smoke coming out of places near his farm in Shejaiya. His loss is estimated at around $500,000. Meanwhile, the Ministry of Agriculture says it can't reach all areas to account for the damage unless the longer cease-fire holds.

The uncle of Sami, Hamad Abu Hadaeid, 80 years old, sustained even more damage than his nephew. For years he has made his living from his dairy and beef cattle.

"It is appalling that even sheep are slaughtered by Israeli machines," he said, giving thanks for one small miracle—his donkey survived the air strikes.

"My donkey must have been terrified. His behavior has changed—he's nervous and just wants to run away from here," he said.

He mentioned animal rights groups. "If the abuse of our human rights is not condemned by the world, then I hope at least animal rights groups will have something to say about this."

Palestinians find shelter at Gaza hospital

With emergency shelters overcrowded, displaced Palestinian families have sought refuge at Gaza City's Shifa Hospital

GAZA CITY—Thin bedsheets provide little comfort to Naima Abu Asar and her three teenage daughters, living in a makeshift tent in the yard of one of Gaza's busiest hospitals.

The family now calls the Shifa Hospital compound home; they lie on the hard ground outside as hospital and ambulance staff rush between patients, and family members frantically check if their loved ones are alive. "The schools [shelters] are bursting with families sheltering [there] already. The only option, for our safety, is here at the hospital," Naima told Al Jazeera.

"Life here is already harsh, but [Israel tries] to crush us more [and more] every day," she said, adding that the family's tent—made from hospital bedsheets and pieces of plastic—doesn't protect them from the scorching summer heat, or the cold at night.

Naima and her three daughters are living within the walled compound of Shifa Hospital with dozens of other families, totalling a few hundred people. They are in the same clothes they were wearing when they escaped the bombings near their home in Shejaiya, a neighborhood in eastern Gaza City that suffered extensive Israeli shelling in July.

"I couldn't retrieve anything from the house. It's all ruined," said 15-year-old Yasmine. "We just managed to escape the artillery shelling, but it killed several of our neighbors. We are lucky to have gotten away with the clothes on our backs."

"We couldn't find anywhere safer or less overcrowded," Naima added, while an elderly man in the makeshift tent next door chimed in, saying that Israel has bombed Gaza hospitals, too.

Unlike Palestinians sheltering at United Nations or government-run facilities, the Abu Asar family and others now living at Shifa Hospital get little support, relying solely on passersby who sometimes share food and other supplies with them.

The UN estimates that about 365,000 Palestinians are living in UN and government emergency shelters or with host families across the Gaza Strip, as at least 16,800 homes have been destroyed or severely damaged since the Israeli offensive began on July 8.

At least 1,980 Palestinians have been killed, and nearly 10,200 others injured, in Israel's operation, according to the Gaza Health Ministry. Sixty-four Israeli soldiers have been killed, along with two Israeli civilians and a Thai worker.

Kefah al-Harazeen, 25, is also from Shejaiya. "Even [during the] cease-fire, as now, I know my home is partially demolished, with much of the stone structure turned to dust and sand which could crash down on our heads," said al-Harazeen.

Sitting at her feet, her two young children have head lice and skin rashes; it's been nearly one month since the family has been able to shower, al-Harazeen said. She now uses a small pot, filled with water from the hospital's maternity ward, to wash her children.

"I never had to live in the dirt like this before the bombing. Now, viruses are spreading among our children while we all shelter at the hospital and still try to stay clean," al-Harazeen said. "We couldn't get into the UN schools and now we feel excluded from any aid, food or water," she added.

Chris Gunness, spokesperson for the UN Relief and Works Agency (UNRWA) for Palestinian refugees, said the group does not turn anyone in Gaza away.

"It is UNRWA's policy to turn no one away, whether refugee or non-refugee, while there is an emergency in Gaza such as we are now seeing. We assist people on the basis of need," Gunness told Al Jazeera.

Eighty-seven UNRWA schools are currently being used as emergency shelters in Gaza. "The number of displaced fluctuates as families discover that their homes are uninhabitable or lack even the basic amounts of water, electricity and food available in emergency shelters," the group stated. "Others are returning because they wish to secure their places in shelters should hostilities resume or because of general insecurity."

Gunness explained that UNRWA is currently trying to prepare its facilities for the upcoming school year, which means clearing out the schools that are currently being used as shelters. "To that end, we are trying to consolidate and regroup, moving people into a fewer number of shelters," he said.

Amal Alaraer, 46, lives at Shifa Hospital with nine family members, including her husband and son, who both sustained injuries when Israeli troops fired on a local market in Shejaiya, killing at least 17 people and injuring 200 others.

"We sit on pieces of old cardboard medication boxes from Shifa Hospital," said Alaraer, as she prepared her children for another night of trying to sleep through loud ambulance sirens. Alaraer told Al Jazeera that her family tried moving to five separate schools being used as shelters, but upon seeing the conditions—overcrowded and lacking basic resources—she decided to go to the hospital instead.

"We gave up and came here to Shifa, where my family was also sheltering," she said. "Children shiver from the cold night air. It hurts me as a mother that I can't make them warm enough."

Despite a five-day cease-fire, which took effect on August 13, holding in Gaza, Alaraer said she is too scared to return home. "We want a long-term truce," she said, "not just these short-pause cease-fires, and then running from Israeli tank shells and missiles again."

Horror, then degradation, confront Gaza residents

Imam survives bombardment only to be stripped naked in front of family, humiliated and used as human shield

KHUZA'A, SOUTHERN GAZA STRIP—Khalil al-Najjar sat in his brother's home with his mother, siblings, in-laws and children—15 family members in all. They were under constant Israeli-artillery fire all night, not knowing what would happen with each passing second, bombs raining around them.

"A tank shell hit, and there was heavy black smoke in the building, so we ran under the staircase to hide and rest for a few minutes," Najjar said.

As the bombing continued, automatic gunfire was heard outside. "We shouted out that we were civilians. But more bullets were fired after we declared ourselves as civilians," said Najjar, who, at 55 years old, is a well-known and highly respected imam in his community.

A few minutes later, a military dog rushed into the home, terrifying the children. The imam shouted out in Hebrew to the soldiers behind a wall riddled with bullet-holes: "We are civilians. We have children and babies with no medicine or milk."

The soldiers shouted back, in Hebrew, ordering him and the family to "get out, one by one."

Outside, the soldiers ordered everyone to get down on the ground—women and children on one side, men on the other—as more neighborhood women were brought to the street corner.

"In front of all these women, I was forced to undress until I was naked, at gunpoint," recalls the imam while walking through the destruction in his neighborhood.

"Making a well-respected man stand, completely naked, in front of everyone was the most humiliating thing of my life," he added as tears began to well up in his normally proud, dark eyes.

The situation would have been embarrassing for any man, but for a deeply religious and conservative Muslim who is seen as a pillar of the community, the act was particularly shameful.

Adding to the humiliation, Najjar said that he and the other men were ordered to stand naked with their arms held up until they hurt. When he could take no more, Najjar told one soldier in Hebrew, "My arms hurt," at which point he was ordered to sit. "This was the only time they listened to me. They brought a chair for me to sit on," he added.

The imam and his family had already been denied sleep by the pandemonium of Israel's attacks, but that fateful morning was the fiercest attack they saw. Najjar now calls it "the Black Tuesday of July 22."

While still naked, he was told to "take the women and children somewhere else." The only option he could think of was his brother's home, two streets away, which he hoped would be safer.

"The bombs and bulldozers left massive holes in the streets, so I carried my elderly mother on my shoulders to my brother's home," he said.

But when the family arrived there, they found that the house was filled with Israeli soldiers lying on their backs, some asleep on mattresses and beds belonging to the family.

"These soldiers were angry that someone had allowed us to come," Najjar said, as if there was a lack of communication and coordination between the different Israeli units in Khuza'a.

The men were then rounded up while the Israelis decided who would be arrested and who they would let go.

Najjar, however, was singled out and marched to the Khuza'a Mosque, which had been badly damaged and defaced by Israeli soldiers. It's here that he was interrogated by the Israeli officer in charge of the men inside his brother's home and repeatedly asked about particular individuals from the Abu Rida family, a very large extended family that is well known in Gaza.

"Yes, I know him from the mosque where Abu Rida says Friday prayers," the imam said.

Still held at gunpoint, he was then questioned further about "where the rockets come from." The imam replied that the "only rockets I know of are the Israeli missiles from the F-16s and drones." But this did not save him.

The officer soon became angry with Najjar, demanding to know about the "tunnels" that Israel had used as a pretext for expanding its military campaign in Gaza.

Najjar stayed firm. "You are Israeli intelligence with all your technology, drones, F-16s, and you don't know where the tunnels are," he said. "Do you think those building tunnels are going to come and tell me where they are?"

This continued for a while, but eventually one of Najjar's brothers was brought to the mosque. He caught a soldier looking at some graffiti on the wall citing Islamic Jihad's term for Operation Protective Edge, "al-Bunian al-Marsoos"—a Quranic term that means "hard-packed structure"—and asked the soldier if it needed erasing. But the soldier dismissed Najjar's brother, simply stating that he would "deal with that." Soon after, a bulldozer came to demolish the whole mosque wall that had the graffiti on it.

In retrospect, the bulldozers should have acted as a warning sign that Najjar's troubles were far from over.

The imam was soon ordered to dress and was ushered outside at gunpoint along with his brother. Najjar was then told to walk ahead of the soldiers down the center of the street, while calling to all young residents to come outside and surrender.

The Israeli troops seem to have selected a well-respected resident, the imam, knowing that the local residents would trust his words and be more confident about their safety, although they also harbored deadlier intentions if this plan failed.

The imam's brother heard the officer tell his soldiers behind them in Hebrew that "if people didn't come out, my brother and I were to be shot."

The soldiers behind them had warned: "You are being observed. Our guns are pointed at your heads, so watch out. If you move from the center of the street, you will be shot."

While walking ahead of the soldiers, people saw the imam. Another brother shouted from a window: "Brother Khalil, brother Khalil." The imam told his brother and everyone around him to come outside and they would be safe.

The young people came out, seeing the imam, but not the troops, who stayed out of sight until the majority of the residents walked outside. It's only then that the soldiers appeared and shouted at them to put their arms above their heads.

Some of the people, however, stayed inside. One soldier told the imam that "there are over 1,000 people still in their homes." The Israelis then marched him back to the mosque, where an officer raised his gun and ordered Najjar to start the electricity generator to the mosque and use the loudspeaker to call all young people out of their homes, insisting that they would be safe.

"I was having problems giving the call to prayer anyway from exhaustion and fasting. My voice was dry, but the soldier put his gun to my head and ordered me to tell everyone to come out," he said.

When the imam finished his message, he was led outside the mosque and saw more people arriving, trusting his words that they would be safe.

The soldier then ordered him, "Take your mother and go. If I hear any of these women speak, I'll bomb your home immediately."

All the young men who surrendered were arrested, leaving just the women, children and elderly behind. The imam was allowed to carry his mother home, finding a way between numerous Israeli tanks parked around the area.

When he reached his brother's house, the same soldiers were still lying around on the floor and furniture. The soldiers locked the family in one room while they kept the rest of the house for themselves.

"I heard an Israeli soldier discussing on a mobile with someone else what they had done in Gaza. The soldier responded that they had 'turned Gaza upside down,'" said the imam.

Najjar now mourns the nearly 2,000 lives lost and the hundreds of thousands who have been made homeless, but the damage and the brutality have not necessarily hurt him the most. Instead, it is his shame that will stay with him the longest.

"I will never live this down. I will never forget," he said.

"401 is not a number"

Family of first ambulance driver to be killed in Gaza can mourn only now, amid the cease-fire

GAZA CITY—Fouad Jaber, the first ambulance crew member killed in Israel's assault on Gaza more than a month ago, is only now being remembered amid a semblance of peace. The five-day cease-fire since August 13 has given his family a moment to reflect on the life of Fouad, who left behind a two-year-old daughter, Hala, his young wife and parents, and a deep sense of loss.

His family recounted his story to *MEE*. Unitl now, the story has not been told by local or international media.

The 24-hour shift for the 28-year-old Fouad Jaber was over. Umm Hala, his wife, would usually hear from him if he was staying late. But this day there was no call.

A ground attack had taken place in the eastern Gaza City neighborhood of Shejaiya, and Fouad's phone seemed to be turned off. His father tried to locate Fouad by calling some ambulance crew colleagues. They said he was working on the front lines, evacuating the injured and dead from buildings wrecked by Israeli tank shells.

"I had an unusual feeling, something deep in my heart," said Fouad's father.

Fouad's mother urged her husband to call his son's number again, but he replied that Fouad was likely busy rescuing desperate people and that they shouldn't bother him.

After some time, with shaking hands he picked up the phone anyway and dialed the number of Fouad's boss at Medical Services, who told him: "You are a strong man, and I must tell you that your son has been killed."

Fouad's father was stunned. He then had to tell his wife and mother.

His mother, Umm Fouad, had felt a deep sense of dread when she heard on TV that an ambulance driver and journalist had been killed together. The journalist was identified as 24-year-old Khaled Hamad, who was working for a local media company.

Fouad's ambulance had been the first to get through to evacuate the injured and dead in Shejaiya. He managed to rescue many people. At some point his ambulance sustained damage from an Israeli tank shell, but he still managed to continue.

He got inside one of the homes where women and children were appealing for help before he, himself, was fatally hit by an Israeli mortar shell.

Israeli troops allowed ambulances through only after a few hours of the humanitarian cease-fire. When another ambulance crew managed to get inside the house and dig people out of the rubble, they saw an orange ambulance vest and realized the body was that of their colleague and good friend, Fouad.

"Oh my God, Fouad, Fouad!" a fellow ambulance driver had cried, trying to wake him. But Fouad had died before they found him.

Abu Fouad says he always wanted to support his son in being a nurse, and was proud when his son received his nursing qualification. But his son then decided to use it to become an ambulance driver and help people who were in emergency distress.

"I will always be proud of him and the work he dedicated himself to," he told *MEE*.

Responding to the desperate calls and pleas of victims and their families kept Fouad on the run; there was never a call for help that he didn't respond to. At the time of his death, he had not been home for two days; usually, Fouad would drop by to quickly pick up some food and coffee for his colleagues. His dedication to his work earned him a strong reputation among his fellow rescue-team workers.

"I won't get home until the war is over," Fouad had told one of his colleagues.

His father, tears running from his eyes, told *MEE*: "When Fouad was killed, I felt the pain of all the families who have lost loved ones. I felt the agony of separation. I felt how parents feel when they bury their children and return home with an empty heart and empty hands."

He continued: "Never think that [Israeli Prime Minister Benjamin] Netanyahu is killing without precision. No, he knows he is killing innocents, including children.

"It's not about an apartment being bombed, or a house being razed to the ground. It's the loss of a dear beloved son that matters to the heart." Israel did not kill just an ambulance driver. It killed a good man, and a kind heart.

Fouad's father, who himself still has shrapnel in his head and leg from injuries in the First Intifada (the Palestinian uprising in the late 1980s and early 1990s) takes comfort from the fact that his son was doing an honorable job. Still weeping, he says: "Even if they kill us one by one, Palestine, Al Quds [Jerusalem], Barbara [a village cleared of Palestinians in 1948] and Haifa will never die in our hearts."

Last contact

One cheerful memory he holds dear is when he said to his son: "Fouad, you have your education, and we gave you the best wedding ever. But when I die, who will pay the debt?" Fouad replied, "Daddy, I will do that."

But now his father must take care of everything, including the debts his son was happy to shoulder. He must also take care of Fouad's wife and child.

Already, Abu Fouad has taken the first painful steps in taking over his son's burdens. He has been to the pharmacy where his son worked and gathered medicine for patients in need. He told them that if Fouad owed any money, he, Abu Fouad, would pay it back.

And yet, "All people told me they owed him money. Fouad was getting medicine for those who couldn't afford it."

One of Fouad's colleagues had asked him what number victim he would be if he was killed by Israeli tank shells. Fouad had replied, "Oh, any number after 400."

As it turned ou, Fouad was victim 401 in Gaza, as confirmed by Shifa Hospital logs.

Earlier, as phone calls constantly came in to the emergency dispatch center from people needing help and rescue, Fouad had asked his boss not to put his body in the morgue if anything happened to him.

That was his wish before he died. After five hours, his body was returned to his family—his forehead cold, his face clear and his still lips saying so much to his family, says his mother.

His wife, Umm Hala, says Fouad was committed to his job.

The night before he was killed, he called his wife and told her: "Say some prayers for me and take care of Hala."

Saying this, she bursts into tears, her sobs filling the silence of a ceasefire that came too late to save her husband and others he had devoted his young life to.

"Your drones see everything. Why kill the innocent?"

Doctor throws down challenge to Netanyahu after epic ordeal with injured patients from wrecked clinic

KHUZA'A, SOUTHEAST GAZA—Kamal Qudeh, a doctor serving this small village near Gaza's border with Israel, is sitting in what is left of his private clinic, surrounded by shards of glass, bloody bedsheets and discarded medical gloves.

He is summoning the energy to rebuild and cauterize the memory of the attacks last month that rained death and injury on his fellow villagers—even on already injured patients as they tried to flee the Israeli onslaught. Among the injured were his brother and sister. Among his patients was the doctor himself, having repaired his own wounds even as he treated others.

The initial attack, when it came, was unexpected. On July 17, Israeli F-16s dropped leaflets ordering people to leave their homes before a ground offensive started on July 20.

"The day [July 20] came, but all seemed normal in Khuza'a. So people returned, thinking the leaflets had been a false alarm. Then, on July 21, in the afternoon, an Israeli F-16 missile hit the main road connecting Khuza'a with neighboring villages," said Dr. Qudeh.

He then detailed a shocking story involving those who survived that day but are now hospitalized with wounds or badly traumatized.

When the Israeli bombardment began, Dr. Qudeh contacted the officials of the International Committee of the Red Cross requesting the evacuation of civilians by ambulances.

"The agreement was that we would walk down the middle of the road, clearly visible, with ambulances escorting us on both sides," he said.

But as the people of Khuza'a waited, neither ambulances nor ICRC personnel appeared.

"We had to make a decision to go by ourselves, without protection, and get to the village entrance. There were around 2,000 of us, walking toward Israeli tanks. . . . I told the Israelis, 'We are civilians, unarmed, and we needed safe shelter. We have women, children and elderly and we want to evacuate peacefully.'"

The Israeli troops replied through loudspeakers that there was no coordination and everyone should return home. "We stayed there, standing, hoping they would have compassion and let us through," said Dr. Qudeh.

But the Israeli troops began firing their weapons, immediately injuring 30 people. The rest of the evacuees started running and screaming, trying to carry the injured with them, Dr. Qudeh said.

"There was no other option. Ambulances were blocked from entering the village, with tanks, F-16s and drones watching the movements of everyone."

The injured and bleeding had to get back to Dr. Qudeh's private clinic, even though it is just one room with only basic equipment and medical supplies such as gauze, bandages, cotton wool, antiseptic and some sutures.

"We carried bodies on our shoulders back to my clinic. I managed to stop the bleeding of some people, sutured some wounds and treated others," said Dr. Qudeh.

Ala Abu Rejela, a youth who helped carry some of the bodies, tells of how the soldiers watched as residents tried to carry the injured and dead evacuees. "Despite this, they still shot at us, near the entrance to Khuza'a," he said.

One of those he tried to carry was a paralyzed 15-year-old girl, Ghader Abu Rejela, who had been unable to run and had been shot. But he was also shot at, and her body lay in the street for three days, until Israeli troops backed off, he said.

In the clinic, Dr. Qudeh's assistants were merely young villagers, who wiped the sweat from his face as he worked to stitch deep wounds. Someone held a phone to his ear as he made urgent calls to the ICRC and to ambulances for assistance. Some of his patients were semi-conscious, suffering from inhaling some form of gas, which he was unable to identify.

As he worked, more villagers came to Dr. Qudeh's clinic to check on relatives and friends, mistakenly believing they were safe when the Israeli ground troops fell back.

"While I was treating victims inside, the outside area of my clinic was hit by two Israeli drone missiles—window glass shattered on those receiving treatment, and scores more people were injured outside," he said.

His own brother—Ahmed Qudeh—and many family members, including his sister, sustained injuries. Dr. Qudeh himself suffered shrapnel injuries to his leg and arm.

"I removed the shrapnel from my leg and arm and continued stitching others," he said.

One of those injured that day, Hussein Abu Rejela, 19, was still at home when he heard people screaming and running from the bombs. He ran with them, but was hit by a bullet and three bits of shrapnel.

"People were running from missiles that were falling like rain," he said later at Nasser Hospital with head and hip injuries. "I only remember Dr. Qudeh treating me, before coming here."

Rejela is waiting for the completion of documentation before he is transferred to Jordan or Turkey for further treatment.

"The soldiers could see we were civilians and I was only wearing a white undershirt," he said.

Rejela was fortunate. One missile fired at the crowd from an Israeli jet killed 22-year-old Rami Qudeh and seven-year-old Bader Emish.

With the clinic no longer safe, Dr. Qudeh, his patients and everyone else had to evacuate and hide in his uncle's basement. A space only 60 meters square now held 200–250 people, including women and children, staying the night while he still tried to treat those he could. Come the morning, the situation became even more dire.

"At 6 am, Israel troops fired teargas, leaving people stunned and in respiratory distress. We had to help each other breathe using mouth-to-mouth resuscitation," he said.

At 7 am, an Israeli missile hit the basement. "The door was blown off and we had to escape. I shouted: 'All of you, come this way to get out of here, come on!'"

About 2,000 people were outside on the street and were met by Israeli tanks. This time, they were allowed to pass, though only for about 500 meters before being led onto a sandy road full of holes and tracks left by Israeli bulldozers.

"The road was covered with cactus thorns and stones crushed by heavy machines, and we were mostly barefoot and naked from top to bottom to show Israeli troops that we were unarmed and just civilians," he said. "We are peaceful men, women and children, young and elderly who want safety"—this was what we told the Israeli troops.

Dr. Qudeh and others carried some 130 injured people on their shoulders. On the way, an elderly man—Ismail Abu Rejela—was killed by random fire. Other patients were pulled onto donkey carts as they made their way to Nasser Hospital, in Khan Younis, about two hours' walk to the west.

Upon arrival at Nasser Hospital, there were 15 critically injured among the 130 civilians. Some are still waiting for surgeries that can't be carried out in Gaza. Their health now depends on paperwork and closed borders.

Back in his clinic, Dr. Qudeh said: "I challenge [Israeli Prime Minister Benjamin] Netanyahu—his drones can clearly see everyone, pregnant women, elderly, youngsters and children, who have nothing to do with militia resistance—to explain why they should be injured or killed."

Gazans prepared for anything despite weight of looming violence

Violence begins again before the expiration of cease-fire talks but many Gazans feel Israel is just "wasting time and offering nothing"

"I used to be able to analyze the situation, read the silence and what lay behind words and positions, but not anymore," says Abu Amjad Saleh, 42, in Gaza.

He feels that the Cairo talks are a waste of time, "like running behind one's own shadow."

"Israel is best at wasting time and offering nothing," says Saleh, frustrated at having had to flee his home and go to relatives when his Rafah neighborhood was heavily bombed recently.

Saleh is not alone in his opinion. As a father of 5 children, he feels unable to resist Israel's war, but finds it even more difficult to just concede to Israeli demands after all the massive loss and destruction in Gaza.

"I have no doubt that Palestinian negotiators are united in Cairo. But I hear the international community calling for cease-fire when the bloodshed still goes on. It is time for Ban Ki-moon to be in Cairo," he says.

Dr. Mukhair Abusada says Israeli Prime Minister Netanyahu seems to be in trouble when it comes to the arena of Israel's internal political arena. He appears to have failed in achieving his goals from this war on Gaza.

"Israel is trying to return to a circle of violence situation, clearly shown in statements from Israeli officials in the past days."

The comments from Hamas spokesman, Fawzi Barhoun, show a lack of progress in Gaza.

"If Netanyahu does not understand the message and demands of Gaza through political language in Cairo, we will know how to make him understand," he said in statement on his Facebook page.

Hamas is ready to deal with all potential developments and possibilities, but says Israel's intransigence would be to blame if the talks failed to create a long-lasting cease-fire.

Islamic Jihad leader, Khaled Al-Batsh, says from Cairo that the Palestinian delegation is willing to sign a cease-fire deal, but not at any cost. "Any deal should meet the people's aspirations, hopes, pain and steadfastness."

However, in statements issued by Islamic Jihad there seems to be no intention of extending the military confrontation.

Before the expiration of the cease-fire, several Israeli F-16 air strikes were carried out in eastern Gaza City, Khan Younis and the northern Gaza Strip. Israel states that these were retaliatory strikes after rockets were fired into Israel from Gaza.

But political analysts say that Palestinian factions usually announce the firing of rockets from Gaza, and no factions have taken responsibility for such rocket attacks.

"Israel has an interest in rockets coming from Gaza, in order to withdraw its negotiators from Cairo without results, before the end of the day," says Abusada.

Israeli drones continue flying over Gaza despite the cease-fire, and the occasional Israeli F-16 flies overhead at low altitude, intimidating the Gazan people.

Meanwhile, Gazans are receiving conflicting reports from Cairo that do not help understand the ongoing events.

Mahmoud Aldermli, 49, father of 11, is staying at a UN school shelter and says: "The resistance should continue as long as it can. It's better that we die in dignity than live in humiliation."

For Aldermli, waiting for the results of negotiations is the worst type of insult: "I have the patience to wait in the miserable conditions we live in, but in the end we want to see those results, so that we can live in dignity," he says.

The recent air strikes are likely to end the peace talks, an Israeli officials say the talks between the Israeli and Palestinian delegations in Cairo have collapsed. Prime Minister Netanyahu and Defense Minister Ya'alon have recalled Israeli envoys from Cairo.

Earlier on, the Palestinian ambassador to Egypt, Jamal Shoubaki, said that the Israelis proposed arrangements for "not (fully) removing the blockade but easing it." Palestinian negotiators say they want an end to the blockade forever.

As Saleh hears more Israeli air strikes hitting nearby, he says: "This is a clear Israeli message, that if you don't accept what we offer in Cairo, we will continue our air strikes."

Palestinian factions, including Hamas, say none of them have fired on Israel and they are committed to a 24-hour cease-fire.

Hamas accuses Israel of "foot-dragging" and Sami Abu Zuhri says this is a well-known Israeli policy, causing the "abortion of cease-fire talks."

The Palestinian Minister of Housing, Mofeed al-Hassayneh, estimates that Gaza needs $6–8 billion to rebuild the Gaza Strip. Twenty thousand homes have been demolished completely and rendered uninhabitable. Forty thousand other homes are partially destroyed, and 2.5 million tons of rubble from demolished homes needs to be cleared away.

Gaza outraged at Israel's use of GBU-28 missile

Palestinian civilians brace for another round of intensive attacks and remain steadfast in their support for the resistance as Israel employs the use of much more lethal missiles

GAZA CITY—"We either die as one or live as one," said Abu Suliman al-Buriem and his 11 family members, as they fled their home in the al-Zannah area of eastern Khan Younis.

Life doesn't have much pleasant news for the family of Abu Suliman; during the cease-fire, he left one UN school shelter in search of another. He said that this time, Israel broke the cease-fire to evade signing a long-term cease-fire agreement.

"If it was just me alone, I'd have known how to cope, but this also involves the lives of my 11 family members—mostly children," he said as he hurried his children to another shelter. This time, he said, he does not feel safe anywhere—the more the war continues, the more Israel wants to test new weapons.

On Tuesday, the Israeli military used a GBU-28 "bunker-buster" missile—sometimes referred to as "Deep Throat"—to kill the Aldalou family. The five-meter long missiles smash into homes and then explode.

Palestinians in Gaza were made to believe that peace was being negotiated, but last night's air strikes tell Abu Suliman that no one is safe.

"Not even a child in his mother's womb," said Abu Suliman, referring to Nabila Allouh, whose home was hit by an Israeli air strike, killing seven family members, including a heavily pregnant woman and her unborn baby.

In Gaza, the public is shocked that all targets, so far, have been civilian. There is a general belief that this is intended to turn Gaza against resistance factions. But Abu Suliman said, "If we let the resistance down, who else will protect us from Israeli missiles?"

He said UN and Arab leaders remain silent on the constant murder of residents in Gaza. Anger is mounting toward Arab states for not supporting long-occupied and besieged Palestinians.

Israel said that one air strike was meant to assassinate Mohammed Deif, the chief of Hamas' military wing, the Qassam Brigades. However, medical sources said that his wife and small baby were killed. Hamas sources said that the apartment that Deif's wife was staying in is known among the public and was not a resistance building.

Anger among Gazans toward Israel is also mounting after Israel tested its GBU-28 missile, apparently more destructive than F-16 missiles.

Meanwhile, it appears that Israel didn't manage to assassinate Deif. Both Ismail Haniyeh and Mohammed Deif became leaders of the resistance after Israel assassinated Sheikh Ahmed Yassin, Dr. Abdelaziz al-Rantisi and Ahmed al-Jabari.

Hamas sees any targeting of Hamas leaders as unlikely to crush the spirit of the resistance, although the Qassam Brigades and many Gazans fear that it will spur more retaliation than ever before.

Abu Suliman said that Netanyahu has tried to justify the war on Gaza to the international community, but that the United Nations has reported that the majority of those killed and injured have been civilians.

During an interview on Al-Aqsa TV, Hamas said that Mohammed Deif is the one who holds the authority to stop rockets fired from Gaza.

Six weeks of fierce bombardment has taken the lives of over 2,055 people and has injured 12,000 people, the majority of whom are civilians—and those numbers are increasing hourly. The public is confused as to what Israel's target could be.

Most of the targets are not informed of strikes beforehand. An eyewitness in Rafah said that he received a call from an Israeli officer, telling him to evacuate a home he had already left in 2009. The apartment was bombed and he didn't have time to tell the family who was living there to evacuate.

Hamas spokesman Fawzi Barhoum said that Israel started this war, as he asked Egypt to note that Palestinian factions did not fire rockets—it was Israeli troops that were called up eight hours before the cease-fire expired in order to murder the wife and child of Mohammed Deif.

Egypt expressed "profound regret" at the end of the 10-day period of calm and said it would continue trying to secure a lasting truce.

It seems that the apparent assassination attempt on Mohammed Deif may explain the intensity of rocket fire coming after the collapse of the Cairo peace talks.

Azzam al-Ahmed, a senior member of the Fatah movement of Palestinian Authority President Mahmoud Abbas, said that Israel is responsible.

"Israel thwarted the contracts that could have brought peace."

Meanwhile, Hamas said the strike was an attempt to assassinate Deif and said Israel had opened the "gateway to hell." Barhoum of Hamas said the coming days were going to be tough, without precedent.

Hamas spokesman Abo Obaida warned that international airlines should stop service into Ben Gurion Airport in Tel Aviv, assuring the public that Deif was not killed.

Sadi Hamd, 39, arrived from the northern Gaza Strip to find shelter, and expressed anger at the displacement of children. He said that he would never direct his anger at the resistance, only toward Israel's occupation and the killing of people in the school where he sought shelter.

"A shelter is supposed to be safe, and I feel America shares much responsibility for providing missiles to kill innocents," he said as he pulled his four daughters into a UN school to seek a safe haven.

"It appears certain that the Obama Administration is satisfied with such massive destruction, using the GBU-28 missile on a defenseless people who can't even find milk for their babies."

"I cheered for Obama when he came to power, thinking he was better than Bush, but now I say that a man who fought injustice is shamefully supplying weapons to the Israeli occupation."

In Gaza, rage is rising against the international community for their lack of reaction to Israel's attacks. "For once he [Obama] should stand up and speak his mind—but maybe he'll just wait until all US-made missiles are tested on our bodies."

Profile: who were the three Hamas commanders that were killed?

Hamas' military wing announced the killing of three of its most senior leaders in an Israeli bombardment on early Thursday in Gaza

The three Hamas military commanders killed early Thursday in southern Gaza are amongst the earliest generation of Qassam Brigade fighters. Here are more details about the three:

Raed al-Attar

Born in 1974, Raed al-Attar joined the Qassam Brigades in his early youth. Over the years, he gained a reputation for building Hamas' military capacity and became one of Hamas' top-ranking leaders.

Since 1994, he had been on Israel's most wanted list. Israel accused him of being able to snap up Israeli soldiers, teaching Hebrew to Qassam Brigades soldiers and drugging Israeli soldiers during military confrontations. Several assassination attempts had been made on his life, including repeated bombing of his home on several occasions. He was known to change his location and never stay in one place for long.

More recently, al-Attar was a member of the higher military council of the Qassam Brigades and was the Rafah Division commander. He was also one of the founders of Hamas' elite commando unit, Nukhba.

He was best known within Gaza as the architect behind the Gilad Shalit prisoner exchange deal and kept Shalit in a secret place for five years in Gaza.

In a video showing al-Attar walking beside Shalit on the day the exchange deal happened, Israeli TV channel 2 said al-Attar was "sharp looking, quiet and ready to deal with any emergency, his eyes filled with determination, and wearing very modern clothes."

During the recent conflict, Israeli intelligence accused al-Attar of knowing the whereabouts of Israeli soldier Hadar Goldin, who was reportedly captured by Hamas during recent fighting and has been reported to be dead. As the commander of Rafah, al-Attar was also accused of supplying weapons to Hamas through the smuggling tunnels underneath the border town.

He was married and had two children.

Mohammed Abu Shamalah

Head of the Southern Division, commander Mohammed Abu Shamalah was one of the most senior leaders in the southern Gaza Strip and was in charge of overseeing the Rafah and Khan Younis areas.

Born in 1973 in Rafah and married with five children, Abu Shamalah was believed to have been the successor to Hamas' former second in command, Ahmed al-Jabari, killed during the eight-day Israeli offensive in November 2012. He is thought to have been one of the founders of the Qassam Brigades and to have directed their fighting strategy.

In the First Intifada, between 1987 and 1991, Abu Shamalah was involved in chasing down alleged Israeli collaborators and planning resistance operations in different parts of Gaza.

In 1999, the Palestinian Authority issued execution orders against both al-Attar and Abu Shamalah, but massive demonstrations held after the orders were released contributed to stopping the executions.

Abu Shamalah worked with al-Attar on the Shalit prisoner exchange deal.

Abu Shamalah was on Israel's most wanted list since 1991 and had survived previous assassination attempts. One of the most high-profile attempts occurred in 2004 when Israeli troops surrounded his home and bombed it with explosives. In 2012, Israeli warplanes bombed his home again. A third home that he built in 2014 was bombed by F-16 missiles a few weeks ago.

Mohammed Barhoum

A close friend to al-Attar and Abu Shamalah, Barhoum was the senior commander of the Rafah Division. In 1992, he left the occupied Palestinian territories after being chased by Israeli intelligence. He continued to travel secretly between different Arab states, but he returned during the Second Intifada to rejoin the Qassam brigades.

Born in 1970 and married, Barhoum is not well-known in Gaza, but he was nicknamed "the gray-haired man."

"Collaborators" publicly executed in Gaza

The policy of executing alleged collaborators with Israel hasn't been used for nearly two decades

GAZA—Friday's execution of 18 Palestinians who allegedly collaborated with Israel during the recent conflict in Gaza is part of the new "show no mercy" campaign that Palestinian resistance groups have announced.

It was not immediately clear on Friday how many of the 18 were alleged to have collaborated with Israel in the recent fighting, or if they had been tried in court.

The new campaign—and the executions—follow an increase in Israeli assassination attempts, after fighting started again this week with the failure of truce talks in Cairo.

On Tuesday, hours after the talks broke down, an Israeli air strike that was thought to be targeting Hamas' military chief, Mohammed Deif, killed his wife and two children. Then on Thursday, three Hamas military commanders were assassinated in Rafah.

The precision of the attacks led many to believe that Israel had been fed credible intelligence. The executions on Friday would seem to confirm that Palestinian resistance groups believe this as well.

"Amidst the dangerous developments on the ground, decisive orders have been issued to start strangling the necks of collaborators, and to deal harshly with suspects and collaborators in the field," said a statement released on al-Majd Security, a website that is close to Hamas and Gaza security affairs.

"Those killed on Friday were responsible for the deaths of many Gazans and the destruction of their homes," the statement said. As part of the campaign, any future collaborators who are discovered will be punished immediately.

"The resistance will show no mercy to any collaborator caught in the field," the statement said.

On Friday morning, masked men ran into the police station in Gaza City, where alleged collaborators, many of whom have been incarcerated for years, are held. Eleven men were shot.

Several hours after the 11 alleged collaborators were shot in the Gaza City police station on Friday, another seven men were publically shot in Palestine Square, one of Gaza's most crowded districts.

As worshippers came out of Friday prayers in Omari mosque, which is situated on the square, a group of masked gunmen dressed in black shot the men, whose faces were covered and hands were bound.

The identity of the men was hidden, as families associated with collaborators in Gaza suffer from discrimination for generations. A child, for example, whose father was caught as a collaborator would be nicknamed "the son of the collaborator" at school.

The bodies of those killed, apparently as an example to the public, were later taken to Shifa Hospital.

The killing was quickly denounced by human rights groups.

"We demand that the Palestinian National Authority and the resistance intervene to stop these extra-judicial executions, no matter what the reasons and the motives are," said Raji al-Surani, the Chairman of the Palestinian Center for Human Rights, in a statement.

These are the first executions to take place in Gaza since the 1990s.

Witnesses on the ground say that most of those killed had been convicted in military courts and were awaiting execution orders, seemingly having exhausted all appeals in the courts.

In recent months, the Palestinian Interior Ministry had offered mercy to any collaborators who voluntarily handed themselves in.

But the security divisions of Gaza's resistance groups have now issued orders to tighten security procedures to protect against collaborators and suspects, and to discourage would-be collaborators, according to a source that preferred to remain anonymous.

Security sources say that another group of people are to be executed, once juridical and legal procedures are completed.

For years, Israel has relied on Palestinian collaborators by either threatening to bomb their homes, blackmailing their businesses, offering alluring exit permits for travel or other incentives.

In his book *He Who Comes to Kill*, Yaakov Peri, the former head of Israeli security agency Shin Bet, stressed the importance to Israeli security of information provided by collaborators.

But in Gaza's culture, working as a collaborator is considered one of the most shameful of acts and can haunt the family of an alleged collaborator for years. In a famous collaborator case, a university student informed Israeli intelligence of the whereabouts of Sheikh Salah Shehdah, former chief of the Qassam Brigades. Due to the intelligence obtained from the collaborator, an Israeli F-16 bombed Shehdah's residence, killing him, his wife, his daughter and 7 members of the Matar family, in addition to injuring over 100 people. The bombing took place on July 22, 2002.

As a result of this, a group of collaborators were executed in the 2008–09 war on Gaza, Operation Cast Lead.

Neither the names nor photos of those executed this morning have been published, as security forces say this would hit Gaza's social fabric. Their identities have not been released in order to prevent offense to the families of those killed.

As prices soar, Gaza food crisis looms

With produce and meat selling at inflated costs, many Palestinians in Gaza are surviving on emergency food rations

GAZA CITY—Ashraf al-Helou knows that whatever chickens he has in stock right now, may be his last.

"Most chicken farms have been destroyed. The livestock was either directly killed by Israel's attacks, or from lack of food and water," al-Helou, 32, tells Al Jazeera from his shop.

On the phone to his usual supplier, al-Helou explains that the farmer does not have enough chickens left to make a delivery; what he has left will last one more week at most. "If there were restaurants open, we would have run out of chicken about two weeks ago," al-Helou adds.

Before Israel's military operation began in the Gaza Strip, one kilogram of chicken cost 10 NIS ($2.83). Today, with his stocks quickly depleting, al-Helou charges his customers 15 NIS ($4.24).

According to the Gaza Health Ministry, at least 2,102 Palestinians have been killed, and another 10,540 others injured, since Israel's operation in Gaza began on July 8. Sixty-four Israeli soldiers have also been killed, along with three Israeli civilians and a Thai foreign worker.

Israeli bombings in Gaza have destroyed much of the local infrastructure, including water and electricity supplies. At least 360 factories and workshops have also been damaged in the shelling, including 126 that were completely wrecked, amounting to $47m in damages.

Many of Gaza's farmers and shepherds have been forced to abandon their crops and animals, paralyzing agricultural and fishing activities and bringing local food production to a halt, the United Nations Food and Agriculture Organization reported.

"Up to now, ongoing military operations have prevented detailed assessments of damages to agriculture," said Ciro Fiorillo, head of the FAO offices in the West Bank and Gaza Strip, in a statement. The FAO estimates that half of Gaza's poultry stocks have been lost, while Gaza's fishermen have seen their annual catch reduced by 9.3 percent.

Mohammed Abu Ajwwa says about 500 cows were killed on his farm in eastern Gaza City, costing him approximately $500,000. "My business used to provide milk and dairy [products] to a local factory, but now neither the factory, nor my cows, exist," he tells Al Jazeera.

When 51-year-old Umm Ghazi usually goes to the market in central Rafah, in the southern Gaza Strip, her youngest son, Osama, goes with her to help carry the groceries home. For the past week, however, she has not had much to buy or carry back.

"It's not only bad [produce], but it is also unaffordable," says Umm Ghazi, inspecting tomatoes that appear wrinkled and dry, a sign of possible crop dehydration. In some parts of the Gaza Strip, the price of eggs has gone up by 40 percent, potatoes by 42 percent, and tomatoes by 179 percent, the FAO found.

"Twenty-three NIS [$6.50] for a box of eggs, which were 11 NIS [$3.11] a few weeks ago," Umm Ghazi adds, as another customer explains that these eggs are smaller than before, since the chicken farmers have lost most of their livestock.

Prior to the ongoing war, 66 percent of households in Gaza were receiving food assistance, and 72 percent of households were vulnerable to food insecurity, according to the UN's humanitarian office (UNOCHA). In cooperation with the local ministry of social affairs, the UN has so far provided emergency food assistance to 415,000 out of 730,000 needy people who do not normally receive food assistance.

According to Hossam Madhoun, project coordinator at Maan Development Center in Gaza, inflation has primarily impacted fresh produce and meat, after eastern parts of the strip—home to Gaza's main agricultural zones—came under heavy Israeli bombardment and military ground incursions.

"[During] the two-week closure of Khuza'a, which [comprises] the main part of the vegetable basket of the Gaza Strip . . . farmers could not cultivate at all. [The vegetables are] rotten," Madhoun tells Al Jazeera, adding that a severe cash shortage has made it difficult for most people, even those with money in the bank, to buy food.

"The canned food is available . . . in the markets at fair prices, but still most of the people cannot buy it," he says. "Even when the war ends, the food situation is deteriorating and I don't see that [this problem] is going to be eliminated unless there is a huge campaign [to have] infrastructure enter Gaza [and] jobs to rebuild."

Gaza war strengthens Palestinian unity

Rival Palestinian factions in the Gaza Strip have united in celebration of the end of the war, but will it last?

GAZA CITY—Raef had never been to a demonstration before. But after the announcement of the latest cease-fire agreement between Israel and the Palestinian factions, the 13-year-old borrowed a green Hamas flag from his neighbors, and ran to the center of Gaza City to cheer on the Palestinian faction at a victory rally.

"I started to know more about Hamas over the last 53 days," he said, explaining that surviving Israel's recent seven-week military operation in Gaza, which killed at least 2,100 Palestinians and injured more than 10,000 others, has made him a Hamas supporter.

"I like them because they defend us," said Raef, adding that witnessing the destruction of the 12-story Zafer apartment tower made him realise the importance of Palestinian resistance fighters.

"My mom and dad support Fatah's Abu Mazen [Palestinian Authority President Mahmoud Abbas] but they have sympathy for Hamas," he added, before disappearing into a sea of green at the rally.

In 2006, Hamas won the Palestinian Legislative Council elections. The victory caused political tension with the PA, which refused to acknowledge the new Hamas-led government because of pressure from the international community and Israel to discount the results.

After the two sides failed to come to a power-sharing agreement, violence quickly ensued, leading to a bloody attempted coup in Gaza in 2007. The occupied Palestinian territories were then divided along factional lines, with the PA controlling the West Bank and Hamas governing Gaza, and political institutions were paralysed as a result of the split.

In June, Fatah and Hamas unveiled a consensus government and announced forthcoming parliamentary and presidential elections. In response, Israel said it would pursue punitive steps, including withholding Palestinian tax revenues and stopping peace negotiations.

According to a recent Palestinian Center for Policy and Survey Research poll, which surveyed 1,270 Palestinians in the West Bank and Gaza after the Gaza war ended, Hamas leader Ismail Haniyeh would win twice as many votes as Abbas in a presidential election. Hamas had an 88 percent approval rating, while the PA had only 36 percent of support.

Despite this, Hamas' rivals in Fatah—the faction that dominates the PA—have garnered increased support in Gaza after the war: yellow Fatah flags and photos of Abbas can be seen throughout the strip. The support for both major factions has contributed to the sense of unity in Gaza, according to Dr. Ahmed Yousef, the chairman of the Palestinian Reconciliation Committee, a body established to urge Palestinian reunification.

"Hamas has now emerged as part of the broader political spectrum, it no longer stands alone," Yousef, who served as an adviser to former Hamas Prime Minister Ismail Haniyeh, told Al Jazeera. "It is the steadfastness and survival of people which gives a flavor of victory. We are not a superpower. . . . The message we are telling Israel is that we love life."

Both Abbas and Khaled Meshaal, Hamas' political chief, met with the Emir of Qatar on August 21, in what analysts described as a sign of Palestinian unity, shortly before the cease-fire agreement was unveiled.

Under the deal, the PA has been charged with administering Gaza's borders and coordinating reconstruction efforts in the Palestinian enclave with international donors like the European Union, Qatar and Turkey. Long-term issues, such as Israel's push to demilitarize the strip and Hamas' demand to reopen Gaza's seaport and airport, will be negotiated next month.

Meanwhile, after the announcement of the cease-fire, Israeli Prime Minister Benjamin Netanyahu said that Hamas had suffered a "very hard blow," and did not achieve any of its demands in the agreement. "I think that Hamas is also isolated diplomatically," Netanyahu said. "I think that we also instilled in the international community the fact that Hamas, [Islamic State group] and Al-Qaeda and other extremist Islamic terrorist organizations are members of the same family."

But according to Dr. Khalil al-Hayyeh, a Hamas leader who was part of the Cairo delegation, the indirect talks between Palestinian factions and Israel was evidence of the end of internal Palestinian divisions.

"Today we are in a new era of unity and have adopted [the rhetoric of] resistance," he said in a speech delivered during prayer last Friday, adding that all the Palestinian factions would continue fighting Israel if it did not respond to all Palestinians' demands.

Addressing the rebuilding of the Gaza Strip following the seven weeks of war, al-Shayyeh said that the only body responsible for the strip's reconstruction, including managing the border to allow the necessary materials in, would be the Palestinian consensus government.

Meanwhile, Mouin Rabbani, a senior fellow at the Institute of Palestine Studies, told Al Jazeera that while Israel's attacks on Gaza backfired, resulting in greater ties between the Palestinian factions, this togetherness could easily fall apart.

"The Palestinians were not defeated, but can yet defeat themselves if they do not invest their achievements into a coherent national project and instead return to the pattern of seeking petty factional advantages," Rabbani said.

"Israel's political leadership was simply too extreme and fractious to identify achievable political objectives, and failed miserably to achieve any objective it did identify, such as reversing recent moves towards Palestinian reconciliation which it in fact strengthened," Rabbani added.

Sixty-two-year-old Fatah supporter Abu Mahmoud Braim, from Khan Younis, said the war had made him feel more compassionate toward Hamas members. "Once you see your brothers murdered by a foreign power, we return to what unites us—Palestine and not just factions," he said, pointing to the killing of three leading Hamas figures and civilians in Israeli strikes on Rafah, in southern Gaza, as a catalyst that caused him to change his views.

Khalil Abdelhadi, a 31-year-old school teacher in Gaza City, said his support for Hamas has been unconditional, but he cheered on the efforts of the other armed groups, as well. "It's odd that aggression unites us, but after today, the pain we suffered makes us focus only on ourselves as one with a common enemy: [the] Israeli occupation," he told Al Jazeera.

Dr. Fayez Abuetta, a Fatah leader in Gaza, said that cooperation exhibited during cease-fire negotiations in Cairo proved that factions are able to work together. "We forgot our internal squabbling and focused on what unites us all. Palestinian blood is most important to us all," said Abuetta, adding that he hoped this newfound unity would last beyond the end of the war.

However, on August 28, President Abbas said on Palestine TV that "as long as there is a shadow government in Gaza, there will be no real unity," in what appeared to be a reference to Hamas. Hamas did not respond to the comment, but many Palestinians are waiting to see whether the Fatah leader will pay 45,000 employees of the previous de facto government in Gaza their overdue salaries.

The PA released a statement on Tuesday announcing that it was making "maximum efforts" to disburse the payments, but gave no specific date for when they would go through.

Gaza-based analyst Ibrahim al-Madoun told Al Jazeera that failure on the part of Abbas and the PA to deliver the wages to Gaza-based employees could lead to another internal conflict. "If Abbas does not provide salaries, then things may blow up again," al-Madoun told Al Jazeera.

Meanwhile, Abuetta said that it remains to be seen whether the consensus government will be able to function properly, but he was hopeful that under the supervision of Abbas, it will continue its mandate. This new atmosphere may make it easier for the government to work, he added.

"We have realized we are stronger together. We [can] rely on this united power to strengthen our resistance . . . [and] better meet to our national aspirations."

Who are Israel's Palestinian informants?

Israel relies on information provided by a network of Palestinian collaborators. But how does the system really work?

GAZA CITY—The public execution of alleged Palestinian informants for Israel in the Gaza Strip, known locally as collaborators, drew international attention recently, a few days before the end of Israel's seven-week military offensive in the coastal territory.

With beige sacks over their heads, several men were positioned on their knees in front of a white wall. Standing over them, their executioners: armed Palestinian fighters, dressed in all black, balaclavas over their faces and AK-47s strapped to their sides.

At least 18 Palestinians were executed on August 22 in Gaza, accused of providing information to Israel during its recent war. But what exactly motivates a Palestinian to collaborate with the Israeli intelligence services, and how does the phenomenon work?

"Under pressure, I gave in to [their] demand," said a former Palestinian collaborator, who spoke to Al Jazeera on condition of anonymity. A resident of the Gaza Strip, the man said that an Israeli intelligence officer approached him in 1995, threatening to revoke his permit to work in Israel if he didn't divulge information about the location and activities of Hamas members, among others.

"I was unhappy and couldn't live [with] that shame, so one day I woke up and told my wife I would no longer work in Israel," the man recalled. He immediately went to the Palestinian security forces to confess what he had done. Imprisoned for a few weeks, he was eventually released on voluntary probation.

For years, Israel has relied on Palestinians to gather information. Often, Israeli officials threaten peoples' families or livelihoods, or offer incentives, such as difficult-to-secure travel permits or cash, in order to get people to collaborate.

Capital punishment is permissible under the Palestine Liberation Organization's Revolutionary Penal Code of 1979, including Article 9, which stipulates that a person can receive the death penalty for acting "against the security and safety and interests of the revolution troops."

Human Rights Watch reported in 2012 that "given credible evidence of widespread and gross violations of due process as well as systematic ill-treatment and torture. . . . Hamas should immediately declare a moratorium on executions in death penalty cases."

According to political researcher Hazem Abu Shanab, several of the men who were recently executed in Gaza had spent about one month in prison, where they confessed during interrogation to giving information to the Israelis or planting surveillance equipment in Gaza.

"One of the methods of recruiting collaborators is by shutting down Rafah crossing [between Gaza and Egypt] and allowing Palestinians to travel through Erez [crossing between Gaza and Israel], so that it can pressure, blackmail and tempt them to work as collaborators," Abu Shanab said.

Shawan Jabareen, director of Palestinian human rights group Al-Haq, said that the men executed in Gaza likely did not have a fair trial, a guarantee under the Fourth Geneva Convention, and called on Palestinian factions to halt the practice of executing collaborators.

He added that sometimes, Palestinians' humanitarian needs are abused in order to coerce them into providing information. "Those peoples' needs and illness have been abused and the [Israeli authorities] force them to work in its military and security apparatuses. [Israel] is responsible for the crime," Jabareen said.

Mohammed Abu Hassira, 30, told Al Jazeera that social media has become a place where Israeli intelligence officials seek out collaborators from Gaza. With an unemployment rate of 40 percent in Gaza—the highest since 2009—offers of money and other perks are tempting, Abu Hassira said. "Many are innocent, naive youngsters who don't know they are collaborating," he added.

Indeed, according to Gaza security services interrogator Abu Ahmed, who didn't give Al Jazeera his full name, the information requested often appears inconspicuous.

"One of my collaborators was asked for simple information: look from the balcony and see what types of clothes are hanging there," he told Al Jazeera. "The request appears very innocent, but in that case, it was an apartment of a Hamas leader and Israeli intelligence wanted to know if men's clothes were drying on the balcony, indicating that the occupant was asleep inside."

In other cases, Gaza security officials have caught merchants asked to bring small bags of sands to the Erez border crossing with Israel. "It turned out he [was taking] this sand to be tested by Israeli intelligence officials . . . to figure out location of [Palestinian] tunnels."

Local journalist Fathi Sabbah agreed. "Collaborators are national traitors and the only solution for them is the execution," he told Al Jazeera. "[But] those people should be given a fair trial and should have the right to defend themselves."

"We demand that the Palestinian National Authority and the [Palestinian armed factions] intervene to stop these extra-judicial executions, no matter what the reasons and motives are," said Raji Sourani, head of the Gaza-based Palestinian Center for Human Rights, in a statement.

But the practice doesn't seem to be stopping, as Palestinian factions in Gaza announced that 13 more collaborators had handed themselves in to the local security services.

"Palestinian resistance groups should be fair and comply with laws," said a Gaza judge, who works on collaborators' cases and who spoke to Al Jazeera on condition of anonymity. "It's enough that Israel kills scores of us on a daily basis."

Gaza airport: hopes that dreams will be a reality again

Gazans dream of the day when seaports and airports will be open once again, allowing the free movement of goods and people and bringing wealth and freedom back into their lives

RAFAH—Gaza International Airport was a reality in 1998. Palestinian children ran to the streets to formally greet US President Bill Clinton. The airport was seen as the gateway to the world, whereby Palestinians could simply hop on a plane traveling out and return back home, freely.

The airport was known internationally by its code, GZA, after which it was renamed Yasser Arafat International Airport, in honor of a man who carried a Kalashnikov rifle in one hand and an olive branch in the other.

Some airport staff members fondly remember when a KLM flight arrived for a test, and then flew a return trip to Schiphol airport. The airport was the proud home of three Palestinian airplanes that had daily flights to Egypt, Jordan, Syria, Morocco, Cyprus and Turkey.

Issam Saleh remembers the day he traveled to Jordan on one of the flights: "It felt like a flying bus, shaking all the way. I was confused as to whether the plane was flying or landing," he laughed, as he recalled the one-hour journey. Now, if he wants to travel, it takes weeks of preparation and paperwork. Ultimately, the success or failure of travel in Gaza depends on whether Egyptian border control authorities are willing to allow people to travel.

"But those shaky flights were better than not being able to travel at all," he said.

For him, the reality of that flight faded and became a distant dream. But after all of Gaza's sacrifices under the present Israeli assault, he says he is determined to make such dreams a reality again.

When the Second Intifada began in 2000, Israeli fighter jets first hit the flight control tower. Then bulldozers tore up the runway. And over the years, until this current Israeli assault, the beautiful Moroccan-designed terminal with colorful marble—where President Arafat received his guests—was still faintly visible.

The project that cost $86 million has now become a place for farm animals, some alive and others dead, left in the ruins of a once-beautiful airport. Chickens peck in the sand and rubble while the flights overhead are ones that never land on the runway—just Israeli F-16s and drones, which continuously circle above, ever-watching and intimidating Gaza's population.

Salman Abu Haleeb, head of the Palestinian Aviation Authority, remained hopeful—even after the airport had been bombed. He said that the Oslo Accords gave the Palestinians a right to an airport.

Indirect negotiations between Israel and Palestinian factions have failed. But among the demands of Palestinians is an open airport and seaport. Both represent dreams that were once a reality.

"This reality existed before, and I feel it will return, as long as the Palestinian resistance continues to demand it," says Abu Sadi, who lives a few minutes from the airport ruins.

"I remember the days when we waved to our loved ones traveling on flights out. Now I look forward to seeing a no-fly zone for Israeli fighter jets," he said.

Nowadays, the seaport and airport have become obstacles for cease-fire talks, with Israel refusing access to both because they would give more freedom and independence to Palestinians.

Israel's air strikes have turned the whole airport terminal and runway into piles of gravel, which is now used to rebuild many homes after Israel tightened the blockade. During the cease-fires, Gazans collected gravel left by Israel's missiles and tank shells to try to rebuild parts of their homes.

Saleh remembers that in the old days, passengers would go through Israeli-controlled crossings to have their passports stamped before boarding their flights.

"But at least there was hope. We had more of a state, and thoughts of flying made me feel free." he said.

The Oslo Accords also allowed the construction of Gaza's seaport. In the late 1990s, a $73 million contract was signed with European partners.

Now, Saleh says, he wants and needs to go back to Jordan for medical treatment. He calculates how many air miles it would take to reach Amman. His dreams of flying are shared by others, including many young Gazans, who want to take a break from Israel's torment.

Gaza economist Dr. Maher Taba'a of the Chamber of Commerce says that a seaport and docks would allow Palestinian traders to import and export goods and materials, which would improve Gaza's economy and provide employment for over 30,000 workers.

"Today there is a chance to have a floating seaport which takes a year to be built," he said, adding that rebuilding the seaport is the most important first step for reviving Gaza's economy.

Importing through Israel since 2002 has cost Gaza's business, trade and economy an estimated $1 billion annually, says Taba'a. Since then, he said, the scale of import requirements has increased at least five-fold.

Palestine's new generation has mostly never been outside of Palestine because of Israel's occupation and restrictions on travel through Egypt and Israel. But that doesn't stop young Palestinians from hoping for freedom of movement, like everyone else.

Dr. Taba'a says that external European monitoring can be used to address Israel's security concerns. "Gaza will be overjoyed the moment we can work and feed ourselves, import and export freely."

He says this will make goods more affordable for customers, and it will be a reliable source of income for the PA budget.

Meanwhile, Egyptian brokers at the suspended Cairo talks between Israel and Palestinian factions have suggested that the airport and seaport demands be deferred for a second round of negotiations in about a month.

"Once we have our airport and seaports open, we can wave goodbye to aid. Palestinians can make paradise from our own air and water."

Israel blows up apartments in Gaza City, sending families fleeing

In the six weeks of Israel's offensive in Gaza, 2,276 homes have been destroyed completely and 13,395 have been partially destroyed, in addition to tens of thousands of other homes that have also been affected

Over the years, the Zafer Towers apartment blocks in Gaza City have become a residential area to most of Gaza's elite. In the 1990s the first people in Gaza to live in high-rise blocks moved into Zafer Towers.

As darkness fell on Gaza on Saturday night, Israeli fighter jets attacked one of the 12-story apartment towers in western Gaza City, completely destroying the tower and bringing the 44 residential apartments crashing down.

The Palestinian Interior Ministry said in a statement on Saturday that targeting residential towers is a "dangerous escalation and continued collective punishment, meant to displace more civilians."

Israel, however, says that there was an operation room for Palestinian resistance groups in the building. Residents dispute this claim, saying there was nothing there that belonged to any resistance groups.

The Interior Ministry says Israel's allegations are baseless and "bankrupt."

"Why would Israel warn us to evacuate the tower building before attacking if it knew there were resistance members inside? It doesn't make sense," says an injured eyewitness at Shifa Hospital.

Abu Salah, 42, says first an Israeli drone struck the roof, then some minutes later he saw people rushing downstairs. He gathered his five children and wife and ran into the street.

"We got outside with in-house clothes on us, leaving all our money and papers behind."

Now the "Al Zafer 4" apartment tower is in ruins.

Including Abu Salah himself, a former Palestinian Authority (PA) employee, residents in Al Zafer are among the elite of Gaza. Some are sons of senior former PA employees who, historically, have not been considered with favor by Hamas because of their long association with Fatah.

Residents say a "knock-on-the-roof" warning missile was fired and then just minutes later the building was bombed, with most residents able to escape just in time.

Gaza's Health Ministry stated that 22 people were injured, including 11 children and five women who couldn't escape quickly enough in the five minutes before two Israeli F-16 missiles struck. For many Gazans this unprecedented attack on a residential tower is shocking, and demonstrates yet again that Israel is willing to attack any building in Gaza, regardless of whether it is strategically important to Israel's "security."

Thick black smoke billows out of huge gaping holes where Israel's missiles struck the tower. The damage to local infrastructure is massive, including to neighboring upscale high-rise buildings in the Tal Al-Hawa neighborhood. People ran outside in fear and shock as the building shook.

"I had thought the explosion was in our building. I ran out of the toilet down the stairs," says a 45-year-man living next to Zafer Towers.

Meanwhile, wheelchair bound Hesham Saqallah, 51, a former PA employee, says he had some assistance in evacuating the building. He has lost everything. "My money, clothes, papers, furniture and everything. I feel I am born naked with my four children today."

Hesham says Israel lied when talking about an operation room for the resistance. "We are a close community, and we know one another very well. No resistance and no strangers live among us," he says.

"Even when beggars come seeking charity, we help them while they stand outside the tower," he adds.

Israel's six-week offensive has caused around 450,000 inhabitants to become displaced in Gaza, seeking shelter either in hospitals or in UN and government-run schools. Some 100,000 Gazans are now also homeless, according to the UN.

Saturday marked the highest number of homes destroyed ever by an Israeli offensive.

Explosives experts in Gaza have said that Israel has dropped 20,000 tons of explosives over the past six weeks. On three occasions over the past 48 hours, Israel has used "cluster bombs," says the department: first at the Abuakleen family home, where the damage reached 1 sq. kilometer, and then at Zafer Towers and a third location in northern Gaza. The destruction caused by these bombs is greater than the destruction in many other areas.

The organization Euro-mid Observer for Human Rights states that during the six weeks of Israel's offensive, 15,671 residences have been targeted, of which 2,276 homes were destroyed completely and 13,395 were partially destroyed. Tens of thousands of other homes have also been affected.

Euro-mid also noted that on Saturday alone, Israel bombed 439 homes, 99 of which were completely destroyed and 340 of which were partially damaged.

On Saturday, Israeli fighter jets also hit four NGOs, raising the number of targeted organizations to 26, all of which provide services to over 200,000 inhabitants of Gaza.

As the Saturday morning sun rose on another part of Gaza, Israeli missiles targeted a home, killing members of the Abu Dahrouj family in Zawyda, in the central Gaza Strip.

Residents say this was not a political or militia area. The home just had family members sleeping inside, who now remain asleep forever.

"The first rocket didn't explode, luckily. But as my aunt and family were about to wake the children and evacuate, they were hit by two more rockets," says Arafat Abu Dahrouj, who lives near his cousin's home.

"Israeli fighter jets shelled the house without giving us time to escape," he says.

Wael Abu Dahrouj, a cousin, says there are still bodies under the rubble waiting to be recovered.

Some of the bodies of the five family members were blown to pieces, scattered to different areas. The bodies are still missing.

Earlier on Saturday, Hamas deputy Mousa Abu Marzouq announced that Hamas had signed a pledge to join the Rome Statute Charter in an effort to endorse any Palestinian bid for membership in the International Criminal Court (ICC). Such a bid could expose Israel, as well as Hamas, to possible war crimes prosecution.

Israeli fighter jets have bombed Qarara Municipality and its cultural center, south of Deir al-Balah. In Rafah, six air strikes hit Rafah Shopping Center, destroying and setting alight 80 shops and also damaging two schools nearby, as well as neighboring homes.

Around the pile of ruins that was Zafer Towers, Saqallah can't restore the feeling of safety to his four children and wife, who are now homeless. He says that when he watched the collapsing tower, he thought of the 9/11 attacks in New York City. When asked what he wants Americans to know, he said: "Your 9/11 is our 24/7 of terrorism practiced by Israel."

Attack on Gaza: "economic warfare"

From shop owners to factory bosses, fishermen to farmers—all count losses and face huge debts as missiles blow livelihoods to pieces

RAFAH—Parents of newborn babies usually come to al-Belbisi for various infant supplies, from bodysuits and pajamas to bedcovers. The shop has become an icon, serving some 180,000 people, mostly refugees in Rafah, in the southern Gaza Strip.

But that is history. Omar al-Belbisi now stands dazed in front of what remains of his shop—one of 80 in Rafah Trade Center that were destroyed by Israeli missiles on Saturday morning.

As a haze of smoke drifts out of Belbisi's shop, he is taking a brief break, his face covered in ash and smeared with soot from digging through the ruins of his property to salvage what he can, despite still being frightened that more missiles may fall.

At least six Israeli missiles were fired on the center, smashing shops, a wedding hall and an attorney's offices. Most people rented the shops from the local municipality after the shopping mall was built with US $2 million in Norwegian-Dutch support in 1998, said the mayor's office.

"We were not expecting this to happen. What could be a threat to Israel's security here, in a shopping center, which only sells domestic products to ordinary families?" said Belbisi.

His shop employed several people, providing them with an income that helped feed and clothe about 40 people in all.

He looks around at what is left—not "rockets" or militia equipment, just pairs of trousers for $30 each and other clothing and household items now burned or torn to shreds.

Belbisi had bought a large stock of clothes for Eid, summer and the new academic year. This was more than double his usual stock, and it had arrived before Israel launched its most recent 50-day attack. Now he has nothing left and must shut down for the rest of the season.

Normally, anything he doesn't sell he can exchange or sell the next season for a discount, an option he no longer has. His business is ruined.

"The loss is too big, because I stocked up for three seasons. That is going to cost me triple losses—many thousands of dollars."

Belbisi's plight is worse than most. He doesn't buy with his own money directly; a merchant buys his stock, and the shop's sales pay back the debt. His merchant will be looking for a check of about $39,500 come the middle of September.

Belbisi does not know what to do—but Majed Hadied of Gaza, who used to own the biggest carnations nursery in town, had a similar experience and said he knows what will happen.

Before Israel's siege of Gaza in 2006, he travelled to the Netherlands to take part in the European Flower Exchange Market and enjoy seeing his products sold to different European Union countries.

Israel's closure of commercial crossings to Gaza blocked the export of Hadied's carnations. As they withered while waiting for Israel to release them, he could only feed them to his cows and camels. Then he had to face suppliers and merchants who resorted to police or the courts to collect their debts.

For Belbisi, the immediate future looks like it will be similar to Hadied's ordeal.

There is no one to support Belbisi with his debts. He and his family can only pray that something will come up so they don't starve.

Gaza economist Dr. Maher Taba'a says the damage caused in this war is three times the damage caused in 2008–09.

While inspecting the damage, the mayor of Rafah, Subhi Radwan, described it as a horrendous image of destruction. As smoke still billowed from the shopping center, his staff tried to assess the value of the damage, thought to be around $10 million.

"This is an unjustified barbaric act, designed to crush what remains of the Palestinian economy," said Radwan.

Early on August 1, Israeli F-16s hit the same shopping center, but damaged mainly the roof. This time, Israeli intelligence called Fouad Zard, who lives next to the center, to tell him he had eight minutes to evacuate.

"I called all the neighbors to evacuate immediately," he said, but before the eight minutes passed, the first Israeli missile hit the shopping center.

The Zard home was not apparently a target, but it was hit anyway, along with the Amina Bint Wahb and al-Khansa UN Relief and Works Agency schools—both shelters for hundreds of families forced to flee their homes in eastern Rafah.

Rafah Trade Center director Riad al-Holy said he could not imagine any rationale for this attack, other than the deliberate destruction of the Palestinian economy. "There is no security pretext, and the loss among shop owners is massive."

Meanwhile, the UN's Food and Agriculture Organization (FAO) said about 42,000 acres of croplands had sustained substantial damage and half of Gaza's poultry stock had been lost due to direct hits or lack of care during the seige. Gaza's fishermen have seen their annual catch reduced by almost 10 percent.

All this on top of the destruction of Gaza's infrastructure, including water and electricity supplies. At least 360 factories and workshops have been damaged, including 126 that were completely wrecked, amounting to $47 million in damages.

The Palestinian Federation of Industries said the majority of industrial plants halted production during the war, causing losses estimated at more than $70 million.

Juda family mourns as cease-fire announced in Gaza

After 50 days of fighting, some 1,800 children have become orphans in Gaza, according to Euro-mid Observer for Human Rights

JABALIYA REFUGEE CAMP, NORTHERN GAZA—As shouts celebrating the cease-fire ring out across Gaza, 10-year-old Thaeer Juda lies in Gaza's Shifa Hospital ICU unit.

He's badly injured and has had his right leg and a few of the fingers on his right hand amputated. His left side is only marginally better off. His hands have been shattered, while his face and chest have been pocked by shrapnel that ripped through his little body after an Israeli strike.

Thaeer will survive, but will have to do so without many of the loved ones he expected to know for the rest of his life. He doesn't know what happened to his mother, Rawia, or his two sisters, Tasnim and Taghreed, nor his brothers Osama and Mohammed. But they are all gone—killed in one fell swoop by the same Israeli strike that landed Thaeer in the hospital and that will keep him there, long after the "victory" cries outside have died down.

Disaster struck this family just before sunset, on a very hot August night.

Rawia Juda, 40, was sitting on her doorstep in the fresh night air, telling stories to her children to distract them from the horror of Israeli missiles and bombs. Just for a few moments, the family expected things to stay quiet.

When she finished, she went into the house to check on her husband, Essam, 45, who had decided to give her a break from the domestic routine and was busy cooking the evening meal.

Taghreed, 12, and her sister Tasnim, 13, were playing with a doll. One had asked the other to fetch a comb to style the hair of the toy bride, in preparation for its wedding.

Mohammed, 9, and Osama, 8, were also nearby playing with a balloon. Each time a missile struck, they would run over to their mother's arms and hide until the smoke disappeared and things were quiet enough to play again.

Rahaf, 11, was visiting a friend next door and playing, blissfully unaware that she would never see her family alive and together again.

Before long, however, the brief lull was shattered.

Out of the sunset, two Israeli drone missiles hit Rawia and her children, shattering their bodies to pieces. The explosion shook the whole neighborhood and people ran to the house hoping to help but instead they were greeted by dead bodies of friends and family members they could no longer recognize.

Essam Juda, the father, quickly ran outside screaming for help: "Help me, neighbors! Help me!" When his daughter Rahaf ran over from next door, all she could do was look at her mother's dead body and scream.

The family insists that they don't know why they were hit. They swear there could not have been any military target nearby.

A cousin, Mohammed, who came to help with the rescue, said that the children were merely playing: "The house was filled with our laughter only. Does that upset Israel?"

He explained that Osama, 8, was excited about starting his first school year and already had his drawing book and paints inside his school bag. He never got the chance to use them.

When the family's bodies were brought to the hospital, a trail of neighbors and distant relatives, young and old, rushed behind the ambulance whizzing to Kamal Adwan Hospital. Most of them were bringing pieces of shattered, burned bodies to be put back together for burial.

An old man wearing a Palestinian keffiyeh wrapped the body parts together in a white shroud so the family could be promptly laid to rest.

"The world cries for dead Jewish child in Israel, but will they cry for this good Palestinian mother and her four dead children?" he said as the small bodies were carried, two on each orange ambulance stretcher.

Usually a mother gets the last look at her deceased children, but this time she was also gone. Her remaining children were either left ravaged by the shrapnel and fighting for their lives, or were broken on the inside by the loss, facing a gaping hole as they realized that they would forever remain separated from their loved ones.

At Shifa Hospital, next to the broken body of Thaeer, many friends gathered to offer their blood for transfusion. Mohammed Alhessi was one of those who donated his blood.

"This was a family, not a military target," he said. "No one in the family is associated with the resistance and they live far from where any resistance rockets are fired," he added, referring to Tal al-Zatar, one of the most crowded areas in Gaza Strip.

The rockets have now stopped falling but tonight may not be any easier for many in Gaza. After 50 days of fighting, some 1,800 children have become orphans in Gaza, according to Euro-mid Observer for Human Rights.

A total of 536 children were also killed in Gaza, comprising almost a quarter of the total Palestinian dead, according to the Al-Mezan Center for Human Rights, which has been monitoring the death toll.

Israel is also believed to have carried out 145 strikes on families.

In total, the 50-day conflict has killed more than 2,145 Palestinians—mostly civilians—and 70 Israelis, of whom 66 have been soldiers.

Children that are left behind are usually taken in by extended family members, but the scars prove hard to heal. The trauma of losing a limb, or a loved one, is likely to endure long after the smell of explosives and decomposing bodies begins to fade.

Gaza's fisherman take advantage of cease-fire

Gaza's fishermen have been hard-hit by the latest conflict but hope expanded boundaries may revive business

GAZA CITY—Abdelsalam al-Essi knows better than anyone that he didn't choose to be a fisherman. It was handed down to him from his father, who got it from his father, who got it from his father before him. The chain goes back generations, acting as a sort of genetic inheritance.

Al-Essi is not alone in this legacy. There are several families living in Shati refugee camp in northern Gaza that share the same family fishing tradition.

"The only job I have ever known is fishing, which I have done since 1967," the 63-year-old said.

"I never thought of changing it. My great grandparents were all fishermen," he said as a smile appeared on his face, prompted by memories of his grandparents' tales of Jaffa, the family's ancestral home before the creation of Israel.

It's memories like this that keep al-Essi coming back to his boat, day after day, despite the prospect of facing heavy bombardments by Israeli warships. Every day since the latest war started on July 7, he has come to check on his equipment and make sure that his nets and boats have survived.

A few times he got news that his friends had lost their boats to Israeli attacks, but he was spared and his boat and livelihood outlasted the 50-day military operation.

Cease-fire announced

When the cease-fire was announced on Tuesday, al-Essi could not wait to get back to his boat. As morning broke on Thursday, he took all his relatives down to the shore with one mission in mind—today, after years of being confined to a three-nautical-mile stretch, he and Gaza's fleet of fishermen could now float out to the new six-mile barrier, a key condition of the latest cease-fire.

Despite the possible dangers, the whole family cheered al-Essi on, urging him to be the first one to sail out and test the new boundary.

Three miles may not seem like much, but when 1.8 million people have been overfishing the same three-mile stretch of coast, even this limited expansion could be the difference between life and death.

The waters are "virtually fished out," said al-Essi, as he prepared his boat for the new adventure.

As a father of four, including two daughters, al-Essi rarely stops talking about his large extended family of 27, including all his grandchildren. They are his pride and joy, but such a large family also means extra pressure to get back out there and start fishing immediately.

Al-Essi lost much of his equipment in an Israeli strike several weeks ago, but his boats and net survived. This means al-Essi now has to tend his remaining equipment even more diligently and fish even harder to make up the shortfall.

But doing so will not be easy. Before the war, the boat had 12 people working on it, and about 70 people living off its proceeds.

The high price of fuel, however, which skyrocketed under the Israeli blockade, forced al-Essi to take out a loan. He then had to take out another loan to keep up with the first.

"I had to take a bank loan in order to pay other loans," he said.

He now has to pay off $200 every month. While he previously managed to cover his debt, this time he cannot pay. After seven weeks of not working, al-Essi is bankrupt, his savings used up on feeding his family during the war.

Nor does the new fishing boundary extension provide much reprieve.

"Even at six nautical miles, the area is virtually fished-out," said al-Essi, sharing the experience he had after a cease-fire deal was reached in 2012, where Palestinian factions and Israel agreed that the boundary would increase to six miles.

There could also be security risks, and no one really knows how Israel will react—will it decide to hit back at Gaza's fishermen? Even within the old three-mile limit, venturing out was risky. Kamal Abu Watfi, a friend of al-Essi's son Subhi, claims that not long ago he was shot at by Israeli marines and then arrested. He was later released but his boat was never returned.

Fishermen, like many Gaza residents, have struggled under the Israeli blockade and the latest war with Israel.

"This is not a war, it is a holocaust, which I have never known before," said al-Essi.

"We have seen many wars but Gaza has never known it as bad as this. I lost my fishing gear in the war. My fisherman's room was burned completely, but thanks to Allah, the children are still alive."

Others said they also had all their equipment destroyed.

When Israeli F-16 missiles hit the fishing wharf in Gaza City on July 27, the damage was beyond belief, said Merhrez Abu Ryala, 37, another fisherman.

"I lost all my equipment, all my fishing nets and my boat engine," Abu Ryala said.

As a father of 10, he and his brothers feed 53 family members with their proceeds from their boat.

"This is our life, and we've suffered around $45,000 in damages," Abu Ryala said as he inspected the ruined boats.

This is "economic terrorism" by Israel. "This was a war to wreck Gaza's economy totally," he added.

All the family can do now is sit and wait for a miracle in a land that has not seen much luck in recent decades, Abu Ryala explains.

Fishing is all he has ever done since he was 10 years old. Abu Ryala says that he can't imagine doing anything else.

His wife Basma has offered to sell her earrings and wedding band so that the family can try to start again, but it is no use.

"I want to begin again, but no one sells these motors. They are all on Israel's banned-goods list," Abu Ryala explains.

Golden age

Things were not always like this. Israel first restricted access back in 1994 when the PA was formed, but even then fishermen felt bold enough to stray out as far as 10 nautical miles, especially when escorted by international activists.

"We could get lots of fish. At one stage, this boat was filled with fish, with no room for more," al-Essi said. "We would catch red mullet, evelan ripple, round sardinella, atlantic sting, aramtan blue, albacore tuna, sea bass, sea bream, farida and shrimp."

It was normal for al-Essi to sell as much as 20,000 NIS ($5,620) a day—a huge income for him. It's more than six times what he gets within three miles these days.

He now calls this "the golden age," when Israeli gunboats would not shoot at fishermen because of the international presence.

When President Mohammed Morsi came to power in Egypt in 2012, al-Essi claims that Gaza saw its second, albeit brief, golden age.

"We could escape Israeli gunfire by crossing the Egyptian maritime border, and then go beyond 20 nautical miles," al-Essi said. There he could fish as much as he liked.

If you ask al-Essi, the solution is simple. He does not call for any big concessions or fresh borders. All he asks for is a 12-mile boundary off the strip.

"At 12 miles or more, we can catch a large variety of fish," he said. "It is our water and sea. We should fish in it and not have Israeli fishermen fishing with Israeli warships following behind."

Gazans sick with thalassemia want to be a priority

Facing untold numbers of wounded, Gaza hospitals have many urgent cases to cope with, but thalassemia patients are not among them

GAZA CITY—Under normal circumstances, Ibrahim Abdullah receives new blood every three weeks. But because of the war in Gaza, he has only had two transfusions in two months. While the truce give him some hope, Gaza hospitals have urgent cases to cope with, and thalassemia patients like him are not among them.

Thalassemia is an inherited autosomal recessive blood disease, usually caused by the destruction of red blood cells. The disease is prevalent among Mediterranean people, caused by a faulty synthesis of hemoglobin (red cells bearing oxygen) or missing chromosomes affecting how the body produces hemoglobin, resulting in a form of microcytic anaemia that requires patients to undergo blood transfusions in order to survive.

Abdullah has been unable to reach the hospital—but now, with the cease-fire, he has a chance. "It was a miracle that I managed to call a nearby hospital, which informed me they would send an ambulance out for me and three other patients."

The patients waited, but no ambulance came. Abdullah called the hospital again, but was told that they couldn't send an ambulance.

"I told them that we are like those injured by Israel's missiles, and that we too would die if we didn't receive a transfusion and dialysis," said Abdullah.

But that didn't change the reality on the ground, and no taxis were available anywhere, he explained.

He was standing in the middle of the road, waiting for any car that could take him to the Gaza-European Hospital in the southern Gaza Strip, when he saw a bus transferring doctors to the hospital.

"The doctors understood and they let me on board—but many patients needing long-term treatment didn't get this chance," he said.

"The risk is that many of over 300 patients in Gaza will die if not given access to hospitals," explained Dr. Bayan al-Saqqa, head of the Blood Disease Department at Shifa Hospital. Israel knows these patients need regular treatment.

The patients are treated by transfusion and dialysis, removing the overload of iron in their blood, he said.

As a result of the war, stocks are low. Doctors can only provide half the necessary amount of essential medications: "Instead of six boxes of tablets, we get only three," said Abdullah, a thin man who seemed to be at a loss for what to do next.

Dr. Saqqa said that major cases of inherited thalassemia require frequent blood transfusions—once every three to four weeks for the rest of the patient's life.

In Gaza, courts determined that for any couple who wants to marry, one of the partners is obliged to be thalassemia free. Otherwise, if both partners carry the gene, the judge will not allow the marriage. This legal step was taken some years ago to reduce the prevalence of thalassemia as much as possible.

At Gaza hospitals, there is an urgent need for blood for those injured from Israel's attacks, causing high demand for already short supplies. Gaza hospitals called on people to donate more blood and hundreds of people rushed to donate despite the obstacles.

Thalassemia patients are scattered throughout the Gaza Strip, and over the last two months of Israeli attacks, only three hospitals had the facilities to offer appropriate treatment.

Dr. Saqqa confirmed that during the war, it was enormously difficult to get patients in to receive transfusions.

Dire conditions caused by Israel's war have put thalassemia patients in a position where they must take extreme measures if they want to survive. Ibrahim risked his life, exposing himself to Israeli artillery shelling just to flag down a bus full of doctors to get to the hospital.

Doctors say that 70 families who have members with thalassemia had to flee their homes in Jabaliya, Beit Hanoun and Shejaiya. Now they are seeking shelter at UN schools. Four of the thalassemia patients have been killed.

On the first day of the cease-fire, Abdullah could access the hospital, but the hospital was overwhelmed and medication was unavailable. Israel said that as part of the cease-fire it would allow humanitarian supplies, so he hopes that his medication is forthcoming.

But others don't have that option. They must silently face the complications of the disease, such as iron overload, bone deformities and cardiovascular illness. It causes pain for Abdullah and his fellow patients to know that they are not a priority when hospitals are overcrowded.

Abdullah says the medication he receives from hospital can't meet his needs. "We appeal to the world, please rescue us," he said. "We want to live."

Gazans ready to rebuild, but key materials are not allowed in

While truckloads of food and other goods have come to Gaza, materials for the Strip's reconstruction, promised in the cease-fire agreement, remain elusive

RAFAH—The moment Mounir al-Ghalban heard about the cease-fire conditions, he called all his staff members on the Palestinian side of the Kerem Shalom border crossing to come back to work.

Soon trucks heaped with goods and some humanitarian aid pulled into the war-torn Gaza Strip. But al-Ghalban is still waiting for desperately needed construction materials and there is no sign they will come anytime soon.

Plastic chairs, soft drinks, candy, cans of food, shoes and toilet paper: al-Ghalban counts off all of the items coming through the Rafah crossing, but these aren't the only things Gazans needs, he says.

Gazans like Abu Khaled al-Jammal are waiting for bags of cement.

Several years ago, al-Jammal lost his home when Israeli missiles struck it. With financing from the UN Relief and Works Agency (UNRWA), he moved into another home two years ago.

This month, that house sustained minor damage from Israeli tank shells.

And now, instead of waiting for help from international organizations and governments, al-Jammal said he wants cement to fix the damage—and the damage on the homes of friends and family—on his own.

"By waiting for the international community's response, my children will suffer the next 10 winters," he said. "Yes, the cease-fire is a good thing. It ends slaughtering us, but we want to rebuild our homes. I can't watch my children freezing cold when winter kicks in."

After seven weeks of the deadliest attacks on Gaza, he heard in the news that construction materials would come. Since Tuesday, when the cease-fire was declared, he has been waiting for al-Ghalban to announce that building materials have arrived.

At the busy Kerem Shalom border, Abu Ahmed Siam, a truck driver, stood in a dusty area filled with trucks. The situation at the crossing has become "slightly easier" since the cease-fire, he said, and some items restricted by the Israelis have been allowed in again.

"We got aid trucks from the West Bank, WFP [World Food Program], and UNRWA [United Nations Relief and Works Agency]," he said as one of his colleagues waved to him from a new truck entering with fruit for Gaza merchants.

Siam said school stationery, too, has been allowed in, but the timing was bittersweet: schools in Gaza were due to start last week, but have been postponed for two more weeks until UNRWA and government schools are able to find shelter for homeless families who have been living inside classrooms and sports clubs.

Seven weeks ago, only fuel and some humanitarian aid came across this crossing. Now commercial goods are entering for the first time—many everyday items like milk, cheese and diapers that Gaza's emptied-out stores need. But not any cement.

"Nothing came through, as far as building materials are concerned," Siam told *Middle East Eye*.

Since 2006, building supplies and various raw materials have been on the list of items banned by Israel. Banned items include cement, steel and concrete. Israel holds the position that these items could be used by Gaza military groups to build military sites.

For years, Gaza has relied on tunnels to get the building materials in. Now the majority of tunnels have been sealed by the Egyptian military in an attempt to crush Hamas, an ally of the Muslim Brotherhood. Last December, after the coup that ousted Muslim Brotherhood President Mohamed Morsi, Egypt declared the group a terrorist organization.

In Cairo, Israeli negotiators agreed to ease restrictions on the border and allow materials in for the reconstruction of Gaza. Al-Ghalban was under the impression that this would start immediately. But it has not.

"Now everyone is waiting for construction materials," he said. "This is Gaza's immediate need."

Al-Ghalban said that during the war, Israel allowed the entry of 200 trucks, but in fact, being the most densely populated place in the world, Gaza needs 600 trucks per day.

According to the Israeli human rights group Gisha, from June 2007 until June 2010 an average of 2,400 trucks per month entered Gaza from Israel, compared to 10,400 trucks per month entering Gaza in 2005.

The Kerem Shalom crossing is supposed to be used for the export of agricultural products, herbs and furniture. According to Gisha, since March 2012, in an exception to the rule, 55 truckloads of goods have exited Gaza for the West Bank and Israel: 49 truckloads of date bars for a World Food Program project and four truckloads of school desks and chairs ordered by the Palestinian Authority to the West Bank, plus two truckloads of palm fronds to Israel.

"During the months of January to July 2014, an average of 12 truckloads of goods exited Gaza each month, or less than one percent of what exited monthly prior to 2007," wrote Gisha in *The Gaza Cheat Sheet* on August 19.

The Kerem Shalom crossing is next door to the Rafah crossing, where hundreds of travelers are waiting to leave Gaza. But Egypt does not grant permission to travelers trying to go through Gaza's point of exit. During the past seven weeks of war, Egypt closed the crossing to everyone except those holding foreign and Egyptian passports, those holding resident permits, and scores of wounded people.

The Rafah crossing is not part of the cease-fire deal signed in Cairo last week. Egyptian officials refused to negotiate the matter with Palestinian factions at the truce talks with Israel, stating that this was an Egyptian–Palestinian matter.

The Rafah terminal arrival, departure and VIP halls are still functioning, despite Israeli air strikes on the crossing last week. The head of border crossings, Maher Abu Sabha, said, "We want to challenge Netanyahu by keeping the crossing open, despite damage."

Among the crowds waiting were students whose classes at universities abroad started while they were trapped in Gaza. Others needed medical attention, but they were waiting too.

"The crossing is supposed to be for Palestinians, and they [Egypt] are only allowing foreigners," said 21-year-old Amjad Yousef while waiting in the summer sun. Yousef came to Gaza after studying for two years in Morocco. He planned to stay for a month, but the war has kept him in Gaza for two.

"I don't want to enter Egypt. Escort me directly to my flight from Cairo to Morocco," he said.

Next to Yousef stands a cancer patient. She has all of the papers required to cross, including a certificate from the Palestinian Health Ministry explaining that she can no longer be treated at any of the local hospitals, which have largely collapsed after heavy bombardment over the past month.

Yousef expressed disappointment with the cease-fire deal, saying, "We were hoping that the treatment would change and humiliation at crossings would end."

"This is why I will support Palestinian resistance demands until we get our own airports."

International NGO: Gaza will take 20 years to rebuild

Shelter Cluster's assessment is based on the assumption that construction materials will be allowed into Gaza as promised in the cease-fire. So far, locals say supplies have yet to arrive

GAZA CITY—Standing in the rubble of his three shops, 20-year-old Mahmoud Nofal in Beit Hanoun said he will be in his forties before his life returns to the way it used to be before the most recent war in Gaza.

"I can't believe it. Israel bombed the shops and the home in less than 30 seconds, but now it will take 20 years to rebuild," Nofal said.

The remains of the supermarket that Nofal ran in his father's absence, including toothpaste bottles, a scattering of baby diapers, pieces of gum and smashed cans of cola, are strewn across the roads in Beit Hanoun. The goods of the three shops alone will cost $50,000 to replace.

All Nofal can do now, he said, is sit in a UN school where he has taken shelter and wait together with his children. At night, he sleeps in the playground of a UN school, while his wife and children are crammed inside a classroom, packed with others like sardines. A few years ago, he was well-off, but now he has no option but to rely on canned goods and other food aid—items he used to sell in his supermarket.

Shelter Cluster, an international housing group involved in post-conflict assessment of reconstruction, agrees with Nofal's assessment: it will take 20 years to rebuild Gaza following the seven-week war, the group said in a report released on Friday.

The group, whose assessment was co-chaired by the UN and the International Committee of the Red Cross, said 17,000 Gaza homes have been destroyed or severely damaged—and there are still around 5,000 homes that were demolished in the 2008–09 and 2012 Gaza wars that have yet to be rebuilt. In Rafah, several families whose homes were destroyed between 2003–05 are still waiting for a Saudi-funded project to be completed so they can return home.

Overall, there is a deficit of 75,000 houses in Gaza, according to Shelter Cluster.

The Palestinian Ministry of Housing estimates that the destruction wrought by the most recent war will cost more than $6 billion.

These are early estimates: those measuring the damage acknowledge that the scale of destruction is massive and it will take more time to have a full assessment.

Palestinian Minister of Housing Dr. Mofeed Al-Hassayna, recently appointed to the Palestinian unity government, told *Middle East Eye* that his staff members are working hard to assess the damage in all sectors. Palestinian President Mahmoud Abbas has assigned Al-Hassayna, together with two other ministers, to further assess the destruction to Gaza, with the hopes of presenting the findings at a future donor conference.

Norway and Egypt have jointly raised the possibility of hosting such a conference, but no details have been confirmed.

Shelter Cluster's 20-year assessment is based on the assumption that 100 trucks of construction materials will be allowed across the Kerem Shalom border crossing.

As part of the open-ended cease-fire agreement announced on Tuesday, reconstruction materials and humanitarian supplies were to be allowed into Gaza. Israel had previously restricted the import of building materials into Gaza, fearing militants would use them to build military facilities.

But so far, Gazans told *Middle East Eye* that they have yet to see any rebuilding material pass through the border in the past week. Many who have heard the 20-year rebuilding figure are in despair.

"It is enough. We are tired," said Nasser Mohammed Al-Najjar, 62. "I lost my wife in the war. I lost my cousins and our homes have been turned into sand."

It took years for Al-Najjar to build his home and now he and six family members are homeless, temporarily sleeping in a UN school. Al-Najjar used to work in Israel, but since 2000 when he was laid off, he has tried to live off his land, which was also damaged when bulldozers ravaged his neighborhood east of Khan Younis.

"No one cares about us," he said.

In another UN school shelter in Khan Younis sits 42-year-old Rasem Abu Zaed. He had been living in Jordan for more than 15 years and working as a taxi driver, which gave him enough money to feed his wife and four children. Then Abu Zaed decided to return to Gaza.

In Gaza, he said he has found freedom to express his views, but he has not found stability, nor security. Yet despite the knowledge that it could be 20 years before his family home is rebuilt—when his one-year-old son, Musbah, will then be an adult—he said he does not want to return to Jordan.

"I felt something fishy the moment the cease-fire was announced," he said. "I asked myself, 'Why would this work when Israel has the position of power to violate cease-fires?'"

Abu Zaed said he and his family had heard about Shelter Cluster's 20-year assessment.

"But we never heard of what they will do to challenge that," he said.

Diana Buttu, Palestinian analyst and former spokesperson for the Palestinian Liberation Organization, told *MEE* that for the cease-fire to be sustained, Palestinian borders must opened. Otherwise, Israel will continue its blockade on Gaza.

"The international community must ensure that Gaza is not returned to its state of being an open-air prison," Buttu said. "Palestinians must be allowed to import and export goods freely, enter and exit freely, travel to and from the West Bank freely and be given the right to open and operate an airport and seaport."

"Without ensuring these basic rights, the international community will be sending a message to Israel that it is allowed to continue its brutal, illegal blockade with impunity, and to Palestinians that statements from their governments condemning the blockade are meaningless," she added.

While he wants to see Gaza rebuilt, Abu Zaed said he is tired of official statements.

"Sympathy can neither feed my children, nor bring them shelter again. The winter is approaching and there is nowhere to go," he said. "If the international community wonders what 24 hours are like for us, they should know it's like a year in their lives."

Gaza's human shields: victims speak out

"The soldier poured liquid on my trousers, saying he would 'burn me alive' if I didn't tell him where the tunnel system was"

KHUZA'A, GAZA STRIP—When an Israeli tank shell hit the outside walls of their home, Sami Al-Najjar was sitting with his sister and brothers in Khuza'a, in western Khan Younis.

"The room was filled with thick smoke and we couldn't breathe, so we ran outside," said Najjar as he began to recall that dark day back in July.

As the family tried to flee the building, Najjar's father found a piece of white cloth. He fashioned it into a makeshift flag and began waving it above his head to signal the Israeli soldiers and let them know that there were civilians inside and that his family was about to start streaming out behind him and away from the smoke.

But despite his father's efforts, Israeli soldiers outside ordered the men and women to separate and then began binding the men's hands.

As soon as they were tied up, the soldiers started interrogating the men, began demanding to know where the tunnels (used by resistance fighters) were. Najjar insisted that he did not know, but the soldiers did not believe him.

Next, one of the soldiers "picked up a chair and slammed it into my back," said 21-year-old Najjar.

He could see his mother and the rest of his family watching him from the house as he was then taken into the backyard alone and told to kneel as a military dog—wearing a metal muzzle and what looked like a camera on its back—approached.

Bottle of water

"I didn't know what would happen next," Najjar said.

"Then one of the three soldiers stood an empty water bottle on my head and aimed his gun at it," Najjar added, before pausing to take a deep breath and calm his nerves.

"The first bullet broke the bottle but then one of the soldiers—who was about my age and was short and stocky, with a shaved head, black combat boots and narrow, almost Asian-looking eyes—held up an M-16 automatic weapon.

"He stood over me as I knelt on the ground."

To the other side of Najjar stood another soldier who wore a mask and conveyed the orders from the rest of the soldiers to the prisoners in perfect Arabic.

After the bullet shattered the bottle, Najjar's hearing was impaired for a while. He couldn't hear what one soldier was saying, but recalls that he heard the Asian-looking soldier scream: "We will show you how you're going to tell us where Hamas rockets are fired from, and give us two names of Hamas leaders."

Najjar replied: "I don't spend much time in Khuza'a; I fix tire punctures in my workshop, that's all."

The soldier then grabbed Najjar by his shirt, pulled him to his feet and slapped him across the face.

"You're a liar," the soldier screamed as he resumed beating Najjar with the chair, which he raised again and again until it finally broke.

Najjar says that after this, the soldiers pulled him up from the ground and the Arabic-speaking soldier removed his mask and began ordering him to reveal tunnel locations.

"Tell me where the tunnels are!" he screamed as he waved his gun at Najjar's neighbors.

Najjar was terrified and in pain, but the worst was yet to come.

"Suddenly bullets were fired at the soldiers from somewhere," Najjar said. "The soldier who had hold of me made me walk in front of him."

As the exchange of fire continued, Najjar claims that he was hoisted up and forced to jump onto the deck of the tank.

"There was random shooting, and the soldiers used me as a human shield," Najjar said.

"When it got quiet, the masked soldier poured liquid on my trousers, saying he would 'burn me alive' if I didn't tell him where the tunnel system was or give him the names of two Hamas members."

The last thing that Najjar saw before the Arabic-speaking soldier blindfolded him and told him to undress was his mother and sisters being led out of the house.

"I didn't know how much to take off, but when I got down to my underwear, the soldier told me to stop," he said. He was later taken to an unknown location, along with a few dozen other young men.

Najjar's testimony is just one of many collected from young men in Khuza'a that day, all of whom have similar stories to tell.

Najjar's cousin, Fouad Al-Najjar, 24, also said he was taken and used as a human shield.

Like his cousin, Fouad was taken away by soldiers. Initially they kept telling him that he would be fine and not to worry, but when he didn't answer their questions and insisted that he didn't know the location of Hamas' tunnels, he too was struck in the face several times by the very soldier who had first told him not to worry.

"He pinned me down on the ground with his combat boots, forcing my neck into the dirt," said Fouad, who recalled hearing the sound of tanks thundering nearby.

Fouad then said that he was taken to join a line of other young men who were also being used as shields.

"Each time an Israeli F-16 hit, an Israeli soldier behind my back—who had dark skin and a light beard and who the other soldiers kept calling 'Rami'—would tell me to be quiet," he said, explaining that the Israeli soldiers seemed scared and were trying not to draw attention to themselves.

The issue of human shields is a complex one. While Israel blames Hamas for using civilians as human shields to try and ward off attacks—an allegation that Hamas consistently denies—testimonies recalling Israel's use and abuse of the practice in both Gaza and the West Bank have appeared consistently throughout the years.

The practice is considered a breach of the Geneva Convention and Israeli courts outlawed it in 2005, although the Israeli army has long contested the decision.

The end result is that even in the very few instances when misconduct is prosecuted—such as an incident in 2009 where a nine-year-old boy in Gaza was made to check a bag for explosives—the punishment is mild and the army insists that these are acts committed by individual soldiers in difficult situations, not army policy.

Detention camp

Once Sami Najjar was blindfolded and stripped at his home, he said that the three soldiers threatened him and forced him to walk ahead of them. He was barefoot as the summer sun shone down on the boiling hot ground.

Najjar estimates that they walked for about 90 minutes before they eventually reached a military detention camp on the Israeli side of the Gaza–Israel border.

Apart from the voices of soldiers, "I could hear the voices of my cousins, Momen and Issa," Najjar said. "I felt relief that I wasn't alone."

The relief didn't last long; Najjar remembers being kept blindfolded in a cage outside, where the sound of rockets burned his ears and he could hear Israeli soldiers periodically dashing to safety in the camp's shelter.

On the second day, Najjar said he was taken into an interrogation room with a soldier he could not see. Once again the soldier kept on yelling, demanding that Najjar give up the names of three Hamas members.

"He put his fingers on my throat, and when I said I didn't know anything, he shouted 'You are liar.' I then collapsed to my knees."

When he fell, the soldier picked him back up, shouting: "Stand up! You're lying to me."

The soldier next told Najjar that he was treating him in this way "because you are a human" and are designed to feel humiliation, fear and shame.

After the interrogation, which lasted for a few hours, Najjar says he was told to remove his underwear and put on a white prison outfit.

He would occasionally be given water and food, but he complains that he was kept in a cell where sewage water was spilling onto the floor.

"I could smell the dirt and the mud underneath me," he said.

On the fourth day, Najjar had his name called and was told to get on a bus. He didn't know where he was going but before long he and several dozen other men were thrown off the bus at the Gaza border. Najjar looked around for his cousins but he couldn't see Momen and Issa. They were not among those released with him.

It has taken Najjar almost two months to be able to recall his ordeal. Even as he does he shakes and his voice crumbles as he explains that he heard his cousin Momen screaming in the camp, but has not seen him since and does not know what happened to him.

"The moment the Israeli soldiers removed the sheets from our eyes—there were about 50 to 55 of us—all of us had been used as human shields on the border of Gaza," said Najjar.

"The moment a Palestinian rocket flies over, soldiers use us as human shields to avoid the resistance's gunfire."

War of wages: Hamas employees pressured into resigning

Forty thousand workers in Gaza have not received their wages in nine months while many others can no longer earn a living via the tunnels to Egypt

Palestinian President Mahmoud Abbas has taken to the airwaves of late to accuse Hamas officials of maintaining leadership roles in Gaza and running a shadow government despite the Palestinian reconciliation agreement in April.

That agreement was supposed to end seven years of Palestinian division. Both sides agreed to establish a Palestinian unity government and prepare for presidential and legislative council elections six months after signing the reconciliation deal.

On the face of things in Gaza, Abbas' accusations are accurate: practically all government work and daily errands are being performed by the same former de facto government led by Hamas, only without ministers.

Following the Palestinian reconciliation agreement, the de facto government ministers resigned, leaving vacant positions that were filled by the deputies of previous ministers running the Gaza Strip.

Only four of the ministers in the new unity government are from Gaza, while the rest are from the West Bank. The latter are reportedly refusing to communicate with their counterparts in Gaza.

Zakria al-Hur, Director General of the Ministry of Education in Gaza, described the problem as the PA's failure to include everyone under one umbrella.

The PA, he said, "refuses to acknowledge that there are ministries and staff members who have been working already for eight years in Gaza."

Around 40,000 workers have not received their wages in nine months, he said.

"Until this moment, the minister of education, within the consensus government, hasn't called us, during or after the war, to check on the progress of work," al-Hur said.

Al-Hur, however, said the problem goes beyond Abbas' claims of a shadow government in Gaza.

"President Abbas should come to Gaza and we will give him the keys to the ministries, with all staff members," al-Hur said.

In the meantime, the four ministerial members of the consensus government in Gaza say they have full control over their ministries, including border crossings.

Al-Hur says Abbas is trying to weaken Hamas by pressuring staff members into resigning and leaving.

"Abbas wanted to achieve the taming of Hamas by telling the world that he is the one who decides. He does not want the outside world to understand that the resistance was victorious in the war," al-Hur said.

The PA still, however, pays the salaries of a few thousand of its people employed by the ministries. But the majority of all ministry staff who used to work under the Hamas-led government, including those working in hospitals, have yet to receive salaries.

Out of the 50,000 staff members, al-Hur said, there are "over 40,000 staff members who have worked for eight months and received no income, while tens of thousands are sitting at home getting paid from international community money."

The PA staff, composed of people who were employed by the government before the Hamas takeover of Gaza in June 2007, are getting paid to sit at home. After the national unity deal, they were supposed to go back to work, but they did not.

As of late June, before the war in Gaza started, many of the government workers had not been paid in seven months, while others had received only partial pay. Hamas officials estimated at the time that the workers could be owed as much as $1 billion in backpay.

As many as 600,000 Gazans—or an estimated 36 percent of the Gaza population—have family members who work for the government. They have been seriously impacted by the pay freeze.

The unanswered question, for international observers, is how the ministries are running after the tunnels underneath the Gaza–Egypt border were shut.

Up until former Egyptian President Mohamed Morsi was ousted, taxes from tunnel operators were collected and used to pay public-sector employees. As tensions between Egypt and Hamas, an offshoot of the Muslim Brotherhood, escalated after the Egyptian coup, Egypt accused Hamas of allowing gunmen to slip through tunnels in the nearby Sinai Desert. In response, Egypt destroyed at least 1,370 tunnels—and with them, a major Hamas revenue stream.

As the enclave recovers from war, the ministries are now running on revenues from taxes and fees collected locally. Revenues come in, for example, when cars are serviced, as they must be checked by a government agency.

Al-Hur says that the education ministry has been forced to cut its running costs and other vital program budgets, including a $100,000 educational project to rehabilitate pupils. The budget for this project has now been cut to only $20,000.

Cuts to fuel coupons have also been made. For example, senior staff members commuting from various areas used to receive 130–150 liters of fuel per month. They are now only allowed 30 litres.

Accusations from both sides ceased during the seven-week Israeli war, replaced by apparent displays of national unity—but all this seems to be crumbling with increased accusations from both sides, which are played out in the media.

Still, the Palestinian public is confident that the planned meeting between the political parties in Cairo this month may yield some common ground. Abu Abdelhadi, a 43-year-old teacher in Gaza City, says that President Abbas and his consensus government should have visited Gaza.

"We were slaughtered. They never thought of asking about us," Abu Abdelhadi said. "No prime minister would not go check on his people after a massive slaughter."

But he said there is no room for naming and shaming right now. National unity has to work, because the Palestinian people should come before Fatah and Hamas.

"After all, we are Palestinians and the blood that Israel spilled should unite us," said Abu Abelhaid.

Abbas has threatened to break off a unity agreement with Hamas if the Islamist movement does not allow the government to operate properly in the Gaza Strip.

Mussa Abu Marzouq, a top Hamas leader, said at a recent seminar in Gaza City that the consensus government has a larger responsibility for Gaza reconstruction. He criticized the PA for establishing a committee for Gaza reconstruction inside the West Bank.

"The Gaza Strip has the ability to manage itself," Abu Marzouq said.

As the back-and-forth attacks continue between the parties, there are concerns on the ground as to who will pay the price for the political squabbling.

Some EU officials who recently visited Gaza met with several leading civil society individuals and alluded to the notion that both the EU and Israel do not object to paying salaries to Gaza staff members.

Hamas, meanwhile, blames Abbas.

"We are heading for a massive explosion in the face of Abbas. The public and media [are] starting to realize that the only obstacle to the payment of salaries is Abbas," says Al-Hur.

Gaza's choice: chase aids groups or starve

Numerous NGOs are distributing aid in the aftermath of the latest war on the Gaza Strip, yet who gets it and why may have little to do with need

The outside of a UN school in Tal al-Hawa, western Gaza City, has turned into a minimarket, where vendors selling goods to homeless families seeking shelter inside UN schools must compete with some of those very families who use the market in an effort to raise desperately needed cash.

Abu Khaled, 54, had a home in Gaza's Shejaiya district before Israel raided the area. Now homeless and destitute, he is deeply unhappy with how aid to those whose lives have been wrecked by the attack is being distributed. Many international NGOs arriving with aid do not have a clear strategy, unlike the long-established UN Relief and Works Agency for Palestine Refugees (UNRWA).

"Our home was completely destroyed, and so far we have received nothing, while others have received many food coupons," he said. And unlike others with a similar plight, his dignity will not allow him to chase food trucks and beg for what he terms a basic right to survive.

The problem is that there doesn't appear to be an overall system for aid distribution that would allow help to reach those who are most in need first. A lot of the operations now underway seem random, with many people who are most in need remaining out of the aid loop.

One of those affected is Hesham Saqallah, a 51-year-old disabled Gazan whose home in Tal al-Hawa's 12-story Zafer Towers apartment building was destroyed by Israel's attacks.

"Distribution is based on personal connections and political affiliations," he said, indicating that some of his fellow homeless families received aid based only on the people they knew and their political loyalties.

Homeless families in Gaza also complain that they have not received good quality aid, some of which is either sold in local markets or given to people who did not lose their homes. This involves what locals have started to call "VIP coupons."

"There is even a VIP coupon, which I heard about from my fellow homeless families. This entitles one to washing machines, refrigerators, dishes and other kitchen stuff," Saqallah said. He received nothing because, he said, he is not affiliated with any political group.

"There is even discrimination in bedding, which is handed out through donation: quality mattresses were donated by Kuwait, but only to those with connections, while ordinary people like us who need help the most get the poorest quality. Some of us get nothing."

Families in Gaza say that aid groups have failed to reach the most marginalized groups.

"There is not the minimum level of coordination between aid groups," said Saqallah. "Some organizations gave us the same food cans five and six times over. We don't need that, but there are other things that we do need." As a disabled man, he needs cash to get other basic goods, such as medication, washing detergent and pay for transport to get his daughter to school.

When the war on Gaza stopped, Saqallah received $1,000 from Qatar, but he said that others with stronger political affiliations received noticeably more financial aid.

"Aid groups turn us into beggars without human dignity," he said as he paused for a moment while pushing his wheelchair.

After a month of war, Saqallah has had to leave his children with various relatives so that they have somewhere safe to shelter and sleep; he knows that a hard winter is coming, though it is a prospect that he does not want to contemplate.

As a disabled father, it is not just food he needs. But he doesn't know who to approach and feels abandoned.

Except for the clothes on his back, all of Saqallah's clothes are under the ruins of Zafer Towers. He has received some secondhand clothes, and he makes do with them, but they only add to his sense of indignity.

"Each time I get the feeling of begging, it makes me feel the terrible pain of being homeless once again," he said.

Feeling excluded

Mohammed al-Jamal, a member of the network Palestinian Human Rights Defenders, said aid distribution has been functioning on the basis of factional affiliation, or has been going to those who live close to NGO offices. Such distribution can leave many feeling excluded.

"There is no doubt that aid distribution is factionalized, as in the case of eastern Rafah, which was very hard-hit yet received no aid. . . . Those who remain at home with dignity get nothing."

Jamal does not see this as a deliberate attempt to marginalize, rather just laziness on the part of international NGOs preferring to give to those who they know and who are close to them.

"Unjust distribution of aid is no new phenomenon, but now with massive aid coming, it is very apparent when one sees some families receiving eight times the amount of help, while families who lost homes and family members receive comparatively nothing."

It is difficult to know who is responsible for addressing this concern. Even assessments of the destruction caused by Israel are not accurate because many homes that were partially damaged have not been officially registered by the Palestinian Authority's aid groups.

Jamal says his house sustained damage, but he has not received even a bottle of fresh water since the war ended. He has friends in even more desperate need after sustaining greater damage, and they have so far received no help either.

"I know some of them would rather starve to death than chase the food trucks around like beggars," he said.

Mouneer Khalil, 37, is an unemployed Gazan whose home in Khirbet el Adas, on the edge of Rafah, is still waiting for aid three weeks after Israel's latest war on Gaza. He wants to know why, although has his own ideas.

"International NGOs work in air-conditioned offices and are unwilling to go outside to the streets, so they wait for people to arrive begging for help and seeking leftovers after factionalized aid has first been given out to affiliated members."

The disparity in distribution and obvious favoritism calls the reputations of aid groups into question.

"This aid should have been primarily for people who had to flee their homes and who sustained massive damage, and that includes myself," he said as trucks carrying mattresses passed by on their way to Gaza City.

Saqallah, in Gaza City, is much better off than many in more marginalized areas. But he too says the work of relief agencies lacks coordination and organization, even in the center where aid distribution takes place.

He had to share the extra food cans he received, and now he can't afford to buy simple essentials.

"I wish we didn't have to receive aid, or be exposed to the problem of abuse of factionalized power in the unfair distribution," he said.

Desperate Gazans lost at sea leave families searching

For many in Gaza, the perilous journey by sea to Europe is a desperate attempt to reclaim normalcy in their lives, but it often ends in tragedy

Zuhair Marouf, 51, is at a loss for words after the disappearance of his son and granddaughter. He has done everything in his power but he has been unable to determine their whereabouts.

His 29-year-old son Mohammed Marouf, who survived one of the deadliest Israeli attacks on Gaza in a long time, took his three-year-old daughter Lana and ran through the tunnels to escape the devastation of Israel's bombardment.

"There is nothing left for me in this place. I am broken and it's time to help my daughter to live," he told *MEE* before he disappeared with Lana.

On September 6, Mohammed called his father to say, "Dad don't worry about us. We are on our way to Sweden."

But, on September 10, the Marouf family received the tragic news that Palestinian migrants had been killed off the coast of Malta, after being smuggled onto a boat to seek freedom. The boat sank and the migrants drowned.

Zuhair is now waiting in limbo to hear if his son and granddaughter were among the victims. With Gaza under Israeli blockade, and with the Rafah crossing blocked, hundreds of Gazans are forced to find alternative ways to flee the Palestinian coastal enclave, often via tunnels to Egypt or boats to Europe. This desperate practice has been common over the past decade, with Belgium and Sweden seemingly the preferred destinations.

Some news did get through to the Marouf family, supposedly from one of the survivors: the 3-year-old girl died when the boat sank, and her father Mohammed swam for a long time before also drowning. But this news has not yet been confirmed, officially or otherwise.

The Guardian reported that the smuggling boat carrying the migrants was reportedly rammed by another vessel carrying traffickers.

Mohammed Marouf ran out of options in his life. As a car technician, he mastered Volvo automobile technology but was forced to abandon that trade when all access to spare engineering parts was blocked by the Israeli siege, causing him to lose his income. Some years later, he moved and got a new job as the head of the Kia motor maintenance department in Gaza, a job that earned him very little money, especially given the extreme shortage of spare parts.

"Get me out of here. I want peace. I want to work and raise my family," he had told *MEE* while working at Kia. "There is no life left here. I can't do anything without spare parts."

His brother Ahmed managed to reach Sweden after Israel's war in 2008–09 and has been living there ever since. He had encouraged his brother to leave and to try to achieve a better life and a better income working as a mechanic in Sweden, raising his children in a violence-free environment.

Security forces in Rafah estimate that several thousand Palestinians fled Gaza through the tunnels during Israel's most recent war on the strip. Hopeful but desperate people pay a hefty fee to be transported via the Rafah tunnels to Alexandria, and then on to Libya and Italy. The whole process is one of danger and luck. The road to freedom is full of many risks.

Tunnels have collapsed on fleeing refugees. Others who manage to get through are often apprehended or arrested by the Egyptian military in Sinai. The Egyptian coast guard boards some boats, while other boats sink at sea, filled with refugees.

But all that risk seemed worthwhile to Mohammed Marouf. To him it seemed like a better option than watching his daughter grow up under oppression, in pain and witnessing the deaths of her family in a homeland blockaded on all sides by the Israeli military. Many of his friends disagreed with him and refused to leave their home of Gaza, stating that it was Israel's plan to make the Palestinian people leave their ancestral home, to empty the land and to colonize it.

His father Zuhair Marouf says that Mohammed's decision was only ever intended to be temporary, just until the situation improved and he was able to return. But now that return seems unlikely.

Sources in Italy and Malta suggest that a few hundred Palestinians drowned seeking asylum. Migrant groups estimate that approximately 2,900 people died this year in the Mediterranean, compared to 700 who died in all of 2013.

Christiane Berthiaume, spokeswoman for the Geneva-based International Organization for Migration, commented on the sunken boat near Malta: "Some 500 people were on board—Syrians, Palestinians, Egyptians and Sudanese. They were trying to reach Europe." But the information Berthiaume provides does not solve Zuhair Marouf's dilemma. He is still unable to get definitive news.

A family in Deir al-Balah had been waiting for news about their son, but when none reached them, they set up a tent of mourning and started receiving condolences. Then someone called from Italy and informed them that their son might be alive after all. They shut down the mourning tent. But two days later, news came in again. It wasn't their son, but someone else who had survived and was receiving treatment in a Malta hospital. The father says his son had to leave Palestine to work and earn money to pay for a surgery for his mother.

His wife is unable to sleep, and the wife of Mohammed Marouf has declared the name of her husband to be among the missing on Palestinian websites. Now she is monitoring the news sites all day and night, waiting for some news of hope.

Dozens of families are missing. Some are complete families with no one left behind in Gaza except extended family members. It was a collective decision to flee a war and die in the sea, to which Israel has limited Palestinian access since 2006.

Dr. Rami Abduo of Euro-mid Observer for Human Rights says it is hard to know the numbers and names of the victims right now.

"The Malta authorities simply don't have sufficient means to search for bodies, and the Italian authorities will bury bodies they find immediately."

If the Marouf family is lucky, they may get a photograph from Italian authorities of their family members before burial, he says.

But this is not enough for Marouf. She will not tolerate not knowing what happened to her loved ones in a strange land where they never thought they would be.

"I want to know if my son and granddaughter are alive or dead," he says.

Also from Haymarket Books

Against Apartheid: The Case for Boycotting Israeli Universities
Edited by Ashley Dawson and Bill V. Mullen, Foreword by Ali Abunimah

Apartheid Israel: The Politics of an Analogy
Sean Jacobs and Jon Soske, Foreword by Achille Mbembe

The Battle for Justice in Palestine
Ali Abunimah

Before the Next Bomb Drops: Rising Up from Brooklyn to Palestine
Remi Kanazi

Boycott, Divestment, Sanctions: The Global Struggle for Palestinian Rights
Omar Barghouti

Diary of Bergen-Belsen: 1944–1945
Hanna Lévy-Hass, Foreword and Afterword by Amira Hass

Freedom Is a Constant Struggle: Ferguson, Palestine, and the Foundations of a Movement
Angela Y. Davis, Edited by Frank Barat, Foreword by Dr. Cornel West

Gaza in Crisis: Reflections on the US-Israeli War Against the Palestinians
Noam Chomsy and Ilan Pappé

Israelis and Palestinians: Conflict and Resolution
Moshé Machover

Lineages of Revolt: Issues of Contemporary Capitalism in the Middle East
Adam Hanieh

On Palestine
Noam Chomsky and Ilan Pappé

Uncivil Rites: Palestne and the Limits of Academic Freedom
Steven Salaita

Mohammed Omer is an award-winning Palestinian journalist whose reporting has appeared in media outlets including the *Washington Report on Middle East Affairs*, Al Jazeera, the *New Statesman*, Pacifica Radio, Electronic Intifada, and the *Nation*.